OF INNOCENCE AND AUTONOMY

This collection is dedicated to Henry Steiner and Martha Minow
– paving the way for a new generation.

Programme on International Rights of the Child
Series Editor: Geraldine Van Bueren

Titles in the Series:

Children's Rights and Traditional Values
Edited by Gillian Douglas and Leslie Sebba

Monitoring Children's Rights
Judith Ennew

The Right of the Child to a Clean Environment
Edited by Agata Fijalkowski and Malgosia Fitzmaurice

Cultural Pluralism and the Rights of the Child
Michael Freeman

Of Innocence and Autonomy
Children, sex and human rights
Edited by Eric Heinze

The Human Right to Education
Douglas Hodgson

The Child and the European Convention on Human Rights
Ursula Kilkelly

Legal Secrets, Cultural and Scientific Truths
Personality rights under the Convention on the Rights of the Child
Katherine O'Donovan

Childhood Abused
Protecting children against torture, cruel, inhuman and degrading treatment
and punishment
Edited by Geraldine Van Bueren

Of Innocence and Autonomy

Children, sex and human rights

Edited by
ERIC HEINZE
Queen Mary and Westfield College, University of London

With a Foreword by Katherine O'Donovan

Ashgate

DARTMOUTH

Aldershot • Burlington USA • Singapore • Sydney

Published by
Dartmouth Publishing Company Limited
Ashgate Publishing Limited
Gower House
Croft Road
Aldershot
Hampshire GU11 3HR
England

Ashgate Publishing Company
131 Main Street
Burlington
Vermont 05401
USA

Ashgate website: http://www.ashgate.com

British Library Cataloguing in Publication Data
Of innocence and autonomy : children, sex and human rights.
    - (Programme on international rights of the child)
    1. Child sexual abuse 2. Children - Legal status, laws, etc.
    3. Children (International law) 4. Children's rights
    I. Heinze, Eric
    341.4'81'083

Library of Congress Control Number: 00-132580

ISBN 1 84014 484 X

Printed in Great Britain by
Antony Rowe Ltd, Chippenham, Wiltshire

Contents

                   and Practical Consequences

            6   Punishing Children and Pleasuring   99
                   Adults: One, Both or Neither?
                   Chris Barton

            7   *Lolita* at the Interface of Obscenity: 124
                   Children and the Right to Free
                   Expression
                   Elena Loizidou

            8   Childhood Sexual Abuse as a Predictor   140
                   of Substance Use and HIV/AIDS Risk
                   Behaviour among Women at
                   Admission to Prison
                   Janet L. Mullings, Victoria E. Brewer
                   & James W. Marquart

Part IV   **Empowering Childhood: Awareness,**   161
                   Development and Education

            9   Sex Education: Child's Right, Parent's   163
                   Choice or State's Obligation?
                   Corinne Packer

            10   Health and Education: Conflicting   179
                   Programmes for Sex Education
                   Daniel Monk

            11   Seeking a Gendered Adolescence: 195
                   Legal and Ethical Problems of Puberty
                   Suppression among Adolescents with
                   Gender Dysphoria
                   Catherine Downs & Stephen Whittle

List of Contributors

Chris Barton *is Professor of Family Law and Director of the Centre for the Study of the Family, Law & Social Policy at Staffordshire University.*

Bill Bowring *is Reader in Human Rights Law and Director of the Pan-European Institute, University of Essex.*

Victoria E. Brewer *is Assistant Professor in the College of Criminal Justice, Sam Houston State University.*

Catherine Downs *is Senior Lecturer in Law at Manchester Metropolitan University.*

Eric Heinze *is Lecturer in Law at Queen Mary and Westfield College, University of London.*

Elena Loizidou *is Lecturer in Law, Birkbeck College, University of London.*

James W. Marquart *is Professor in the College of Criminal Justice, Sam Houston State University.*

Daniel Monk *is Lecturer in Law, Keele University.*

Janet L. Mullings *is Assistant Professor in the College of Criminal Justice, Sam Houston State University.*

Corinne Packer, *a Consultant for The Themis Foundation, has been a Consultant for the World Health Organisation, the United Nations High Commissioner for Refugees, and the Council of Europe.*

Christine Piper *is Senior Lecturer in Law and Associate Director of the Centre for the Study of Law, the Child and the Family at Brunel University.*

Margherita Rendel *is Reader Emerita in Human Rights and Education, University of London.*

Stephen Whittle *is Senior Lecturer in Law at Manchester Metropolitan University.*

Table of Publications

JCSA	Journal of Child Sexual Abuse
JCSTP	Journal of Communist Studies and Transition Politics
JDB	Journal of Deviant Behaviour
JLE	Journal of Law and Education
JLS	Journal of Law and Society
JNMD	Journal of Nervous and Mental Disease
JP	Justice of the Peace Reports
JSA	Journal of Substance Abuse
JSP	Journal of Social Policy
KB	King's Bench
LLR	Liverpool Law Review
LNOJ	League of Nations Official Journal
NF	New Formations
NILR	Netherlands International Law Review
NJIL	Nordic Journal of International Law
NSPCC	National Society for the Prevention of Cruelty to Children
NZULR	New Zealand Universities Law Review
PB	Psychological Bulletin
PCNA	Psychiatric Clinics of North America
PHR	Public Health Reports
PJ	The Prison Journal
QBD	Queens Bench Division
RSSR	Russian Social Science Review
SI	Statutory Instruments
SLC	Scottish Law Commission
SMT	Sexual and Marital Therapy
SLPS	Studies in Law, Politics and Society
SLT	Scots Law Times
SLULR	Saint Louis University Law Review
SSM	Social Science and Medicine
SW	Social Work
SWHS	Social Work & Human Sexuality
UNICEF	United Nations International Children's Fund
UNTS	United Nations Treaty Series
UPLR	University of Pennsylvania Law Review
SA	South Africa Reports
SLS	Social & Legal Studies
SMT	Sexual and Marital Therapy
VW	Violence against Women
WLR	Weekly Law Reports

Foreword

This book of essays celebrates ten years of the United Nations Convention on the Rights of the Child. If rapid and almost universal ratification of an international treaty is a measure of success, then the Convention deserves celebration. What international adherence shows is the acceptance that being a child is different from being an adult; that special protection is required. The Convention's task is to reflect that acceptance whilst leaving space for plural visions of childhood.

These essays examine sexual expressions of personality. They show that adults are uneasy about children as sexual persons. Adult constructions of childhood preclude acknowledgement that sexuality is part of personality throughout the lifecycle, including the period of childhood. Children are agents, do act, and sometimes in ways that upset adults' conceptions of childhood. Laws are made by adults and legal uneasiness about children's agency can be seen in legislation in which beneficence towards children in civil law jostles with criminal responsibility.

Claims about shared understandings of childhood must be treated cautiously. Comparative law studies record the constricted legal space of childhood in most if not all legal jurisdictions. Children's agency is largely denied. Treated as lacking legal capacity, children are defined as incompetent. Some writers suggest that it is as compensation that 'special rights' are accorded to children.

It is a truism that law cannot easily accommodate the continuum that growing from infancy to maturity entails. Some persons classified as children may be more mature than those classified as adults. But law requires some line between the two. English law tries to overcome this obstacle by setting different ages of competence for matters such as consenting to medical treatment, refusing medical treatment, driving, consent to heterosexual intercourse, consent to homosexual intercourse, voting in elections. Given the cultural confusion that underlies definitions of childhood in a single jurisdiction, perhaps we should accept, and even welcome, international diversity of interpretations. Historical studies show that adult views of children have changed in the past and may change again in the future.

In his introductory article Eric Heinze notes the critique that the Convention universalises culturally specific ideas about children. The child subject is transnational and yet nowhere to be found. Socio-scientific models created by adults influence contemporary Western legal concepts of childhood. The children subjects of the Convention do not speak for themselves. Adults make laws for the children they themselves once were and for the children to come. The love expressed in this law-making is also an expression of power. And that power operates on theories about childhood. Yet in the revisions of our narratives of our own childhoods, in our constructions of our identities, we already look back from an adult vantage point. Childhood is a country we once inhabited and now cannot find.

A consensus that the concept of childhood is constructed by adults is evident in these essays. From the certainties of Freudian and developmental or structural theories, we move to uncertainty. Once the variety of constructions created to house concepts of childhood is revealed, it is no longer clear what we should be building into our legal structures. Uncertainties stem from an awareness of the inaccessibility of what it means to be a child. Adult anxieties about children will always be based on falsifiable generalisations, because in these discourses children are 'the other'. If we mean to 'do good' for children within legal structures which separate them from adults, we are inevitably imprisoned in our own preconceptions and theories. Whether our claims about childhood are built on empiricism, on intuition, on developmental beliefs, or on our present revisions of our own biographies, the critiques of deconstruction level our edifices.

What then may be salvaged from the ruins of theories about childhood? Attempting to protect the vulnerable is surely worthwhile. International consensus that children are to be loved and respected, with their best interests dominating official decisions, opens a space for action. The Convention creates a place from which the analyses contained in these essays can speak. The critiques of these essays deepen our understandings of the limitations of law, particularly where universality is the goal. Some scholars resist the writing of a mythical legal subject, inevitably contained in the Convention. The fear is that the universal child traps all other children, denying their diversity and excluding those who cannot fit. Yet might not these fears also be based on subsequently falsifiable theories? Illusion and myths play their part in motivating human actions.

What then will follow after deconstruction? Will there be a retreat from writing subjects into law? If so, there will be a retreat from law-making. I foresee a return to genetic accounts of childhood, with claims to scientific certainty. A somewhat different universal child may take the place of the present inscription. Yet scientific theories are open to falsifiability, and will surely be subjected to critiques in their turn. Is this a counsel of passivity? Surely not. Our humanity demands that we express our concerns for children in our legal texts, however imperfect. We need, however, to be simultaneously aware of the provisionality of our theories. Above all, we must be open to hearing the voices of childhood.

Katherine O'Donovan
Queen Mary College, University of London
Spring 2000

Preface

Children, sex, human rights: three terms as uncertain in their meanings as they are controversial in their applications. *Surely* we know what childhood is — a time to learn and play until adulthood is reached. Yet views about the status and needs of children have been as varied as human societies themselves. To seek a constant concept of childhood within the vicissitudes of human culture and history is to seek something elusive indeed. *But surely* we know what sex is — a physical and emotional state that brings joy often, pain sometimes, and children frequently. Yet sex is one of the prime factors differentiating cultures and historical periods: if you want to know what makes the norms of one society different from those of another, the mores of one epoch different from those that have preceded or followed it, look at its sexual life. *But surely* we know what human rights are — those interests so fundamental that existence as a human being is unthinkable without them. Yet, while all societies have had their codes of justice, *ubi societas ubi jus*, the ideal of universal human rights in the form of legally enforceable entitlements held by individuals against the collectivity is historically recent and remains controversial.

A substantial legal literature now surrounds all three of these terms. Rare, however, is the legal scholarship that combines them. With family and social relationships in transformation, and increasing pressure on law to respond, these concepts will be intersecting with increasing frequency. Within the University of London, they first met at a conference held at Queen Mary and Westfield College in April 1998, as part of a series sponsored by the College's Programme on the International Rights of the Child. The contributions to that conference are gathered in this volume. While the purpose of a prefatory remark might ordinarily be to provide some unifying context for these contributions, such an effort would be futile. If anything unites the chapters, it is a sense of the diversity of approaches which must be considered if the law is to come to grips with childhood sexuality. I will not try to improve on it.

Acknowledgements are due in several quarters. Ongoing discussions with my colleagues Roger Cotterrell, Peter Fitzpatrick and Katherine O'Donovan have continued to stimulate my approach to the theoretical dimensions of human rights law, and, I hope, will continue to do so for many more years. A small grant provided by the Nuffield Foundation was of great value in funding research for Chapter One. Departmental funding, provided by the Law Faculty of Queen Mary and Westfield College, was helpful in facilitating completion of the project, which was sponsored by the Programme on the International Rights of the Child, under the direction of Geraldine Van Bueren. I would also like to thank Bob Burns and Eilis Rafferty of the College's library for their research support, and Brian Littlechild of the College's Computer Services Department, for solving every technical problem that could have arisen. Above all, I would like to express my warmest appreciation to Penny Stockwell of the Law Department for her able assistance in organising the conference and preparing the chapter submissions for publication.

Eric Heinze
Queen Mary and Westfield College, University of London
Autumn 1999

Series Preface

The concept of international children's rights has come of age, and the Programme on International Rights of the Child Series is the first series of volumes dedicated to exploring specific aspects of international children's rights. The series comprises both sole authored and edited volumes, and single disciplinary and multi-disciplinary monographs, all considering issues which are at the rapidly expanding boundaries of international children's rights.

Geraldine Van Bueren, Series Editor
Programme on International Rights of the Child
Queen Mary and Westfield College, University of London

Part I

Constructing Childhood:
Theory and History

1 The Universal Child?*

ERIC HEINZE

Introduction

To universalise children's rights is to universalise a culturally specific idea of childhood. Contemporary children's rights movements are the product of models of childhood proliferated through Western social science, itself the product of post-Enlightenment views of personality and society. These models have become instruments of a dual process of globalisation: they form the basis of a growing children's rights regime at the international level, which, in turn, reflects increasing domestic practice within multicultural societies. Lawmakers and activists have a knack for plucking from the social sciences the models that best suit their arguments, while ignoring those models' historical genesis and consequent intellectual limits. If conflicting models are of little significance in the campaign to end gross forms of child abuse, malnutrition, slavery or disease, they nevertheless acquire a key role in efforts to solve the morally textured problems of sexuality.

Starting with some characteristic assumptions about childhood embodied in leading international human rights instruments, this chapter examines a sampling of socio-scientific models which have influenced contemporary concepts of childhood. It does not offer an exhaustive review; that would be a work of volumes. Nor does it embrace any model of its own; that would suggest finality to a process that has barely begun. Instead, it considers some representative 'snapshots' from 20th century social science,

* Thanks are due to the Nuffield Foundation for having generously provided a small grant, and, in particular, to Ms. Louie Burghes, for her constant support in administering the funds. Roger Cotterrell, Peter Fitzpatrick and Katherine O'Donovan offered valuable criticisms on an earlier draft. Mark Napier contributed exceptional research skills throughout the duration of the project. Also of great benefit was the research assistance of Josefin Bengtsson, Mark Kelly, Jo King, Jennie Roberts and Nicky Winstanley-Torode. At an earlier stage of the research, scholarly support was also provided by Michael Caswell, whose untimely death came as a great shock. It is to him that this chapter is dedicated.

with a view towards their relevance to the political processes which shape law and policy governing child sexuality.

The Global Child

By the time of the UN General Assembly's adoption of the Universal Declaration of Human Rights (UDHR) in 1948,[1] human rights instruments were not new to the international community.[2] The Universal Declaration nevertheless represented the first major step within international law towards a comprehensive catalogue of individual rights. With the translation of the Universal Declaration into two binding Covenants[3] — the International Covenant on Civil and Political Rights (ICCPR)[4] and the International Covenant on Economic, Social and Cultural Rights (ICESCR)[5] — one might have expected the norm-creating task of the international community to have been completed.[6] The remaining work would consist of urging States to respect and promote these three instruments (commonly known as the 'International Bill of Rights'[7]) in practice.

Yet it is the opposite that has occurred. The notion that the interests of all human beings could be formulated within three instruments spanning but a few dozen pages has continued to spark controversy about the adequacy, inclusiveness and cultural assumptions of the International Bill of Rights. Subsequent developments have sought to move away from the high level of generality of these three founding instruments, towards increasing attention to human differences. In the same year as the adoption of the ICCPR and ICESCR, the United Nations General Assembly also approved the International Convention on the Elimination of All Forms of Racial Discrimination (CERD).[8] Since that time, pressures to recognise other more specific human rights issues have increased. Women,[9] minorities,[10] indigenous peoples,[11] the disabled,[12] or workers[13] have all been subjects of international instruments. Despite continued affirmation of the universality of the three founding documents,[14] it is no exaggeration to say that one is not a fully recognised beneficiary of human rights until one is a member of some subset of humanity that can boast an instrument 'of its own.' To receive such an instrument is to be recognised as bearing an identity sufficiently distinct to entail specific normative consequences[15] — which may explain why even those, such as indigenous peoples, who might be expected to challenge the legitimacy of State-centred intergovernmental organisations, have nevertheless solicited those organisations for the promulgation of instruments representing their interests.[16]

Children have been the subject of numerous instruments. A first Declaration of the Rights of the Child (DRC 1924) was promulgated within the League of Nations,[17] and a host of instruments have followed. What, then, is the distinctive character of children which justifies or requires a separate set of international instruments? What special identity do these instruments attribute to children? Article 1 of the Convention on the Rights of the Child (CRC) defines children in exclusively chronological terms: 'a child means every human being below the age of eighteen years unless . . . majority is attained earlier.'[18] That definition, however, only begs the question as to what makes persons under the age of 18 different. The treaty's very existence assumes that these individuals are sufficiently distinctive to warrant a separate regime.[19] The 1959 Declaration on the Rights of the Child (DRC 1959) had noted children's needs for 'special safeguards,'[20] and the CRC proclaims that protection and assistance must be afforded to all members of society, but 'particularly children.'[21] And it is not only instruments specific to children which assume children's distinctiveness. The Universal Declaration provides that 'childhood [is] entitled to special care and assistance.'[22] The ICCPR permits States Parties to impose the death penalty, except upon persons under the age of eighteen.[23]

At first glance, the DRC 1924, consisting of only five brief articles, suggests significant differences from the more recent instruments. Certainly, as a non-binding instrument, it was intended only to proclaim aspirations rather than to confer rights.[24] Yet even within that more limited, hortatory mandate, it does not set individual rights as a goal, even for the long term.[25] Despite its titular reference to rights, its language alludes to children's moral deserts, not to their legal entitlements. Its terse preambular paragraph states that 'mankind owes to the child the best it has to give,' and not that children should have affirmative rights *vis-à-vis* the States, communities or families in which they live. Article 1 emphasises children's needs; article 3 notes that children should 'be the first to receive relief in times of distress.' In poetic, quasi-religious terms, article 2 provides that:

> The child that is hungry must be fed, the child that is sick must be helped; the child that is backward must be helped; the delinquent child must be reclaimed; and the orphan and the waif must be sheltered and succoured.

While omitting any enumeration of rights, the Declaration sets the stage for a legal regime that will be defined by children's biological, psychological and emotional distinctiveness. Such views did not enter law by chance. They coincide with socio-scientific movements brimming with theories of childhood. How persuasively, then, do those theories actually support the concepts of childhood accepted not only in international law, but, increasingly, in domestic regimes?

The Essentialised Child

Some universals appear to be dictated by common sense. Human infants enter the world with bodies and emotions different from those of adults. They must be fed and clothed; they command neither language nor other accoutrements of the Aristotelian social animal. These differences alone appear to represent objective indicia of a distinctive phase of human existence. The diverse cultural manifestations of childhood might thus be construed as sheer derivatives of this finite set of physiological and psychological constraints.

Such a view is commonly associated with early psychoanalytic and developmental approaches to childhood. Freud's schema of psychosexual development, for example, still stands as a landmark of early socio-scientific attempts to formulate a schematic progression of 'stages' inherent to child development,[26] independent of social factors. The child's passage from 'oral' to 'anal' to 'genital' stages of development are elaborated in general terms, with no attention to cultural variation.[27] Indeed, Freud's allusion to Greek antiquity in the Oedipus complex[28] serves not as a cultural limitation on the theory's (Western) reach, but rather to reinforce a sense of the theory's universality.[29]

Different assumptions, but also for purposes of producing a generalised model, are adopted by Jean Piaget.[30] For Piaget, too, children develop by traversing a series of stages. Progression to a new stage depends upon successful completion of the preceding one. Each completion is a positive achievement.[31] The overall structure of these stages is universally shared.[32] Piaget does not correlate these stages to narrowly defined age groups (although he does offer general averages). Their sequence, however, is invariable. (The only significant variation, apart from flexibility in age-correlation, is that some adults will fail to attain the highest stage, thus persisting in states of arrested development.) Emotional and mental maturity are goal posts guiding child development teleologically. Each developmental stage is successfully completed when the child has learned to function in the manner appropriate to that stage. Childhood is an apprenticeship; adulthood is its logical conclusion. Child development is a process of 'successive equilibrations of cognitive structures, each structure and its concomitant equilibrium state *deriving logically and inevitably* from the preceding one.'[33]

While Freud and Piaget focus upon psychological development, sociobiologists espouse a more physiologically determined progression, emphasising genetic predispositions and concomitant adoptive behaviours. Linda Pollock, for example, proposes a socio-biological model of child rearing: the surface cultural and historical diversity of child-rearing practices can be seen as manifestations of fixed, underlying similarities, dictated by the biological imperative of survival of the human species. For Pollock, *homo sapiens* is a 'K-selected species.' It produces few offspring, but invests commensurately more time, effort and resources in that offspring, through, for example, the latter's longer gestation period, prolonged post-natal care, or extended immaturity.[34] K-selected species actively care for their offspring in order to maximise their chances of survival: 'there is no reason to assume that parental care must vary according to developments and changes in society as a whole .... [Cultural differences] should be investigated against this background of continuity.'[35] Childhood is a stage of physical immaturity and dependence: '[t]o adults all over the world, children represent something helpless and weak, something to be protected, supervised and trained and also something which is a valuable asset to their society.'[36] Appealing to a universal sense of childhood, Pollock stresses shared, constant elements of human development.

Much more could be said about these three, and other, essentialist schools. Such summary treatment is not meant to be dismissive, but rather to keep our eye on a common problem arising once such models are confronted by concepts of rights — in particular, by an internationalised regime purporting to define a subset of humanity called 'children.' The concept of international children's rights runs into an impasse when confronted with these essentialist approaches. On the one hand, its purportedly multicultural orientation should be instinctively suspicious about absolutist tendencies — indeed, these three models have not exercised much direct influence in the international children's rights movement. On the other hand, how can the international children's rights movement, or domestic movements in multicultural societies, dismiss these models *precisely because of their essentialism*, while maintaining their own universalised concepts of the distinctiveness of childhood, a concept without which such specific regimes of children's rights would make no sense? The international children's rights movement may indeed reject essentialist socio-scientific models. To do so on behalf of children's rights, however, is to do so in the name of a regime which, by definition, has already universalised a concept of childhood.

The Socialised Child

Essentialist models do not dismiss culture. Cultural influences are, however, inevitably relegated to derivative positions. The Freudian superego, while assimilating social processes into the architecture of the individual psyche, never enjoys the primacy of the unconscious. It is above all the latter which the analyst is after in the work of deciphering neuroses, dreams, 'everyday' pathologies (*Fehlleistungen*), and indeed cultural productions such as religion, literature and art. Freud's later work *Das Unbehagen in der Kultur* elevates society to a kind of equal partner with the unconscious, transforming the primacy of the latter into a dialectic between the two.[37]   That shift, however, does not entail a re-evaluation of the fundamental assumptions in classical psychoanalysis of an essential, universal psychic apparatus. It was for sociology and anthropology to bring society and culture into the foreground. While the hierarchy in the relationship between the superego, the ego and the unconscious, would remain open to challenge, Freud's idea of an inevitable, irresolvable tension between the individual and society, as a basis for defining human behaviour, proved influential in theories about child socialisation.

Sociologists sought to be able to explain how it was that disparate individuals could come together to bond into something that was intelligible as society. Ideas of *socialisation* emerged, pointing to a system which led to the regularisation of the desires of participants in society so that they came to embrace common norms and customs.[38]   In 1956 Talcott Parsons defined socialisation as 'the internalisation of the culture of the society into which the child is born.'[39]   In 1978 Frederick Elkin and Gerald Handel characterised it as 'the process by which we learn the ways of a given society or social group so that we can function within it.'[40]   While not dismissing the possibility of biological or innate psychological components of behaviour, these approaches would again consider patterns of development in children, but now with an emphasis on environmental determinants. The family, already occupying centre stage in Freud's work as a fixed background within which individual psychic processes would go to work, would now become a set of active, and thus variable, agents in child development. Early models of socialisation commonly emphasised the parents as primary agents of socialisation, imbuing their offspring with cultural knowledge in much the same way that they give physical sustenance. The family now came to be seen as the primary locus of socialisation, with the mother as the pre-eminent socialiser within this unit.

Parsons depicts the family as the crucible within which the proto-adult is formed. The family is not merely a distinct force in socialisation, acting in tandem with others. It is the socialisation unit *par excellence*. Socialisation counts among the family's 'basic and irreducible functions'; the family is a factory for the production of personality.[41] Parsons situates socialisation at the same point at which physical intervention and nurturing take place. The family, seeking to ensure the welfare of the child, provides shelter and sustenance, but, in so doing, also provides the example by which the child will learn its social role. The parents have already internalised community norms, and thus reproduce them within the child.[42] Yet the naturalist, biological orientation of this model of socialisation is emphasised, for example, by the clearly delineated gender roles that are assumed to exist within the family. Parsons argues that the family unit requires gender distinctions: it is natural for a male leader of the family to develop, and for the female to adapt her role accordingly. Through her nurturing function, the mother acquires the 'expressive' role.[43] Culture, as a phenomenon of socialisation, is thus taken into account, yet in a naturalised form.

Margaret Mead's 1950 analysis of the American family takes a similar approach. It is within the family, and above all through the parents, that children learn behaviour. Crucial to that process is the transmission of gender roles. The young boy learns male conduct through rough-and-tumble play, reinforced by his parents:

> [F]rom his father he learns that relationships with men require putting forth all your strength, taking buffets good-humoredly, getting in and pitching in, small as you are — and that this is fun. Both father and mother demand that he should act up to — and a little beyond — his full strength, and he is always a little anxious for fear the strength that is demanded isn't there.[44]

Through the rewards of the mother for his physical prowess, the boy learns the way in which he will interact with his future wife. In the same way, daughters are taught to be gentle and demure. The father's tendency to indulge his daughter sows the seeds of the daughter's conflicts with the mother in adolescence.[45]

Of course, Mead had come to prominence largely through her studies of non-Western societies. She showed how non-nuclear family structures required less emphasis on the primacy of (biological-)parental influence. Child-rearing, she noted, is shared within the community as a whole. It is through 'group activities [that] the normal group standards assert themselves.'[46] Nevertheless, a similar model of socialisation-through-transmission is at work. Mead describes the Arapesh peoples, for example, as being passive due to being highly coddled as children and from being breast-fed even when not demanding food. By contrast, the Iatmul people, who as babies must fight for attention, are described as being more assertive.[47] Danziger notes the influence of Freudian theory on the early theories of socialisation and the tendency that this produced to stress infant processes, such as weaning and toilet training, as in Mead's work, or to focus sharply on the family unit, as in Mead's or Parsons's studies of American culture.[48] More recent socialisation theory has introduced such factors as the media, schooling and peer groups.[49]

The early socialisation models share a notion of childhood as a training ground for adulthood. Children serve out an apprenticeship, internalising the mores of society, rehearsing them until their performance is sufficient for them to be deemed an adult. Children's experiences and activities are meaningful only in relation to adult values. Adults have *attained* their position; they are functional members of society. The onus is then upon children to achieve this standard. This role of adulthood as *telos* retains the 'stages' of the essentialist theories of Freud and Piaget. The child remains a passive receptacle: activity is confined to channels of successful progression towards adulthood. Children do not actively create their world. They develop within a pre-existing world.[50] Initiative on the child's part, not to mention resistance or revolt, occurs only *within* the developmental framework, and not as a creative challenge *to* it.[51]

More recent socialisation theory has criticised constructs of an essentially passive child, arguing that children do not merely copy adult practices, but formatively and constitutively engage with them (we will return to this point). If the child is indeed an active, constitutive agent, however, the question then arises as to whether the very concept of socialisation can be retained as an accurate characterisation of childhood. Socialisation still means socialisation from the child's world into the adult world. The child's social world remains a sheer rehearsal: when children play doctors and nurses, they are emulating grown-ups rather than embarking on an enterprise with a non-mimetic significance of its own.

The early socialisation models bore direct consequences for law and policy. Unlike innate capacities, environmental influences could be modified. Society carried an affirmative burden to create means for improving children's prospects for satisfactory socialisation, as well as means of dealing with those whose socialisation was unsuccessful — who were, so to speak, deviant. School, in particular, would become a site for reform. The role of the school could no longer be seen as only, or even primarily, educational. It inculcated grammar and arithmetic, but also social values. Jo Boyden characterises schools in Western societies as entrusted with the pre-eminent task of initiating children into the practices of capitalism. The process of increasing industrialisation had 'highlighted the need to foster socially responsible and economically useful individuals to supply a skilled and differentiated labour force . . . . Schools then became a training ground for industrial workers and a place for containing childhood.' Schooling would ensure new generations of consumers and labourers.[52]

The primary responsibility of the State for the socialisation of children through its institutions has emerged as a hallmark of contemporary approaches to child welfare, and certainly has left its mark in the area of children's rights. (The Convention on the Rights of the Child, as a treaty, is by definition State-centred; and even non-biding instruments inevitably emphasise State obligations and programmes.) In addition to schools, institutions such as medical facilities, social welfare agencies, or correctional establishments are expected to carry out programmes of socialisation. Article 5(d) of the European Convention of Human Rights, for example, provides for the detention of juveniles, but 'for the purpose of educational supervision'[53] — a modernist ambition of Foucauldian proportions. The Court has noted the positive obligations that may arise for States under the Convention, in order to assure the promotion of 'normal family life.'[54] (Positive obligations may also arise in such areas as placement of children in psychiatric care[55] or the power of the state to take children into custody.[56])

Socialisation models are conspicuously tailored to the capacities and limits of the contemporary administrative State. The bureaucratic State is designed to implement generalised, standardised, 'macro' *programmes* for classes of individuals. It is not designed to interact with individual experiences. Childhood is a programme of the contemporary State. Yet the same socialisation models by which States have promulgated children's rights regimes can be invoked to deny children's rights: if the State holds primary responsibility for successful socialisation, a process which remains incomplete until adulthood, then children can be seen as not yet having acceded to that full participation in society which is the classical prerequisite of status as a rights holder. Children do not bear full responsibilities, and thus cannot bear full rights.[57] Even the most progressive children's rights instruments do not entirely eschew an image of the still-imperfect, unfolding and developing character of the child and of the child's correlative legal interests.[58] CRC article 5 provides,

> States Parties shall respect the responsibilities, rights and duties of parents or, where applicable, the members of the extended family or community as provided for by local custom, legal guardians or other persons legally responsible for the child, to provide, in a manner consistent with the evolving capacities of the child, appropriate direction and guidance in the exercise by the child of the rights recognized in the present Convention.

While this provision has not been viewed as an open-ended license to limit children's rights, it accepts that children can exercise rights only to the extent of their 'evolving capacities.' [59]

The Constructed Child

While law was increasingly adopting socialisation models of childhood, social science was moving on. By 1960 Philippe Ariès had already published his landmark *L'Enfant et la vie familiale sous l'Ancien Régime*.[60] For Ariès, childhood was not a natural phase, but a product of history, a social construction. Drawing upon a range of sources, including art, dress, pastimes, social activities and schooling practices, Ariès argued that the middle ages lacked any significant or detailed concept of childhood.[61] As soon as children were not absolutely dependent on adults, they moved into the adult realm. Children's dress was the same as adults', with no notion of specialised dress appearing until the 18th century. Children participated in festivals and social gatherings alongside adults. No effort was made to create a separate and distinct world for children insulated from the adult world. '[C]hildhood was a period of transition which passed quickly and which was just as quickly forgotten.'[62] What had long been held to be a natural fact of human development was, for Ariès, a modernist invention. The great preoccupation with childhood, the lavishing of care and attention, the investment in children of all our fears and hopes, are modern developments, not universal constants. Through the combined efforts of moralists and pedagogues, along with demographic and economic shifts and decreasing infant mortality, 'the child' of modern Europe was born.[63]

Ariès inspired subsequent scholarship, including the work of Lawrence Stone, Lloyd de Mause and Edward Shorter. Shorter argued that maternity had not inevitably involved a sense of children as being 'human beings with the same capacities for joy and pain as themselves.'[64] 'Good mothering is an invention of modernisation.'[65] For Stone, parental perceptions of children varied according to class:

The key to the story of the evolution of child-rearing is the principle of stratified diffusion, by which new attitudes first take hold among those classes which are most literate and most open to new ideas; and which are neither so very poor that economic circumstances often compel them to neglect, exploit or abandon their children; nor so very rich that their social and political life is too time-consuming to allow them to devote much time or trouble to child-rearing, and whose enormous economic assets encourage them to compel their children to marry persons selected for them on strictly economic or political grounds.[66]

De Mause takes an even more strident tone: 'The history of childhood is a nightmare from which we have only recently begun to awaken. The further back in history one goes, the lower the level of child care, and the more likely children are to be killed, abandoned, beaten, terrorised, and sexually abused.'[67] De Mause adopts a 'psychogenic' theory of history, which he characterises as the analysis of history in which personality change is the primary dynamic factor in human history, rather than the political, economic or social factors generally associated with historical analysis.[68] He argues that the history of childhood has been marked by the gradual development of parental empathy. Parents gradually developed the emotional maturity necessary to see children as individuals. It is this emotional maturity that has led to the modern concept of childhood.[69]

Ariès and his followers have not been without their critics.[70] *L'Enfant et la vie familiale* has been criticised for anachronism or 'presentism': from the premise that the *modern* concept of childhood was not current in earlier times, it does not follow that *no* concept of childhood existed at those times. David Nicholas writes that 'no medievalist still takes seriously [the] idea that people before the modern period had no notion of childhood as a distinct period of human development.'[71] Ariès is also criticised for relying on incomplete evidence. Sherrin Marshall argues that the historical scope of Ariès's work can lead only to tentative conclusions because there is insufficient evidence, and virtually none from children themselves.[72] While Ariès succeeds in relativising a particular concept of childhood, it would be implausible to take the further step of suggesting that medieval Europeans (or anyone else) would simply have had no awareness of differences between children as such and adults. Ariès's success in relativising the modernist discourse of childhood nevertheless remains significant for our purposes, as it is the post-Enlightenment, social scientific discourse of childhood that he relativises. That discourse cannot be seen merely as the savant articulation of intuitive understandings of childhood shared in all places and at all times. It is an active construction of a culturally specific version of childhood.

It is not only historical analysis in the spirit of Ariès or Foucault which announces the deconstruction of the post-Enlightenment child. Similar conclusions were to be anticipated from anthropology, indeed rather early on. From Mead's observation of differences in patterns of socialisation, the implication of correlative differences in concepts of childhood did not require a great logical leap. On the basis of her studies of child-rearing in Samoa, for example, she had argued that the emotional turbulence associated with adolescence in contemporary Western culture is not inevitable; it is not fixed by underlying biological or cultural laws. In demonstrating this point she aimed to support Franz Boas's idea that environment was a key factor in producing character:[73] 'the social stimulus is infinitely more potent than the biological mechanism.'[74] While working within a socialisation paradigm, she was setting the stage for later anthropologists' acceptance of the view that childhood is socially constructed.[75]   Today, it is widely accepted that '[c]hildhood, as distinct from biological immaturity, is neither a natural nor universal feature of human groups but appears as a specific structural and cultural component of many societies.'[76]

If the reification of childhood presupposed by contemporary law and policy raises difficulties, it is not through the postulation of childhood as such, but rather because any suggestion of a sufficiently fixed concept of childhood can suggest equally fixed sets of values and norms. Is it possible to preserve the concept of childhood, to retain the universal child, without definitively stipulating what that child may and may not be and become? Can the formalism and finality of law make way for a plasticity and heterogeneity of models?   Having assimilated socio-scientific models of childhood, law cannot ignore socio-scientific re-assessments of those models. Boyden insists that Northern concepts are gaining a global hegemony. She argues that ideals of children's sanctity and purity, of the 'safe, happy and protected child,' are the product of Judaeo-Christian beliefs merged with demographic trends that accompanied the rise of capitalism, and are thus 'culturally and historically bound to the social preoccupations and priorities of the capitalist countries of Europe and the United States.'[77] As definitions of what is acceptable become narrower, reactions to lifestyles that differ become harsher, leading even to the criminalisation of certain working class practices.[78]   Child-rearing practices that stray from the dominant Western norms become seen as harmful to children and as retarding normal development. Child street workers are treated as anti-social vagrants and are penalised as such. Of course, the children's rights movement invariably condemns such treatment. On Boyden's view, however, it is only, then, reacting to the consequences of its own assumptions of childhood purity. What begins as a seemingly benign concern for the welfare of children and the belief in their innate purity has the potential to be transformed into stringent policies that have the effect of negatively interfering in children's lives.[79]

The Contextual Child

Syntheses and correctives of earlier socio-scientific approaches have led to models of childhood which draw upon broader and more fluid sets of variables — geographic, economic, psychodynamic, including class, gender and race, and including children's own active, constitutive shaping of their world.[80] This greater number of variables means less certainty of result. As tidy models and schemes fade, childhood becomes childhoods· the concept is simultaneously retained and exploded. The problem is neither that the concept is unduly static, nor that it does not exist at all, but rather that it never can be grasped in one comprehensive gaze. Childhood is undermined by children, who, in so doing, do not destroy it, but reaffirm their *own* childhood. There is indeed a universal child, but that child can never be known. The multiplicity of childhoods does not guide us progressively towards the eternal, Platonic idea of the Child; the concept of the Child, however, can guide us towards the multiplicity of childhoods.

Martin Woodhead has applied social constructionism to concepts of children's needs, which, he argues, flow from 'a complex of latent assumptions and judgements about children.'[81] The uses to which the ostensibly neutral and benign idea of needs are put tells us as much about 'the cultural location and personal values of the user' as about childhood itself.[82] The concept of needs attributes an absolute quality to any given trait, rather than allowing it to be seen as merely desirable or advantageous. It implies that something is empirically verifiable, having a universal and innate quality rather than merely being culturally favoured.[83] Woodhead notes four types of needs. Of these, only one type can be called absolute in character, namely the kind of need which is immediately required for survival, such as the need for food or shelter. This category of 'the needs in children's nature' is not drawn over-narrowly; Woodhead includes, for example, the need for emotional nurturing and the need to seek out human relationships. Even here, however, he argues that there is no fixed way in which such needs can be met.

Two further categories are more clearly culturally determined. Under a category of 'needs and social adjustment,' Woodhead locates traits depicted in universal terms but which are culturally specific. These include the notion that children are predisposed to create a primary attachment to one major figure, in particular the mother. This assumption is based upon prevalent Western norms, as other cultures display different patterns of child-rearing and hence of child attachments.[84] Another category includes needs associated with psychological health. These, Woodhead argues, emanate not from within the child, but rather from judgements about future mental health and social adjustment.[85] A final category is even further removed from the idea of innate needs, yet still tends to be described in terms that imply innate necessity. These fall under the heading of 'cultural prescriptions,' and include professionalised assessments of children, representing the 'value-position' of adults projected onto children, including the need for imaginative play and the need to communicate through music.[86] By demoting such cultural desiderata from the status of needs, Woodhead is not perforce condemning them or seeking to remove them from the ambit of law and policy. Rather, on his view, a more critical use of the concept of need, a franker admission of its cultural contingency, can actually liberate the ways in which more culturally specific values are applied, particularly in global and multicultural contexts.

In a framework of more fluid and tentative models, the factor of child agency comes more prominently to the fore. Earlier essentialist and socialisation models, in Danziger's view, had failed to account for the child's capacity to distinguish, and to make constitutive choices among, the situations they encounter.[87] More recent models analyse society and social practices in terms of children's own interpretations of and interactions with them. Play, for example, has been studied not in terms of developmental models, but in terms of its meanings for the participants themselves. Play situates children as actors in complex social worlds governed by their own meaning and legitimacy, quasi-autonomous of adult norms. One early study by Iona and Peter Opie, *The Lore and Language of Schoolchildren*, had examined children's rituals in terms of the ways in which children made sense of their surroundings. It concluded that 'the scraps of lore which children learn from each other are at once more real, more immediately serviceable and more vastly entertaining than anything they learn from grown-ups.'[88] Other important practices included verses which are intended for consumption solely by peers, or an inherited folk wisdom generated by children among themselves (including, for example, mystical lore). Traditional developmental models construed such phenomena as crude imitations of adult practices — incorrectly rendered, but providing starting points for subsequent progression towards the polish of adult performance. The Opie study, by contrast, stressed the ways in which children make intelligible the social structures and conventions which surround them. Through this approach, children could be said to inhabit a quasi-autonomous 'minority' culture which is both transient (as its members soon move on) yet permanent and resilient to change. Such is the tenacity and vibrancy of this culture that the Opies observe that younger schoolchildren take the rites of older children more seriously than the practices of adults and parents.[89]

The Opie study has exercised considerable influence on recent theory. In one study, Paul Connolly examines masculine identity among British school boys raised in a working class, high unemployment, inner-city area. He observes the reactions of teaching staff to a group that was designated as being the 'bad boys.' Teachers viewed the boys as stubborn, aggressive and moody, and, in an effort to assert their own authority, singled out the boys for discipline. Such attitudes reinforced teachers' and other pupils' perceptions that the boys were disobedient and recalcitrant. The 'bad boys' were often challenged by their male peers and forced into fights with them, further entrenching their negative image. The boys had assimilated the labels they had been given, translating them into a distinct, virile, defiant masculine identity. They had become simultaneously victims and architects of their social roles. External pressures and stimuli were actively interpreted, assimilated and acted upon by the children.[90]

The Opies had noted that children use charms and talismans in an effort to appease an irrational world.[91] Traditional developmental models would depict such practices in terms of children's not-yet-complete development — as a retreat into superstition spurred by their inability to appreciate the complexity of events around them. In contrast, an interactionist model declines to define the phenomenon in fundamentally teleological terms. Developmental teleology condemns children to a perpetual twilight zone in which their conduct can never be understood as anything other than developmentally adaptive, hence correct, or developmentally defective, hence incorrect. Connolly, however, refuses to define children in terms of what they lack.[92] Childhood is not incomplete adulthood. It is a set of experiences neither more nor less internally coherent than those of adults.

The drafting and interpretation of law and policy have, no doubt, revealed increased attention to models of interactive, constitutive, contextualised children. But what are the consequences of these models for the legal regulation of child sexuality?

The Sexual Child

The sentimentalised, Victorian image casts childhood as a period of innocence and sexual ignorance. Childhood purity is extended as long as possible. The child/adult distinction is crucially a distinction between sexlessness and sexuality. Sexual knowledge pollutes childhood innocence, shoving children into the realm of adults before they are able to cope.[93] Such attitudes presuppose a developmental view: sexuality is an accomplishment of maturity. It is the preserve of the adult world; the knowing child is unnecessarily, even dangerously precocious.[94]

More recent research has challenged these attitudes. Developmental models assumed sexuality as a constant drive innate to all people, manifested in a variety of fashions, but innate to our psychological makeup.[95] Social constructionism, however, views sexuality as culturally acquired: 'what is sexual in one context may not be so in another: an experience becomes sexual by application of socially learned meanings. Our heads, it has been said, are our most erogenous zone.'[96] Caplan notes that ideas of sexuality are commonly conflated with ideas of gender, each gender possessing a natural sexuality. She argues that research should more carefully distinguish between ideas of sexuality and gender in order to understand how physiological sex relates to the culturally learned gender.[97] Allison James examines relationships between gender and sexuality in a variety of cultures in order to demonstrate that accepted male/female dichotomies as defined in the West are not universal. She notes that other peoples have accepted interchangeability in gender, or ideas of a third gender, in ways now uncommon in the West.[98] The constructed quality of sexuality and gender suggest that childhood is neither naturally asexual, nor naturally gendered. Theories of childhood agency allow us to understand children as active in the development of their sexuality.

Even in the world of adult sexuality, questions about how sex should be regulated and how the incidents and consequences of sexual activity — sexual health care, contraception, abortion — should be managed, have faced dramatic challenges in recent years. Where children are concerned, these controversies reach their peak. In areas concerning, for example, sexual orientation[99] or gender dysphoria,[100] the willingness of lawmakers and courts to revise earlier assumptions about children's welfare and autonomy has emerged only recently, with great caution, against the broader, global backdrop of ongoing diversity of cultural attitudes. Female genital circumcision and infibulation provide an important example. These practices have been compared to the most extreme forms of torture in their physiological and psychological effects. Demands to outlaw them, however, have met with reluctance among those same States which actively seek international intervention in other areas of health care. The strategic human rights activist (or supervisory body) will invariably frame the problem as an issue of children's physical integrity, psychological integrity, even gender integrity, but never as an issue of sexual integrity.[101] Ideals of physical integrity are widely accepted; and ideals of psychological and women's integrity, increasingly so. The ideal of sexual integrity, however, remains taboo.

As a number of contributors to this volume examine *Gillick v. West Norfolk and Wisbech AHA*[102] as a benchmark of recent law and policy in Western Europe, a brief mention of the case, in terms of the issues thus far raised, is instructive. This case, concerning the right of children to seek contraceptive advice and treatment, illustrates a conflict between two competing ideas of childhood. It was brought by a mother seeking to determine the scope of her parental rights over her children, and the extent to which she had to be consulted on matters relating to her children while they were still minors. A memorandum of the Department of Health and Social Security had instructed doctors that in exceptional circumstances it was permissible to give contraceptive advice and treatment to girls under the age of sixteen without parental permission. Mrs Gillick argued that such guidelines unlawfully superseded her rights as a parent, thus advocating the primacy of parental authority. In the House of Lords, it was determined that the agency of the child was crucial to the rights of the concerned parties, and that the child had a central role in deciding what courses of action were most appropriate. Lord Justice Frasier wrote,

> It is, in my view, contrary to the ordinary experience of mankind, at least in Western Europe in the present century, to say that a child or a young person remains in fact under the complete control of his parents until he attains a definite age of majority ... and that on attaining that age he suddenly acquires independence .... [T]he degree of parental control actually

exercised over a particular child does in practice vary considerably according to his understanding and intelligence.[103]

While advocating a cautious recognition of the right of the child which relies on a test of competency, Lord Scarman emphasised the fact that children can be fully capable of determining the point at which they are sexually mature.[104] This ruling takes a step towards broader acceptance of childhood agency, but does not entirely confirm the children's constitutive role in shaping their social world. While the Lords maintain a socialisation-based view that the child is evolving towards the rationality and judgement capacity of adulthood, they acknowledge that children are capable of independent decision-making and of appreciating the personal and social consequences of their decisions.   The complexity and controversy surrounding such a judgment within the limited context of the United Kingdom[105] augurs the multiplication of obstacles that will confront the regulation of child sexuality in international and cross-cultural perspective.

Conclusion

Law is stability, constancy, predictability.   Human rights, for all their progressive aspirations, become assimilated to that tendency from the moment they become law. For many rights, that is no bad thing: stability, constancy and predictability in the extinction of genocide, torture or starvation would be most welcome. In areas of sexuality and childhood, however, law and human rights, with their vast, State-centred, programmatic ambitions, cannot proceed with such certainty. Having drawn upon post-Enlightenment socio-scientific models of childhood in the regulation of sexuality, law cannot now overlook substantial socio-scientific re-assessments of those models. The universal child is a contextual being.

Notes

[1] UNGA res. 217A (III), UN Doc. A/810 at 71, arts. 25, 26 (1948).
[2] See, e.g., H. Steiner & P. Alston, *International Human Rights in Context* 59-116 (1996).
[3] Not all instruments adopted by international organisations or conferences are intended to have legal force. Many are adopted merely as expressions of a consensus achieved for purposes of addressing a problem of international concern, perhaps with

an eye towards the drafting of a binding instrument at a later stage. Regardless of whether a binding instrument is subsequently adopted, some non-binding instruments have come to acquire authoritative status, particularly in the area of human rights, and may come to be recognised as statements of customary international law. The most remarkable example is the Universal Declaration. Few instruments adopted in expressly non-binding form have enjoyed such widespread recognition as a statement of universally binding law. See, e.g., *id.* at 132-147.

[4] 999 UNTS 171 (*entered into force*, 23 Mar. 1976).

[5] 993 UNTS 3 (*entered into force*, 3 Jan. 1976).

[6] On the genesis of these three instruments, see Steiner & Alston, note 2 *supra*, at ch. 3.

[7] See *id.* at 117.

[8] 660 UNTS 195 (*entered into force*, 4 Jan. 1969). The reasons for this step cannot be found in anything qualitatively different about the norms themselves. While CERD certainly contemplates the consequences of racial discrimination in greater detail — perhaps a sufficient purpose for a separate instrument — it in no way articulates qualitatively different kinds of rights or norms. It does not, for example, adopt group rights. It rigorously maintains an individualist, integrationist, equal protection ideal. See E. Heinze, 'The Construction and Contingency of the Minority Concept,' in *Minority and Group Rights in the New Millennium* 25 (D. Fottrell & B. Bowring, eds., 1999).

[9] See, e.g., Convention on the Elimination of all Forms of Discrimination against Women, 1249 UNTS 13 (*entered into force*, 3 September 1981).

[10] See, e.g., Declaration on the Rights of Persons Belonging to National or Ethnic, Religious or Linguistic Minorities, GA res. 47/135, annex, 47 UN GAOR Supp. (No. 49) at 210, UN Doc. A/47/49 (1993).

[11] See, e.g., Convention concerning Indigenous and Tribal Peoples in Independent Countries (ILO No. 169), 72 ILO OB 59 (*entered into force*, 5 Sep. 1991).

[12] See, e.g., Declaration on the Rights of Disabled Persons, GA res. 3447 (XXX), 30 UN GAOR Supp. (No. 34) at 88, UN Doc. A/10034 (1975).

[13] See, e.g., Employment Policy Convention (ILO No. 122), 569 UNTS. 65 (*entered into force*, 9 July 1965).

[14] See, e.g., Vienna Declaration and Programme of Action, World Conference on Human Rights, UN Doc. A/CONF. 157/23 (1993).

[15] Thus, for example, the refusal of United Nations bodies to adopt an instrument addressing the specific problems of sexual minorities, despite substantial evidence of those problems, signifies a refusal to acknowledge minority sexual identities. See E. Heinze, *Sexual Orientation: A Human Right* 10-22 (1995).

[16] See E. Heinze, Book Review, 46 NILR 269 (1999) (reviewing I. Schulte-Tenckhoff, *La Question des peuples autochtones* (1997)).

[17] Records of Fifth Assembly, LNOJ Supp. 23 (1924).

[18] GA res. 44/22, annex 44 UN GAOR Supp. (No. 49) at 167, UN Doc. A/44/49 (1989) (*entered into force*, 2 Sept. 1990).

[19] Cf. J.S. Cerda, 'The Draft Convention on the Rights of the Child: New Rights', 12 HRQ 115 (1990) (noting the CRC's inclusion of 'new rights' required to meet problems specific to children).

[20] GA res. 1386 (XIV), 14 UN GAOR Supp. (No. 16) at 19, UN Doc. A/4354, preambular paras. 3, 4 (1959).

[21] Preambular para. 5. See also preambular paras. 4, 8, 9.

[22] Art. 25(2). Cf. ICESCR art. 10(3).

[23] Art. 6(5). See, e.g., Comments of the Human Rights Committee on the Report of the United States of America, UN Doc. CCPR/C/79/Add 50, at para. 14 (1995) (noting the Committee's view that a general reservation to art. 6(5) is incompatible with the object and purpose of the Covenant). See also *id.* at para. 16.

[24] See note 3 *supra*.

[25] By contrast, as non-binding instruments, UDHR and DRC 1959 were not intended to confer positive, individual rights. That limitation, however, did not preclude the language of positive, individual rights.

[26] See, e.g., S. Freud, 'Drei Abhandlungen zur Sexualtheorie,' in 5 *Gesammelte Werke* 27 (1942) ['Three Essays on Sexuality,' in 7 *The Standard Edition of the Complete Psychological Works of Sigmund Freud* 123 (J. Strachey, trans., ed., 1953) (hereinafter *Standard Edition*)].

[27] See E. Heinze, 'Discourses of Sex: Classical, Modernist, Post-Modernist,' 67 NJIL 37, 50-56 (1998).

[28] First exposed in detail in 'Die Traumdeutung,' in 2, 3 *Gesammelte Werke*, note 26 *supra* ['The Interpretation of Dreams,' in 4, 5 *Standard Edition* note 26 *supra*].

[29] See Heinze, 'Discourses of Sex,' note 27 *supra*, at 51.

[30] See, e.g., *La Psychologie de l'enfant* (1966) [*The Psychology of the Child* (H. Weaver, trans. 1969)].

[31] Cf. J.H. Flavell, *The Developmental Psychology of Jean Piaget* 19 (1963).

[32] Cf. *id.* at 24.

[33] *Id.* at 36. See also R. Cotterrell, *The Sociology of Law* 141-142 (2nd ed. 1992) (discussing Tapp and Kohlberg).

[34] L. Pollock, *Forgotten Children: Parent-Child Relations From 1500-1900* 34-36 (1983).

[35] *Id.* at viii. Pollock acknowledges scepticism about sociobiological explanations of industrialised societies. Nevertheless, she defends their applicability to preliterate societies. See *id.* at 36.

[36] *Id.* at 38.

[37] 14 *Gesammelte Werke*, note 26 *supra*, at 421 ['Civilisation and its Discontents,' in 21 *Standard Edition* note 26 *supra*, at 57].

[38] See K. Danziger, *Readings in Child Socialization* 2 (1970).

[39] T. Parsons, 'The American Family: Its Relation to Personality and to the Social Structure,' in *Family, Socialisation and Interaction Process* 3, 17 (T. Parsons & R.F. Bales, eds., 1956).

[40] F. Elkin & G. Handel, *The Child and Society: The Process of Socialisation* 4 (3rd ed. 1978).

[41] Parsons, note 39 *supra*, at 16.

[42] *Id.* at 17.

[43] *Id.* at 22-23.

[44] M. Mead, *Male and Female: A Study of the Sexes in a Changing World* 276 (1950).

[45] *Id.* at 276-277.

[46] M. Mead, *Coming of Age in Samoa* 115 (1928).

[47] Mead, note 44 *supra*, at 65-70.

[48] Danziger, note 38 *supra*, at 4.

[49] *Id.* at 18. This point is further examined below.

[50] In *Mythologies*, Roland Barthes's had argued that children are rarely given things which allow them to create, but are rather given 'reduced copies of human objects' ('reproductions amoindries d'objets humains') which are already invested with a meaning given to them by adults. R. Barthes, *Mythologies* 58 (1957) [*Mythologies* 53 (A. Lavers, trans. 1972)].

[51] Danziger, note 38 *supra*, at 4.

[52] J. Boyden, 'Childhood and the Policy Makers: A Comparative Perspective on the Globalization of Childhood,' in *Constructing and Reconstructing Childhood* 184, 186-87 (A. James & A. Prout eds., 2nd ed. 1990) (hereinafter *Constructing*).

[53] Convention for the Protection of Human Rights and Fundamental Freedoms, 213 UNTS. 222 (*entered into force*, 3 Sep. 1953).

[54] Marckx v. Belgium, 31 Eur. Ct. H. R. at (ser. A) (1979).

[55] Nielsen v. Denmark, 144 Eur. Ct. H. R. (ser. A) (1988).

[56] Olsson v. Sweden, 130 Eur. Ct. H. R. (ser. A) (1988).

[57] See, e.g., L. Purdy, 'Why Children Shouldn't Have Equal Rights,' 2 IJCR 219 (1994). Cf. M. Freeman, 'The Limits of Children's Rights,' in *Ideologies of Children's Rights* 29 (1992).

[58] See text accompanying notes 18-21 *supra*.

[59] See, e.g., D. Fottrell, 'Children's Rights,' in *Human Rights: An Agenda for the 21st Century* 167, 173 (A. Hegarty & S. Leonard, eds. 1999).

[60] See P. Ariès, *L'Enfant et la vie familiale sous l'Ancien Régime* (2nd ed.1973).

[*Centuries of Childhood* (R. Baldick, trans., 1962) (hereinafter *Centuries*)].

[61] Ariès, *Centuries*, note 60 *supra*, at 125.

[62] *Id.* at 32.

[63] *Id.* at 129-130.

[64] *Id.* at 169.

[65] E. Shorter, *The Making of the Modern Family* 168 (1975).

[66] L. Stone, *The Family, Sex and Marriage in England 1500-1800* 449 (1977).

[67] L. De Mause, 'The Evolution of Childhood,' in *The History of Childhood* 1 (L. De Mause, ed. 1976).

[68] *Id.* at 3.

[69] *Id.* at 16-17.

[70] See, e.g., Pollock, note 34 *supra*, at 43-65.

[71] D. Nicholas, 'Childhood in Medieval Europe,' in *Children in Historical and Comparative Perspective* 31 (J. M. Hawes & N. R. Hiner, eds.) (hereinafter *Historical and Comparative*).
[72] S. Marshall, 'Childhood in Early Modern Europe,' in *Historical and Comparative*, note 71 *supra*, at 53, 54-55.
[73] Mead, note 46 *supra*, at 139.
[74] M. Freeman, *Margaret Mead and Samoa: The Making and Unmaking of an Anthropological Myth* 51 (1983).
[75] Cf. *id.* at ch. 4 (criticising Mead's reliance on Boas).
[76] See A. Prout & A. James, 'Introduction', in *Constructing* note 52, at 1, 3-5.
[77] Boyden, note 52 *supra*, at 186.
[78] *Id.* at 187.
[79] *Id.* at 204.
[80] See, e.g. A. Prout & A. James, 'A New Paradigm for the Sociology of Childhood? Provenance, Promise and Problems,' in *Constructing* note 52, at 7, 8-9, 15.
[81] M. Woodhead, 'Psychology and the Cultural Construction of Children's Needs,' in *Constructing* note 52, at 60.
[82] *Id.* at 60.
[83] *Id.* at 65.
[84] *Id.* at 70.
[85] *Id.* at 67-69.
[86] *Id.* at 71-72.
[87] Danziger, note 38 *supra*, at 3.
[88] I. Opie & P. Opie, *The Lore and Language of Schoolchildren* 1 (1959).
[89] *Id.* at 209.
[90] P. Connolly, 'Boys Will be Boys? Racism, Sexuality and the Construction of Masculine Identities among Infant Boys,' in *Debates and Issues in Feminist Research and Pedagogy* 25 (J. Holland *et al.* eds., 1995).
[91] Opie & Opie, note 88 *supra*, at 210.
[92] Connolly, note 90 *supra*.
[93] See S. Jackson, *Childhood and Sexuality* ch. 4 (1982).
[94] See C. Piper, 'Historical Constructions of Childhood Innocence: Removing Sexuality,' in this collection.
[95] Jackson, note 93 *supra*, at ch. 2.
[96] P. Caplan, *The Cultural Construction of Sexuality* 2 (1987).
[97] *Id.* at 2.
[98] A. James, *The Contribution of Social Anthropology to the Understanding of Atypical Gender Identity in Childhood* 81-88 (1998).
[99] See D. Monk, 'Health and Education: Conflicting Programmes for Sex Education,' in this collection.
[100] See C. Downs & S. Whittle, 'Seeking a Gendered Adolescence: Legal and Ethical Problems of Puberty Suppression among Adolescents with Gender Dysphoria,' in this collection.
[101] See Steiner & Alston, note 2 *supra*, at 240-254.

[102] AC 112 (1986).
[103] *Id.* at 171 (Fraser, LJ).
[104] *Id.* at 176 (Scarman, LJ).
[105] See, e.g., J. Pilcher, 'Contrary to Gillick: British Children and Sexual Rights Since 1985,' 5 IJCR 299 (1997) (noting limitations on children's sexual rights in British law subsequent to *Gillick*).

2 Historical Constructions of Childhood Innocence: Removing Sexuality

CHRISTINE PIPER

Introduction

Harry Hendrick argues that the image of childhood predominant today had already emerged by the beginning of the 20th century, having developed largely throughout the 19th:

> [T]he concept of childhood in 1800 was not that of 1900. In 1800 its meaning was ambiguous; nor was there a popular demand for an unproblematic conception. By 1900 the uncertainty had been more or less resolved and the identity of childhood determined . . . . [B]y the end of the century reformers of all hues had a fairly clear perception of what they felt was the nature of childhood . . . . Consequently, reformers also knew what they expected of children in terms of behaviour, performance and development. These expectations . . . would be broadened and deepened well into the twentieth century, but many of the fundamental stereotypes were in place around the early 1900s . . . .[1]

Yet that view has been contested. For Cunningham, the most rapid historical change in the conceptualisation of childhood has been a weakening of the adult/child distinction during the second half of the 20th century.[2] Cox argues that '[t]he story of the bourgeois child is now also the story of the fall of the bourgeois child,'[3] and the title of Postman's work on American childhood — *The Disappearance of Childhood* — conveys a similar message.[4] Cunningham, however, includes no detailed discussion of sexuality in relation to constructions of childhood,[5] and Cox concedes that the 19th century notion of childhood innocence 'has come to haunt us and often to mock us in the late 20th century.'[6] This chapter examines Hendrick's view in relation to the way that conceptions of childhood treat innocence and, above all, sexual innocence.

Contemporary Images

The images of child sexuality which underpin the policies of Blair's Britain were in place by the time of Lloyd George. This statement may, at first, seem odd. Surely the Freudian revolution in thinking about children and sexuality in the 1920s — that they have an innate sexuality — might be seen as the main influence on our thinking. As Rex and Wendy Stainton-Rogers argue, '[i]t was Freudian theory which gave childhood sexuality its particular place in modernist thinking.'[7] Without entering into the debate about the validity and influence of Freud's theories,[8] however, it is possible to argue, with Cunningham, that the 19th century construction of childhood has withstood numerous challenges, not least that posed by Freud.'[9] Despite the different meanings constructed for childhood sexual activity and the resulting swings of child rearing theories, '[t]he adult gaze on the sexuality of the child still renders them "subjects of study" or "objects of concern."'[10] Whatever may be the reasons, and the specialist knowledge, used to categorise, supervise, and regulate manifestations of child sexuality, the public image of the child, which has served both to encourage and to justify social policy, is of an 'un-sexualised' person who is vulnerable, weak and innocent.

In the dominant images of 'deserving' children available in 1900, children and sexuality simply did not go together. That is still the case today. Consider two examples. A recent NCH Action for Children (formerly, National Children's Home) leaflet, entitled 'Sexual Abuse and the Whole Child,' refers to Amy, who had been abused by her father. The leaflet states: 'One of our specially trained counsellors is helping Amy to trust again and is trying to give back a little of the childhood her father stole from her.' This statement makes sense only if the message is that Amy has lost her trust in adults because her father no longer comes to see her (he is not allowed to), and that she has 'lost' her childhood because of her engagement in sexual activity. Because that engagement was not her responsibility, she is still treated as a child, but also as a victim because of the loss of 'real' childhood.

A second example of the non-sexualised, 'deserving' child can be seen in the fact that young people who solicit as prostitutes are often processed as criminals under the Sexual Offences Act 1956 and the Street Offences Act 1959, rather than being treated as victims. The child prostitute may be denied the status of victim, despite the fact that the client has committed an offence (by law, a woman under 16 cannot give consent to sexual intercourse). Between 1989 and 1995, approximately 4,000 young people under the age of 18 were convicted or cautioned for offences relating to soliciting.[11] The fact that the criminal act involves sex offered by a minor can negate ideas of child protection and welfare.[12] We find it difficult to sustain an image of a child who is both sexualised *and* deserving of protection.[13] Being sexualised undermines 'merit.' Like the Poor Law, it leads to a distinction between those who are deserving and the undeserving.[14]

These difficulties are implicitly addressed by the Department of Health in its consultation paper entitled 'Working Together to Safeguard Children': 'The Government believes that children who become involved in prostitution should be seen primarily as children in need [of] welfare services and in many instances protection under the Children Act. [...] Views are invited on other ways in which guidance might raise the profile of the issue of children involved in prostitution.'[15]

Frameworks for Analysis

Before beginning an analysis, two important caveats are required. First, this chapter is about constructions and images of childhood. It is not about 'real' children. A socially prevalent image may not determine private action, but is important because it influences and encourages public action and justifies state policies. As Cunningham notes in relation to the influence of romanticism on images of children, '[m]uch of what we have been describing operated as a fantasy appealing especially to adult males' who often had little to do with child rearing.[16] Yet adult males — and particularly those middle class males who were aware of the new ideas about childhood — had much to do, in the 19th century, with the financing of charitable projects and the organisation of campaigns for legislative reform.

Second, the focus of this paper is not whether children *should* be protected from actions perceived as harmful by adults. My concern is why, in some situations, the child is accorded victim status, deserving of protection, whilst in other situations she is not. Where the child chooses to engage in sexual activity, the status of victim is apparently precluded. This is the corollary to the notion established by 1900 that a child is incapable of consenting to sex with adults (or indeed with other children): those 'children' who, by their actions, apparently proclaim that they are capable of giving consent lose their status as children. By 1900, and still today, the only available alternatives are either that 'Child + Sex = Abuse'[17] or 'Child + Sex = Adult.' For the 20th century, the image of the child that had emerged by

1900 has precluded the possibility of the equation 'Child + Sex = OK.'

The last 40 years have seen the publication of influential texts, based on a variety of methods and sources, in areas relevant to this chapter.[18] There is no shortage of material analysing the development of concepts of childhood, the genesis and development of legislation relating to the welfare and protection of children, and the development of attitudes towards, and the regulation of, sexuality. The renewed preoccupation with child abuse, particularly sexual abuse, and with juvenile delinquency has increased interest in historical accounts of the origins and motivations for such concern. For the purposes of this analysis, three strands of historical and sociological research are important: those delineating change or continuity in relation to the concept of childhood, those analysing the genesis of child protection and delinquency systems in terms of moral and symbolic 'crusades,' and those which have analysed, from a feminist perspective, the pressures for and results of law reform concerning women. Feminist perspectives stress 'how the category of Woman is constructed in relation to the category of the Child.'[19] These different bodies of material shed light on adult expectations and fears for children, on the moral frameworks within which reform was conceptualised, and on the ways in which laws operate to regulate women, particularly the sexuality and gender roles of women. Historians of childhood point towards continuities and inconsistencies in attitudes to nature and innocence in relation to children. An analysis of campaigns for state intervention to prevent parental abuse of children reveals the importance of the reformers' concern for the sexual 'corruption' of children.

This chapter therefore aims to bring together these different insights to see how sexuality came to be removed from authoritative images of the deserving child, and how the protection of children became bound up with the regulation of women. Again, however, there must be a caveat. I will take for granted the existence of adult, and particularly parental, fears about the sexual activity of children. There is considerable literature on this issue. A recent book by Gittins, for example, contains a chapter entitled 'Children's Sexuality: Why Do Adults Panic?', which examines the destabilising of conceptions of the family by sexual relations within the family unit (particularly in reconstituted families), the inherent potential of the 'pure and innocent' child to create sexual feelings in adults, and the conflation by parents of sexual activity by their child and parental loss of control.[20] As Rex and Wendy Stainton-Rogers observe, there is now 'a cultural equation' of which the terms are: 'Children + Sexuality = Visceral clutch'[21] — a gut reaction of horror and dismay. At another level there are explanations of parents controlling their offspring's sexuality in order to control the age of, and partner for, marriage and pregnancy and, therefore, control the inheritance of property and the availability of the child's labour. I shall therefore take for granted that there are unarticulated adult fears about childhood sexuality which lay the groundwork for historical constructions of children, but cannot by themselves account for the particularity of constructions at any particular time.

Innocence

The conflation of innocence with lack of knowledge, and specifically with lack of knowledge about sex, has a long history. In the Judaeo-Christian tradition, the Garden of Eden presents a man and woman eating from the forbidden Tree of Knowledge. Before that event they were naked and unashamed. From that point onwards they 'knew' that they were naked,[22] that there were particular parts of their bodies used for particular activities which were innately 'wrong.' The connection — subsequently philosophised into many different forms — between sin and sex (either the sexual activity of the individual concerned or that of his parents at his conception) and, by analogy, between innocence and sexlessness, became an important strand of Christian theology. It reflected pre-existing ideas, notably those of Aristotle, and fed into medieval Western European thought: preaching manuals from the 13th century onwards exhorted those entrusted with the care of children to keep them innocent of any sexual knowledge or activity.[23] Later incarnations of this idea can be found in the theology of the Puritans of the 16th and 17th centuries, and of the evangelicals of the 18th and 19th centuries.

　　Linguistic evidence of this double conflation, of general knowledge with sexual knowledge and of sin with sexual intercourse, is found in the use of the verb 'know' to refer to carnal knowledge.[24] In *The History of Sexuality,* Foucault refers (tongue in cheek, given that he later refutes the repressive hypothesis which he is illustrating) to the 'knowing children' who 'hung about' adults in the early 17th century, when 'sexual practices had little need of secrecy.'[25] Explanations for this long relationship between sin and sex are not, however, necessary for the purpose of this analysis. For at least two millennia theologians and philosophers have been concerned with the nature of evil and of sexuality. Incest early became a taboo because of religious prohibitions on non-procreative sex and because of the social disruption it could precipitate. I will take for granted that knowledge of and engagement in sexual activity has always been socially and morally problematic and bound up with questions of innocence and evil in relation to children.

Historically, the western Judaeo-Christian tradition has agonised over the nature of childhood innocence because of its theological implications for adults and its practical implications for parents. St Augustine's modification of the doctrine of 'original sin' meant that children, though born evil, could be 'made' innocent by the (infant) baptism which was the responsibility of parents and the church. The Reformation, however, brought ideas of salvation by faith and by good works, rather than by infant baptism and sacraments, so that, theologically, childhood became a stage in which the child needed to be trained to withstand the temptations which his evil nature would inevitably place before him.[26] However, to see theology as a dominant and consistent influence on the development of concepts of sexuality, particularly childhood sexuality, would be misguided.[27] As is now well documented, the writers of the Enlightenment from the second half of the 17th century — notably Locke, Kant and Rousseau — have added particular glosses on childhood innocence. Whilst they by no means all came to the same conclusions, they have had a lasting influence on our conceptions of childhood.

A non-religious strain of anti-sensualism, where the senses are deemed to be culturally and environmentally, not biologically, shaped, has been evident in writings since the 17th century. For Locke, the child was a *tabula rasa* so that 'innocence in the sense of not knowing, is therefore innate.'[28] Rousseau's Emile lived in 'original innocence'[29] and was encouraged to learn from nature. Itard's Victor — the 'wild boy of Avreyon,'[30] found living in a purely physical environment in central France at the end of the 18th century — became the focus of intense discussion on the nature of man. The emergence of romanticism at the end of the 18th century added further ideas about the child.

The 18th century had therefore seen a 'chicken and egg' type of discussion about the relationships between signs, senses, and ideas but leaving for the 19th century an unresolved debate on the nature of sexual knowledge and innocence. The images of innocent and natural childhood resulting from the romanticisation of childhood were powerful but not without challenge from the continuing Puritan Christian emphasis on original sin (reinforced by the evangelical revival at the end of the 18th century), by the proliferation of educational and moralising literature and toys aimed at 'training' children, and by a growing consumerism which promoted such goods and which allowed children to be seen as objects of status.[31] Cox therefore talks of 'the tortuous journey the doctrine of innocence travelled, the blind alleys it went up, and the often disturbing lines of thought and expression it traversed.'[32] That Victorian constructions of children included 'contradictions and ambiguities' is important.[33] It points us to the fact that there is no linear development of philosophical ideas about childhood and that the primacy of one particular construction of childhood by 1900 is therefore unlikely to be explained by the 'progress' of philosophy or science. It suggests instead that power issues cannot be ignored.

Corruption

'Childish innocence is very beautiful but the bloom is soon destroyed.'[34] The idea that the essence of childhood is innocence and dependence, and that innocence not only needs protecting but is inherently fragile, was of great utility to reformers seeking to ameliorate the lives of children. Its fragility was a spur to demand immediate action by Parliament and through charitable efforts yet the success of the campaigns for child-related reform depended on keeping the image 'pure'. Those societal ideas of justice and deserving cases that are reflected in legal concepts of contributory negligence and of the need to appear before a judge with 'clean hands' are relevant here. The one deserving of full help and protection must be 'blameless' — there must be no hint of wrongdoing in the one seeking justice. The child has to be presented as separate and different from the adult: the possibility of independent action, particularly of actions that are not childlike, undermines images of vulnerability and dependency. The more clearly the child is constructed as innocent, weak, and dependent, the more powerful the image as a force to legitimate protective action.

Yet, as we have seen, innocence has historically been conflated with ignorance of sexual matters. An increasingly important part of the special 'otherness' of children was perceived as their lack of knowledge of adult sexuality.[35] Because of this conflation, childhood innocence is a state which can be corrupted, above all, by sexual knowledge. This very fact may result in childhood being eroticised: innocence and beauty can 'create a subversive echo.'[36] Childhood innocence is a 'blank image waiting to be formed . . . . Purity, it turns out, provided just the opening a sexualising tendency requires: it is the necessary condition for the erotic operations our cultures have made central.'[37] The natural successors of the Victorian pictorial and literary portrayals of the idealised child are in 20th century advertising: 'Markers of childhood — gym-slips, a wide-eyed "innocent" gaze, thumb-sucking, a gangly pubescent stance — have become recognisable markers of latent and inviting, yet forbidden . . . sexual allure.'[38] Paradoxically, the stronger the image of the innocent, asexual child, the more likely it is to encourage fear and guilt in the adult who acknowledges sexual feelings aroused by such an image of a child. Notions of 'sexual latency' and 'asexuality' therefore put children in danger from adults; but they also become a danger to adults, feeding into a stronger imperative to protect the child from adult sexuality.

Another set of prevalent ideas about the source of corruption of childhood innocence ultimately merged with the above set of ideas: those constructing the city street as evil. The 18th century philosophers and the Romantic poets had forged an enduring link between childhood and nature — a link evident in what Cox refers to as a 'line of beautiful children.'[39] The development of these images of beautiful children in the 19th century show a transition from the 'natural' life of the innocent child of Wordsworth's poetry, echoing Blake and stressing 'emotion and purity,' to the more domesticated and urban but also morbid and sentimentally innocent child, victimised by an uncaring society, in the novels of Dickens.[40] The rural setting, the child-rearing site closest to nature, became viewed as a better place for children, in contrast to the corruption and evil of the urban setting. To quote Lord Ashley, writing in 1846:

> Every one who walks the streets of the metropolis [London] must daily observe members of the tribe ... the foul and dismal passages are thronged with children of both sexes .... Their appearance is wild ... and the barbarian freedom from all superintendence and restraint will fill the mind of a novice in these things with perplexity and dismay.[41]

The image reflected and solidified by Dickens responded to growing concern about the dangers for children caused by the city street,[42] a concern also evident in North America. As Gordon's research found, '[t]he Victorian conviction that children should be domestic and unseen, and the fear of [sexual] "precocity" in children, were part of the characteristic anti-urban bias of so many reformers of the time.'[43]

Concern about the depraving effects of adult public space led to a variety of reforming efforts: for example, to criminalise the use of child performers in theatres or on the streets,[44] to reduce the incidence of street trading by children,[45] and to close public fairs.[46] Such a concern is still with us as Bar-On's critique of recent research on street children in African countries reveals. The public visibility of children on the streets 'challenges bourgeois society which governs in the expectation that children will intrude as little as possible on the adult world ... so generating calls that street children will disappear.'[47] The child's independence is a threat to images of childhood and to expectations of dependent and asexual behaviour.

Paradoxically, it led to the use by reformers of an image of an ever-more dependent, vulnerable, and invisible child, placed firmly in the home and, later, the school. The child should be visible only in those non-adult sites reserved for children and their mentors but not on the streets and not in the factories and mines.

These images lay behind successful campaigns for legislation to protect children from the loss of their innocence and therefore their childhood. The factory system was presented as 'unnatural' and so not a place for children; those who worked in factories were, therefore, 'children without a childhood,'[48] and children of all ages were conceptualised as frail and dependent: 'these little ones,' as Sadler referred to them in the debate leading up to passage of the Ten Hours Act 1832.[49]

The Supervision of Sexuality

One of the most influential works on 19th century sexuality is that of Foucault. His concern is to document the emergence of new discourses of sexuality[50] located in science and medicine and reaching fruition in the course of the 19th century, which affected the way sex is talked about[51] and children's sexuality is supervised.[52] In that sense, sex was not repressed by the Victorians but 'was driven out of hiding and constrained to lead a discursive existence.'[53] As examples of the prevalence of a discourse of childhood sexuality he gives examples ranging from the architectural layout of schools[54] to the increase from the 18th century of published advice by doctors and educators about schoolboy sex.

There occurred what Foucault has referred to as 'a pedagogization of children's sex': 'Children were defined as "preliminary" sexual beings, on this side of sex, yet within it, astride a dangerous dividing line.'[55] The 'truth' constructed, stemming from two bio-medical innovations of the time — the 'medicine of perversions and the programmes of eugenics' — was that practically all children engage in sexual activity and that this poses a threat: the child was constituted as being in danger of compromising the moral fibre and line of descent.[56]

By the closing decades of the 19th century, the aim of rearing children was that they would be 'clean, adequately clothed, fed according to medical norms, and taught to eschew habits — excessive consumption of alcohol, sexual excess and promiscuity and so forth — which were now regarded not only as morally undesirable, but also as damaging to health and constitution.'[57] The neo-hygienist movement had added yet another gloss to existing sources of concern about the sexuality of children. The conflation of sin and sexuality developed into a conflation of sexuality and a more general moral and physical deterioration. Such knowledge added fuel to parental and professional fears about sexual precocity. Masturbation, perceived as an early sign of corruption, became the focus of parents' fears. By the end of the century, child care manuals carried pictorial advertisements for devices which controlled such aberrant behaviour[58] — evidence of the depth of those fears which had been made explicit over a century earlier in two texts, *Onania or the Heinous Sin of Self-Pollution* (1710) and a *Treatise on the Disorders Produced by Masturbation* (1760).[59]

Fascinating though Foucault's analysis is in its description of the minutiae of the diffusion and operation of power in society — how the discourse of sexuality operated as a technology of power and what were 'the effects of power generated by what was said'[60] — what is important for this analysis is why certain medical opinions, not always held by the generality of the profession,[61] fed into those notions of the sexuality of men, women, and children which had most social and political influence. As Rose points out, '[a] scientific discourse is not a mere register of effects from elsewhere. It consists of a set of complex ways of conceptualising the objects of attention,' and '[s]cientific discourses do not only *seek* truth, they also *claim* truth.'[62] Not only is truth constructed in these conceptualisations, but particular objects of attention are selected to generate truths. We are then left with a crucial question: why, in the second half of the 19th century and especially in the closing decades, was sexuality constructed and controlled in those particular ways which Foucault describes and what effects did that have on images of children?

What become useful at this point are those texts which have analysed the passage of contentious legislation as moral or symbolic campaigns. The question then changes to asking whose moral and social beliefs, aspiration and power were under threat and what particular ideas of sexuality fed into those campaigns. To answer this question it is helpful to return to issues of class and gender.

Class Issues

Foucault was concerned to move the debate from juridical and negative notions of power to a focus on the relationships between power and knowledge and the diffusion of power through techniques of surveillance and regulation. In relation to sexuality he analysed how the 'technology of sex' was 'deployed' in society[63] through his 'four great strategic unities' which, from the 18th century, 'formed specific mechanisms of knowledge and power.'[64] He makes the point that '[t]he working class managed for a long time to escape the deployment of "sexuality,"'[65] and outlines how the deployment of sexuality will eventually replace the previous regulatory techniques referred to as the 'deployment of alliance.'[66] His functional analysis of such deployments argues that the deployment of the technology of sex occurs first within the middle- and upper-class families which feared the erosion of particular ideas of family and gender roles.

Victorian middle-class perceptions of the vulnerability of its status and norms led to 'symbolic crusades' to 'rescue' the victims of men not upholding the sanctity of the home and sex within it. As Cox notes, '[t]he bourgeoisie as a class was one that always sensed a threat from within, in terms of a failure of its own cultural reproduction, and from without, through the external threat of mass society.'[67] Gittins would argue that the proliferation of material for parents on masturbation, for example, is a signifier of the widespread anxiety caused by changing definitions of roles and boundaries and fears that dominant moral and religious frameworks were under threat.[68] Specifically, there were fears that Victorian ideas of family and women were not shared by sections of the working classes — the 'unrespectable poor' — and thus needed to be imposed on them. Those fears found a focus in the issue of prostitution — 'The Great Social Evil'[69] and the 'fear that starts at shadows'[70] — which united diverse groups within the 'Social Purity' movement[71] and which, by raising the question of the age of consent, had such an enduring influence on the concept of childhood. The 'Maiden Tribute of Modern Babylon' — the four-part series about child prostitution in the *Pall Mall Gazette*, arising from W.T. Stead's 'purchase' of a virgin for five pounds — 'exaggerated the role of children in the social economy of prostitution and misrepresented the way young girls were recruited for the streets'[72] but this representation influenced constructions of the sexuality of men, women and children.[73]

These campaigns used the image of the innocent, vulnerable child that had become so strong in relation to other successful campaigns for children's welfare. Yet, when these 'innocent victims' of 'the white slave trade' were 'saved' from a life of 'depravity' they were, in effect, punished by the harsh regimes of the 'rescue homes' and by the pressure to 'confess' the evil of their former lives. These contradictory messages were both necessary; one to ensure success of campaigning, the other to ensure the solidification of a particular set of norms about sexuality and the dependence of children. In that sense, as Cox points out:

The symbol of the child was being used, not simply to legislate in the child's own defence, but also to assert the right of a moral majority to regulate the behaviour of all children in the interests of a particular ideology. It was . . . an episode driven less by moral reformers with a radical edge and more by groups who saw in child prostitution a sign of general moral decline.[74]

The theoretical framework for reform movements as symbolic, so that the focus becomes the potentially declining power of the successful campaigning group[75] and the class-based nature of the norms imposed,[76] has, therefore, links with moral panic theory. Both require a focus on the social and economic conditions which led to a very generalised state of anxiety. Elsewhere I have argued that the existence of a national moral crisis in the 1880s was a major factor in the shift in the moral framework which allowed what had previously not been morally and politically possible — state intervention in the family to protect the parentally-abused child.[77] It is clearly also a factor here. The 'condition of England' question had resurfaced: there was economic recession, a sudden loss of confidence in the ability of environmental measures to solve social problems, and the emergence of new bio-medical ideas which allowed the poor to be labelled and treated as 'outcast' and 'a race apart.' As a result, it was, as Walkowitz points out, 'no historical accident' that the Criminal Law Amendment Act 1885 was rarely used to prosecute 'corrupt aristocrats and international traffickers' (despite their featuring in the public outcry which preceded the passage of the Act). Instead the passing of the Act 'coincided with a new interventionist approach to working-class culture.'[78]

Class must, however, be linked with gender in discussion of these middle-class moral campaigns. In Hooper's words, '[t]he potential for "protection" to become control of female sexuality is a recurring theme.'[79] When Jane Tyrell was (unsuccessfully) prosecuted under the Criminal Law Amendment Act 1885 section 5, Lord Coleridge, C.J. stated that the Act 'was passed for the purpose of protecting women and girls against themselves,'[80] meaning that their sexuality must be controlled for their own good.[81] Thus whilst the Governor of the Millbank Penitentiary for Convicts, in London, might write, '[c]ould we but raise the standard of morality among men to that which is established among the respectable portion of the other sex,'[82] as Booth noted, the 'social burden of fornication' was borne almost solely by women and their daughters[83] and the idealised vision of the middle-class woman to which the governor referred was to be the norm imposed on all working-class girls.[84]

Female Sexuality and Sex Roles

Protecting Daughters

It is in any case clear from the legislation itself that gender is an issue: the Offences Against the Person Act 1861 criminalised the procurement for defilement of a girl under 21, setting the age of consent to 12 for girls; and the Criminal Law Amendment Act 1885 raised the age of consent for girls to 16, but for boys to 14.[85] That the sexuality of girls was a more important site for intervention than that of boys was self-evident to the Victorians: 'each unprincipled, impure girl left to grow up, and become a mother, is likely to increase her kind three to five fold,' wrote a Mrs Wardner in 1879.[86]

For the same reason, the image of the child was often bound up with the image of women in moral campaigns for children's welfare. Analysis of the passage of the Factories Acts shows that much of the campaigning for the welfare of children employed in factories was aimed in large part at the protection of female children. According to the Sub-Commissioner of the 1842 Children's Employment Commission:

> The employment of female children . . . has the effect of preventing them from acquiring the most ordinary and necessary knowledge of domestic management and family economy, that . . . when they come to marry, the wife possesses not the knowledge to enable her to give her husband the common comforts of a home . . . .[87]

That the classifying together of women and children — exemplified by the 'women and children first' norm of rescue — stems from 'chivalrous' precepts, integral to social structures of patriarchal power and to legitimating particular gender roles, is a well-rehearsed argument but its effects in terms of the children concerned is rarely the focus of such analysis. Fears of unregulated sexuality and physical deterioration arising from the exploitation of women and children in the new workplaces were conflated with fears of disruption of gender roles — notably the role of women as mothers and home-makers *and* of girls as potential mothers and home-makers. Regulating employment and prostitution thus equated to enforcing particular segregated gender roles. The regulation is via the criminal law to punish the 'visible'[88] and via philanthropic activity to secure the 'redomestication of apparently eroticised women.'[89]

Such state intervention in the lives of women and children upset no moral code: it occurred only when the state was supporting a paternal role or itself taking on the paternal role. 'The state gradually became a sort of moral husband through the development of forms of "protective legislation.'"[90] In the factories women and children were beyond the protection of the head of the family and the state could justifiably intervene to exert the moral authority and discipline of the father. In that process, children's sexuality is regulated: 'Victorian women — respectable Victorian women — were idealised as asexual, domestic, and pure, and such ideals were also applied to children.'[91] Not only were 'proper' women 'pure', so were their children.[92] As Hendrick says of the confusion in the minds of reformers, stemming at least partly from their ignorance of adolescence as a particular stage of development: 'The logic of the thinking seemed to be that if the sexuality were removed, then so would be the "evil" — the girl-child would be restored to a state of purity in which she could exhibit a comforting and non-threatening self-sacrificing love.'[93]

Gender and Childhood

'In their state of unawakened sexuality, chaste women and all children shared a common nature,'[94] but the alignment of images of child and woman was at least partially dependent on the androgenous or even distinctly female conception of children which was constructed by the middle of the 19th century. Erasmus and Locke had thought of the child as a boy but by the third and fourth decades of the 19th century advice books for parents were blurring gender distinctions, notably in dress, and '[i]f anything, people were more likely to imagine the Romantic child as female rather than male.'[95] The image of the female child persisted to the end of the century but by then, according to Cox, Little Lord Fauntleroy had been joined by Action Man.[96] Nevertheless, the lack of a dominant image of a male child as macho man in the making had allowed for dominant ideas of female sexuality to become part of the image of childhood.

Conclusion

It is not surprising that, notwithstanding the influential writings of men like Locke and J.S. Mill, a discourse of children's rights developed, historically, much later than a discourse of, and indeed, campaigns for, children's welfare. The images of children which sustain a discourse of rights are those of 'knowing' and, in some measure at least, autonomous people with a sufficient level of understanding to exercise rights. Such images are threatening to adults and particularly so when they include the possibility of sexual independence. In contrast, the image of the child as a victim, vulnerable and dependent, is one which sits more happily with adult perceptions and concerns and which has made possible the passage of child welfare legislation.

Yet, 'the child as victim' is itself a particular construction. Historically it has included dominant images of the child as voiceless and, above all, innocent, not simply of the ways of the world and of human potential for evil but, more specifically, sexually 'innocent.' There is a sense in which the price paid by children over the last 150 years for the presumed benefits of child welfare legislation and provision has been their 'de-sexing.'

The child is now conceptualised as a victim in a range of circumstances which has been narrowed to encompass little more than abuse by parents (physical and now, in the discourse of divorce,[97] psychological and emotional abuse) and sexual abuse (that which most corrupts childhood innocence). Constructions are not fixed. It may be that the economics of heath care will allow of the construction of the child as a victim of environmental pollution. What is still apparently authoritative is an image of childhood and child victimisation which has no conceptual 'room' for a child whose sexual activity is, to a lesser or greater extent, self-willed. That image, in place by the beginning of this century, is lasting evidence of the 'success' of Victorian child-saving campaigns in relation to children at home, at work, and on the streets.

Notes

[1] H. Hendrick, *Child Welfare, England 1872-1989* 37 (1994).
[2] H. Cunningham, *Children and Childhood in Western Society since 1500* 187 (1995).
[3] R. Cox, *Shaping Childhood* ch. 6 (1996).
[4] N. Postman, *The Disappearance of Childhood* (1982).
[5] The book's index provides five page references under the heading 'children, sexuality and' (but none in regard to 'childhood'), and these are all references to brief mentions and assumptions. See Cunningham, note 2 *supra*, at 204, 206.
[6] Cox, note 3 *supra*, at 203.
[7] R. Stainton-Rogers & W. Stainton-Rogers, *Stories of Childhood* 165 (1992).
[8] See, e.g., R. Webster, *Why Freud Was Wrong: Sin, Science and Psychoanalysis* (1995).
[9] Cunningham, note 2 *supra*, at 190. See also *id.* at 170. Archard argues that 'the idea that before Freud children were viewed as sexless is contestable.' D. Archard, *Children, Rights and Childhood* 40 (1993).

[10] Stainton-Rogers, note 7 *supra*, at 166.

[11] The Children's Society, 'The Children's Society, Child Prostitutes — Victims or Criminals?' 141 *Childright* 15 (1997).

[12] See Archard, note 9 *supra*, at 74-81 (discussing the child's 'right to sexual choice' and the relationship of that right to issues of consent and child protection).

[13] Currently we are also apparently unable to sustain images of the child who offends and is also deserving of protection, as illustrated recently in the United Kingdom by the treatment of the 10-year-old boys who killed the infant James Bulger. This non-fusion however is not a product of a consistent strand of thinking over the last two centuries as is the non-fusion of the sexualised and deserving child. See C. Piper, 'Moral Campaigns for Children's Welfare in the 19th Century,' in *Moral Agendas for Children's Welfare* 33 (M. King ed., 1999) [hereinafter *Moral Agendas*].

[14] I am grateful to members of my LL.M. class on Child Law and Policy for raising this link.

[15] 'Working Together to Safeguard Children: New Government Proposals for Inter-Agency Cooperation,' para. 5.40 (1998). In line with this Government initiative is the campaign launched by Barnardos, the children's charity, in 1998, aimed at changing public perceptions of child prostitution so that the children and young people involved are accorded victim status.

[16] Cunningham, note 2 *supra*, at 76. See also D. Monk, 'Health and Education: Conflicting Programmes for Sex Education,' in this collection.

[17] R. Stainton-Rogers & W. Stainton-Rogers, 'What is Good and Bad Sex for Children?' in *Moral Agendas,* note 13 *supra*, at 179, 184.

[18] See Cunningham note 2 *supra*, at ch. 1 (reviewing the literature from the 1960s to the 1980s).

[19] C. Smart, 'Introduction,' in *Regulating Womanhood* 1 (C. Smart ed., 1992).

[20] D. Gittins, *The Child in Question* 6 (1998).

[21] Stainton-Rogers & Stainton-Rogers, note 7 *supra*, at 162.

[22] Genesis 3: 7 (King James).

[23] Cunningham, note 2 *supra,* at 34.

[24] See, e.g., Matthew 1:25 (describing Joseph with reference to Mary: ' . . . and he knew her not.') (King James).

[25] M. Foucault, 1 *The History of Sexuality* (R. Hurley, trans. 1990).

[26] See Gittins, note 20 *supra*, at 146-52, 186-191.

[27] See Cox, note 3 *supra*, at 131 (arguing that '[o]n the one hand, evangelicalism could on occasion ally itself with progressive thought and give weight to anti-sensualism, but on the other hand religious fervour was never far away from eroticism').

[28] Gittins, note 20 *supra*, at 150.

[29] 'Everything is good as it leaves the hands of the Author of things; everything degenerates in the hands of man.' J.-J. Rousseau, *Emile* 37 (A. Bloom, trans., 1979). See discussions in Cox, note 3 *supra*, at 64; Archard, note 9 *supra*, at 38.

[30] See N. Rose, *The Psychological Complex* 12 (1985) (describing this boy as 'the

first psychological subject').

[31] Cunningham, note 2 *supra*, at 70-72. See also Archard, note 9 *supra*, at 37-40.

[32] Cox, note 3 *supra*, at 76.

[33] *Id.* at 134.

[34] W. Booth, *In Darkest England and the Way Out* 64 (International Headquarters of the Salvation Army, eds., 1st ed. 1890) (appearing in a chapter entitled 'The Children of the Lost').

[35] See Gittins, note 20 *supra*, at 174. See also *id.* at 145 (arguing that '[e]xperience of adult sexuality seems now to be taken as the boundary that distinguishes childhood from adulthood, regardless of the age at which it is experienced by children').

[36] J. Kincaid, *Child-Loving: The Erotic Child and Victorian Culture* 5 (1992). See also discussion in Cox, note 3 *supra*, at 135.

[37] See Kincaid, note 36 *supra*, at 13. See also discussions in Cox, note 3 *supra*, at 136; Archard, note 9 *supra*, at 40-41.

[38] Stainton-Rogers & Stainton-Rogers, note 17 *supra*, at 194. See also Stainton-Rogers & Stainton-Rogers, note 7 *supra*, at 28 (arguing that '[c]ertainly the attributed quality of 'innocence' to the state of childhood makes children thereby targets for those for whom the *corrupting* potential of sex is a key to gaining sexual relief') (original emphasis).

[39] Cox, note 3 *supra*, at 136.

[40] Gittins, *supra* note 20, at 164-6. See also Stainton-Rogers & Stainton-Rogers, note 7 *supra*, at 27.

[41] Quoted in G. Behlmer, *Child Abuse and Moral Reform in England 1870-1908* 47 (1982).

[42] Rose, note 30 *supra*, at 47.

[43] L. Gordon, *Heroes of Their Own Lives* 40 (1988). Cf. Behlmer, note 41 *supra*, at 89 (quoting from evidence given to the 1882 Select Committee about girl street sellers in Liverpool: '. . . though she may carry a basket, there is very little difference between her and a prostitute.')

[44] Gordon, note 43 *supra*, at 40-42.

[45] For example, the 'Cruelty Act' passed in 1889 for England and Wales included sections prohibiting street trading by children between the hours of 8pm (10pm in summer) and 5am.

[46] J. Walkowitz, *Prostitution and Victorian Society* (1980) (examining the Contagious Diseases Acts in the United Kingdom with reference to the cities of Southampton and Plymouth).

[47] A. Bar-On, 'Criminalising Survival: Images and Reality of Street Children,' 26 JSP 63, 68 (1997).

[48] See Cunningham, note 2 *supra*, at 144 (quoting *Punch* editor Douglas Jerrold).

[49] Quoted in J. Ward, 2 *The Factory System* 102 (1970).

[50] Foucault, note 25 *supra*, at 27.

[51] *Id.* at 30 (noting that children were deprived of 'a certain way of speaking about

sex . . . as being too . . . crude').
[52] *Id.* at 13-14.
[53] *Id.* at 33.
[54] *Id.* at 27.
[55] *Id.* at 104.
[56] *Id.* at 118, 121, 153.
[57] Rose, note 30 *supra*, at 85.
[58] R. Stainton-Rogers, 'The Social Construction of Childhood,' in *Child Abuse and Neglect: Facing the Challenge* 23, 25 (W. Stainton-Rogers *et al.*, eds, 1989).
[59] See Gittins, note 20 *supra*, at 191-2.
[60] Foucault, *supra* note 25, at 11.
[61] See M. Mason, *The Making of Victorian Sexuality* (1994).
[62] Rose, note 30 *supra*, at 7-8.
[63] Foucault, note 25 *supra*, at 77-96.
[64] *Id.* at 103.
[65] *Id.* at 121.
[66] *Id.* at 106.
[67] Cox, note 3 *supra*, at 201.
[68] Gittins, note 20 *supra*, at 193 (noting that '[m]asturbation defied clear heterosexual codes, while at the same time undermining rhetoric of the family and notions of childhood innocence').
[69] See, e.g., W. Logan, *The Great Social Evil: Its Causes, Extent, Results and Remedies* (1871) (arguing that destitution constituted one third of the 'fourth principal cause' of prostitution). For a critique of Victorian views on causation, see F. Harrison, *The Dark Angel* chs. 12-14 (1977).
[70] W. Acton, *Prostitution Considered in its Moral, Social and Sanitary Aspects* viii (2nd ed., 1870) (reprinted, 1972).
[71] The social purity organisations arose out of public debate about the repeal or extension of the Contagious Diseases Act (the first being passed in 1864), by which medical examinations of prostitutes near military depots could be enforced. See Cox, note 3 *supra*, at 149 (noting that, in the middle of the century, child prostitution as such was not an issue). The Act was repealed in 1886.
[72] J. Walkowitz, *City of Dreadful Delight* 83 (1992).
[73] *Id.* at chs. 3, 4 (examining how this ordering of subjectivities occurred through the use of narrative).
[74] Cox, note 3 *supra*, at 152.
[75] J. Gusfield, *Symbolic Crusade* (1963).
[76] See A. Platt, *The Child Savers: The Invention of Delinquency* (1969). As Platt argues in relation to the movement to establish juvenile courts

> Child saving may be understood as a crusade which served symbolic and ceremonial functions for native, middle-class Americans. The movement was not so much a break with the past as an affirmation of faith in traditional institutions. Parental authority, home education, rural life, and

the independence of the family as a social unit were emphasized because they seemed threatened at this time by urbanism and industrialism. *Id.* at 98.

[77] See Piper, note 13 *supra*.
[78] Walkowitz, note 46 *supra*, at 250-1. It would be mistaken, however, to view the passage of the Act as inevitable. See A. Stafford, *The Age of Consent* 196 (1964) (arguing that publicity generated by the *Pall Mall Gazette* feature 'resurrected' a Bill which was 'as good as dead').
[79] C. Hooper, 'Child Sexual Abuse and the Regulation of Women: Variations on a Theme,' in *Regulating Womanhood,* note 19 *supra*, at 57.
[80] R v Tyrell C.C.R., 1 QB 710, 712 (1894).
[81] The concern about the age of consent continued well into the 20th century. In 1922 it was raised from 13 to 16 for indecent assault. While notions of adolescence have changed, sexuality remains a focus of control over older 'children.' See Hooper, note 79 *supra*, at 60.
[82] Letter of 1843 to William Logan, quoted in Logan, note 69 *supra*, at 17.
[83] Booth, note 34 *supra*, ch. 4.
[84] But see L. Bland, 'Feminist Vigilantes of Late-Victorian England,' in *Regulating Womanhood* note 19 *supra*, at 33 (arguing that efforts 'to encourage the working class into a middle-class "decency"' offer only a partial explanation of the activities of middle-class feminists in the 1880s and the 1890s).
[85] See K. O'Donovan, 'With Sense, Consent, or Just a Con?: Legal Subjects in the Discourse of Autonomy,' in *Sexing the Subject of Law* 47 (N. Naffine & R. Owens, eds., 1997).
[86] Quoted in Platt, note 76 *supra*, at 27. Interestingly, one of Acton's suggestions for preventative work to eliminate prostitution was 'instruction in household work' for working-class girls. He argued that they learnt only sewing and migrated to the cities for work where low wages were supplemented by prostitution. If they had learnt housework they would have filled numerous vacancies for domestic servants in the country and the colonies, free from temptation in the cities. See Acton, note 70 *supra*, at 295-9.
[87] Quoted in C. Cannan, *Changing Families, Changing Welfare* 52 (1992).
[88] See A. Diduck & W. Wilson, 'Prostitutes and Persons,' 24 JLS 504 (1997) (discussing the current operation of criminal laws in relation to prostitution).
[89] C. Smart, 'Disruptive Bodies and Unruly Sex: The Regulation of Reproduction and Sexuality in the Nineteenth Century in Smart,' in *Regulating Womanhood,* note 19 *supra*, at 7.
[90] *Id.* at 25.
[91] Gittins, note 20 *supra*, at 167.
[92] See Smart, note 89 *supra*, at 29.
[93] Hendrick, note 1 *supra*, at 64.
[94] Cox, note 3 *supra*, at 138.
[95] Cunningham, note 2 *supra*, at 75.

[96] See Cox, note 3 *supra*, at 137.
[97] See C. Piper, 'Divorce Reform and the Image of the Child,' 23 JLS 354 (1996).

Part II

Legislating Childhood: International and Comparative Perspectives

3 Sexuality and the United Nations Convention on the Rights of the Child

MARGHERITA RENDEL

Introduction

The myth of childhood as a period of innocence is relatively recent. It has come after centuries when children in Western cultures were characterised as limbs of Satan, whose will must be broken before they could become part of the civilised adult world of skills, sex, power and violence. Children, sex and children's sexuality can be seen from two standpoints: what the child wants or perceives, and how adults perceive children as sexual beings (or not). Contemporary attitudes see children as needing protection, particularly from exploitation of their labour and of their bodies. In education, a further approach has emphasised the importance of educating children, not merely to fill their place in the adult world, but to develop their creativity. Article 12(1) of the UN Convention on the Rights of the Child 1989 ('the Convention') is innovative in recognising children's autonomy according to age and maturity:

> States Parties shall assure to the child who is capable of forming his or her own views the right to express those views freely in all matters affecting the child, the views of the child being given due weight in accordance with the age or maturity of the child.[1]

This chapter examines the historical background of the Convention and other international instruments relevant to children, sexuality, and human rights, including the drafting of the articles most relevant to these topics, and the work of the UN Committee on the Rights of the Child.

Drafting the Convention

The historical background of the Convention reflects a desire to protect
children dating back some 70 years. The first Declaration of the Rights of the
Child, the Declaration of Geneva 1924,[2] was based on the draft of Eglantyne
Jebb, founder of the British Save the Children Fund (SCF). Neither this
Declaration nor subsequent Declarations of 1948[3] or 1959[4] contained any
forerunner of article 12. While these Declarations stated that children should
be protected from exploitation, none of them referred to sexual abuse or
sexual exploitation, child pornography or child prostitution. Only the 1959
Declaration (DRC 1959) refers, in Principle 9, to trafficking. These forms of
abuse all figure in the Convention. Similarly, trafficking and prostitution are
included in the Anti-Slavery Conventions, but not sexual abuse or
pornography. For example, the Supplementary Convention on the Abolition
of Slavery, the Slave Trade, and Institutions and Practices Similar to Slavery
1956 includes practices whereby a woman can be sold into marriage without
her consent, transferred to another for value received or inherited on the death
of her husband.[5] Clearly these provisions apply equally to girls. They are not
included in the Convention.

The Convention deals with children's rights through the so-called
'four Ps': protection, prevention, provision and participation. This chapter
will examine how issues concerned with sex, sexuality, prostitution,
pornography, incest, abuse, and children's innocence and autonomy were
inserted into a document that at first had little to say about these issues in a
form appropriate for an international legal instrument, and in a context of
differing legal, cultural and religious systems. (Curiously, the Convention
says nothing about marriage, an issue affecting both protection and
participation.) The Convention resulted from a process by which issues
expressed in general terms in the Declaration on the Rights of the Child 1959
are reformulated, added to and re-ordered into a more precise and coherent
structure.

In 1978, the Polish Government put forward a draft Convention
based on the 1959 Declaration and hoped that a Convention could be agreed
during the UN Year of the Child in 1979. Many Western governments
lacked enthusiasm for such a Convention considering that children's rights
were already adequately covered in national and international legislation.[6]
The open-ended Working Group began work on a Convention in 1979. It
considered that the draft based on the Declaration, which had attracted many
criticisms from governments, was unsuitable: too vague, too many
omissions, inadequate provisions for implementation and enforcement.[7] The

Polish Government submitted a revised draft in October 1979.[8] It was a significantly different document, consisting of 19 articles, and took account of the comments on the first draft. The Convention has 54 articles so it is not surprising that it took 11 years to complete. Once completed, it entered into force in less than a year, in 1990.

The composition and methods of work of the Working Group contributed significantly to its success in creating a radical Convention, radical in including civil, political, economic, social, and cultural rights within one instrument, as did the Convention on the Elimination of All Forms of Discrimination Against Women,[9] and in recognising children as subjects rather than merely objects of international law in need of protection and welfare. The Working Group was composed of all members of the Commission on Human Rights who wished to participate; all other member States of the UN could send observers, as could intergovernmental organisations, UN specialised agencies and non-governmental organisations (NGOs); and all were allowed to speak. The proceedings were at first dominated by the North, but with active participation from Algeria, Argentina, Senegal and Venezuela. These four States, together with seven European States including the United Kingdom and the USSR, maintained stable representation, which assisted both the negotiations and the atmosphere. In the last stages of drafting, in 1988, there was far greater participation by governments from the South, including Islamic States. With the exception of the International Labour Organisation for the articles concerned with child labour, and UNICEF from 1986, international organisations were largely absent.[10]

The NGOs, in contrast, were of crucial importance, especially after 1983. Before 1983, they had argued among themselves about protecting the foetus, but were advised that if they wanted to exercise any influence, they should work as a group. As a result, the Ad Hoc Group of NGOs was set up and received logistical support from UNICEF. The Group prepared a joint draft for the 1984 meeting and circulated it to governments. It produced annual reports on proposals and topics, and later organised briefing meetings and materials for government delegates to increase their awareness of the issues. These initiatives were well received and, increasingly, government delegates put forward NGO drafts for articles. Cantwell considers that NGOs were in fact responsible for article 34 (sexual abuse of children, exploitation of children in prostitution or pornography), article 35 (trafficking, sale, or abduction of children), and article 39 (recovery and re-integration of abused children) and had a large impact on article 19 (protection of children from physical or mental violence or abuse within the home or its equivalent), article 24(3) (abolition of traditional practices prejudicial to the health of children), article 44(6) (reporting obligations of States) and article 45 (methods of implementation by the Committee), among others.

The Working Group was chaired by Professor Adam Lopatka of Poland who showed great skill in urging States to arrive at agreed drafts.[11] In the early stages, the climate of the Working Group was adversely affected by Cold War animosities in another Working Group nearby and aggressive Soviet and American representatives. When there was a problem that could not be resolved in the Working Group, Lopatka sent the principal dissenters away with one or two neutral members, and sometimes NGO representatives, to discuss among themselves and come back with an agreed draft. They did.[12]

Children who travelled to Geneva, including indigenous children from Canada, were able to lobby States[13] — a contribution to children's autonomy unless it was entirely stage-managed by adults — but it seems that the Working Group may not have welcomed intervention by children.[14]

Article 12

Article 12 is the most important of the articles on participation.[15] In discussions on the first draft, the Colombian Government remarked that children should be considered as active and participating members of society in general and of the family in particular. The French Government — more precise — had suggested it would be desirable to add provision for consulting children:

> As soon as the child is capable of understanding, his consent must be sought when decisions have to be taken that may seriously affect his personal situation, such as those relating to adoption or the granting of custody.[16]

In the revised Polish draft, article 7, the forerunner of article 12, provided that States:

> shall enable the child who is capable of forming his own views the right to express his opinion in matters concerning his own person, and in particular, marriage, choice of occupation, medical treatment, education and recreation.

In the course of negotiations, the list was deleted, and 'age and maturity' were added, an objective and a subjective test of the child's capacity. In effect, the Convention requires attention to be paid to the child's way of expressing her/himself, not merely by words, but in all relevant aspects of the child's behaviour.[17]   Lücker-Babel draws attention to the possible conflict with article 3 on 'the best interests of the child.'[18]   This conflict will be resolved in practice by adults, family, social workers, and ultimately by the courts. A second paragraph was added at a late stage, after much discussion about the procedural rules of national law,[19] to ensure that children can be heard in any judicial or administrative proceedings either directly or through a representative or appropriate body.

Articles 19, 24(3), 34, 35 and 36

These articles deal with sexual abuse in the family, female genital mutilation, exploitation, including prostitution and pornography, and sale and trafficking of children and other forms of exploitation.[20]   The origins of these articles are complex and lie in articles VI and IX of the first Polish draft. Article VI dealt with the child's need for a loving family and the need for society and public authorities to provide care for children without a family. Greece considered that the problem of child abuse (non-accidental injury which could include incest) required a duty to be placed on the State to protect children whose families would not be able to care for them even with financial or other assistance from the State.[21] This issue is partially covered in the second sentence of article 9(1) of the present Convention.

Article IX(1) of the first Polish draft provided that:

> The child shall be protected against all forms of neglect, cruelty and exploitation. He shall not be the subject of traffic, in any form.

Spain proposed the addition of education to protect the child from 'manipulation, whether in regard to information, consumption, sex etc.'[22] This comment was addressed in article 9 of the revised Polish draft which provided that parents and the State shall protect the child against harmful influences in the media. This provision is also relevant to pornography. The Society for Comparative Legislation added 'trade' to 'traffic'[23] and France added 'commercial transaction' to the second sentence.[24] Other comments proposed the addition of humiliating and degrading treatment, and that children should not be punished for the actions of parents, relatives, or other persons.[25] The revised Polish draft took account of these comments in a less specific form.

Article 19(1) of the revised Polish draft provided:

the child shall be protected against all forms of discrimination, social exploitation and degradation of his dignity. He shall not be the subject of traffic and exploitation in any form.

Article 20 dealt with penal procedure, provided for special treatment and re-education for children and banned capital punishment. The notion of re-education is discussed below in connection with article 39 of the Convention.

In 1982, the United States submitted a long amendment, draft article 8 *bis*, which seems not to have been discussed. Article 8 *bis* (1) included a reference to sexual abuse or exploitation whether by a child's parent(s), guardian(s) or any other person responsible for the child, and set out in 8 *bis* (2)(a)-(i) methods and procedures for dealing with such eventualities. Article 8 *bis* (2)(h) provided for the appointment of a legal representative for the interests of an abused or neglected child in any judicial proceedings. This proposal in amended and broadened form became article 12(2) in 1989.[26]

The basis for the Working Group's deliberations was a short draft proposed by Canada, which, after additions and amendments, became article 19 of the Convention. The Canadian draft of one paragraph included a reference to sexual abuse as well as listing other forms of abuse and neglect when the child was in the care of the family or of others. Following a proposal from the Defence for Children International Movement, the Swedish delegation proposed that a second paragraph be added to the article to deal with measures that States should take to secure the protection of such children. These included measures to support the family. Discussion, especially between the United States and the Ukrainian SSR, centred on how far the phraseology should emphasise judicial and punitive as opposed to social programmes for children in need. These two delegations, together with that of the USSR were asked to meet informally to agree a text. They produced the text which now forms article 19(2) of the Convention.[27] The contributions to the debate were overwhelmingly from the North.

Article 24(3)

Article 24 on health (originally article 12) deals in paragraph 3 with 'traditional practices injurious to the health of children,' the code phrase for genital mutilation. This provision was proposed by Rädda Barnen on behalf of the Informal NGO Group in 1986.[28] It was debated the following year by representatives of Senegal and Western governments. Discussion centred on phrasing and on the scope of traditional practices. Some States argued for a specific reference to female circumcision, opposed by the International Movement for Fraternal Union Among Races and Peoples and by Senegal on the grounds that there were other traditional practices, such as preferential care and feeding for male children, and this was agreed.[29]

Articles 34, 35 and 36

Articles 34, 35 and 36 originated in a brief and wide-ranging article proposed by France and the Netherlands requiring States 'to protect the child against all forms of exploitation, particularly sexual exploitation, as well as against all degrading treatment and all acts prejudicial to the moral, spiritual, mental, and physical integrity of the child., The Informal NGO Group proposed two more specific articles, one dealing with child prostitution and child pornography and the second with the sale or traffic of children.[30] The three drafts, together with variants proposed by sub-groups at the request of the Chairman, were discussed together.[31] It seems clear that States wanted draft articles that were both precise and broad in their scope.

The draft article on the sale or traffic of children (article 35) was agreed first. A proposal to limit the provision to sale or traffic for sexual purposes was objected to by the ILO and others on the ground that sale or traffic occurred for many other purposes, for example for economic exploitation, labour, or adoption, and required bilateral and multilateral measures.[32]

The draft which became article 34 on sexual exploitation and abuse acquired three sub-paragraphs. The first deals with 'the inducement or coercion of a child to engage in unlawful sexual activity.' 'Unlawful' was retained, after discussion, because the age of consent is under 18 in many States. The second paragraph concerns the exploitative use of children in prostitution and other unlawful sexual practices; and the third with the exploitative use of children in pornography. Norway sought unsuccessfully to add 'the distribution and sale of child pornography.' The list of prejudicial acts in the original draft was replaced in article 36 by the phrase 'prejudicial to any aspects of the child's welfare,' on the grounds that the list was not comprehensive and that 'integrity' was not clear in this context.[33]

Article 39

In 1987, a new article on the rehabilitation of exploited children was considered by the Working Group. This article was introduced by Norway and supported by Venezuela on the basis of a proposal put forward by the Informal NGO Ad Hoc Group. The Working Group was sympathetic to the proposal. Discussion centred on the best wording to use including the best translations into French and Spanish: 'recovery and re-integration,' a broader formulation, was preferred to 'rehabilitation.' 'Neglect,' 'torture or any other form of cruel, inhuman, or degrading treatment or punishment; or armed conflicts' were added to forms 'of exploitation and abuse,' as the Working Party wished to cover the range of situations from which recovery was needed.[34] By the end of the discussions, the first sentence of the article was weakened from States 'shall take all measures to ensure the . . . recovery' of a child victim to 'shall take all appropriate measures to promote the . . . recovery' on the grounds that States could not ensure the recovery and that 'all measures' imposed too great a burden on States.[35]

Provisions for Implementation and Enforcement

The first Polish draft provided in articles XI and XII for 'periodic reports' to be considered by ECOSOC which might make observations and refer them to the General Assembly. Comments from States and NGOs showed that importance was attached to establishing an effective system of monitoring implementation of the Convention. To meet this need the Convention provides for a Committee on the Rights of the Child of 10 experts serving in their personal capacity, elected by States Parties from among their nationals, and having regard to geographical distribution and the principal legal systems (art. 43). The provisions are similar to those found in other Conventions.[36]

States Parties undertake to submit a report on their compliance with the Convention and any difficulties they may have encountered within two years of ratification and thereafter every five years. These reports should be made widely available to the public in their own countries. No provision was made for any form of individual petition, nor a right for children to approach the Committee directly. Specialised agencies, UNICEF, and other UN bodies are entitled to be present at the consideration of reports relevant to their mandates and may be invited by the Committee to submit reports on these topics. A unique provision adds to this list 'other competent bodies.' This phrase refers to NGOs. They had earned inclusion by their valuable contribution to the drafting of the Convention. The Committee may make comments, suggestions, and general recommendations as a result of the information received (art. 45), and reports on its work to the General Assembly through ECOSOC every two years (art. 44).

The Convention on the Rights of the Child came into force more quickly than any other Convention, within a year of being opened for signature. It is also the Convention which has been the most widely ratified. By April 1998, 191 States had ratified the Convention. Switzerland and the United States have signed, but not yet ratified.

Assessment

Before turning to subsequent events, let us assess the process of negotiating the Convention. Cantwell lists 13 major innovations, many of which had not previously appeared in any binding international treaty.[37] Those relevant to our topic include the best interests of the child (article 3), article 12 and article 39. There have been very few reservations to these articles.[38]

The negotiations on these substantive articles of the Convention are interesting for several reasons. Delegates seem to have had a genuine concern to arrive at an effective and workable Convention which would not place too heavy a burden on States, thus avoiding the risk that it would either not be supported or that its provisions would be disregarded. Proposals were supported by varying groups of governments. The final draft was arrived at by consensus. Of the developing countries, only Senegal was an active participant throughout the 11 years of negotiations — at least on these articles. A very long amendment, article 8 *bis* put forward by the United States, served the purpose of reminding delegates of many specific issues which might not otherwise have arisen in such specific form.

Even more important was the role of the NGOs and the effectiveness of their work in raising issues and drafting proposals that became the basis of discussion. The UN Secretary-General in 1994 wrote that NGOs provide 'the closest approximation to direct popular participation in the intergovernmental machinery.'[39] In these negotiations they demonstrated the value of that participation.

As we shall see, in the next chapter it is clear from the reports that the Committee is well informed and able to ask searching questions of government representatives. In this they have been helped by NGOs. The Committee's criticisms are phrased in plain, but most diplomatic, language.

Developments Prompted by the Convention

The NGO Group on the Committee on the Rights of the Child

The Informal Ad Hoc Group of NGOs originally intended to dissolve itself once the Convention had been achieved. Instead, it decided to reconstitute itself in order to raise awareness of the Convention, and to promote the full implementation of it by providing a source of information for the Committee on the Rights of the Child, for other UN bodies and NGOs and to offer a channel of communication between the Committee and the NGOs. In 1995, the Group had 37 members, not all of them concerned exclusively with children. The Co-ordinator, based in Geneva, provides a very valuable service for them by making possible the pooling of information and ensuring that the Committee is well informed. The Group meets twice a year to develop joint strategies. In 1995, the seven sub-groups included one on sexual exploitation.[40]

Children's Rights Information Network (CRIN)

In 1992, two years after the Convention had come into force, Defence for Children International (DCI), with support from Rädda Barnen (the Swedish SCF) and UNICEF, called a meeting with NGOs to consider what information was needed by NGOs, the Committee on the Rights of the Child and other bodies to secure effective implementation of the Convention. A Facilitating Group was appointed and in 1995 more than 50 national, regional and international organisations met in Paris. They agreed to set up the Children's Rights Information Network to provide information to NGOs at all levels, from local to international, and to help NGOs to develop their systems of information and their data-bases.

Regional Conventions

Two further developments were the drafting of the African Charter on the Rights of the Child, adopted in 1990 but which had received only six ratifications by the end of 1996. 20 are needed for the Convention to come into effect. A European Convention on the Exercise of Children's Rights, concerned simply with the representation of children in legal proceedings, was adopted on 25 January 1996.[41]

The Work of the Committee on the Rights of the Child

At its first session, the Committee on the Rights of the Child drew up rules of procedure according to which meetings would normally be held in public and representatives of UN bodies and NGOs could participate in public or private meetings when invited to do so. Because there were so many early ratifications and initial reports due within two years, the Committee requested and obtained approval for additional sessions. The Committee also drew up the General Guidelines in 1991 to advise States Parties on making their initial reports.[42]

The Guidelines are detailed and set a pattern for using the reporting process to improve the treatment of children throughout the world in so far as moral pressure is able to do this. We know from the experience of the Convention on the Elimination of All Forms of Discrimination Against Women that international legislation does influence national legislation, and bring about legal improvements which legitimate the activities of national and local NGOs to secure their implementation. The Guidelines also reflect the experience of other comparable Committees.[43]

The reports are intended to form the basis of a meaningful dialogue with the Committee and so should include difficulties in complying with the Convention as well as measures for compliance. States should also facilitate popular scrutiny, both in the compilation of the report and in its circulation. States are asked to provide information on policy, or measures, for monitoring and co-ordinating policy as well as on legislation. The Committee identified four principles of interpretation in the Convention and reports on all articles should show how these principles are implemented in relation to them.[44] These principles are non-discrimination (article 2), the best interests of the child (article 3), respect for the child's views (article 12), and the right to life, survival and development (article 6). Hammarberg, a member of the Committee, points out that 'survival' is unusual in human rights instruments and indicates the importance of the dynamic aspects of the right to life, such as immunisation.[45] States can be asked to supply additional information in response to the Committee's questions, and are examined on their reports some six weeks to two months after they have been submitted so that the members of the Committee have time to study the Government's report in the light of the comments of the NGOs.

On the specific articles we are concerned with, States are required to report on the steps they have taken to ensure that children's views are sought in relation to questions of abuse and neglect whether within or outside the family, and the steps taken to secure the recovery and re-integration of a victimised child. The statistics provided must be disaggregated by sex, geographical, urban or rural area, ethnic or national background, so that it becomes possible to find out whether any specific group is disadvantaged.

In addition to examining States' reports, the Committee devotes one day of each session to a public seminar on a topic arising from the Convention. Topics have included children and armed conflict, the girl-child, and children and the media. At the seminar on the girl-child a large range of topics was discussed including 'harmful traditional practices,' the code phrase for female genital mutilation, preference for sons, early marriage, and lack of access to education and health services. The Committee stressed the importance of education for changing ideas, and that leaders, including religious leaders, should promote girls' rights.[46]

Representatives of UN bodies and of children's NGOs and media attended the discussion on children and the media on 7 October 1996. Three issues were discussed: participation by children, protection of children from harmful influences expressed in and through the media, and protection of the integrity of children when reported in the media. The role of the media in exposing the exploitation of children was recognised — child prostitutes in Bucharest were willing to talk about their work for a price. The Internet has proved to be safe and convenient for paedophiles; an English paedophile was convicted with 9,000 images of sexually exploited children which he had exchanged around the world. Twelve recommendations for good practice for journalists were drawn up which included guidelines on reporting child abuse and for training on children's rights.[47] On 25 March 1998, the Committee held a debate on the sexual exploitation of children at which NGOs explained their policies and work,[48] thereby contributing to the expertise of the Committee.

The Committee members also make field trips each year, for example in October 1995 they split into groups for their visit to south Asia. Members met children, parents, neighbours, political thinkers, and community and NGO leaders, as well as government officials, and they visited institutions and attended meetings to discuss the obligation of States — all within seven days.[49]

The Committee agreed General Guidelines for periodic reports in November 1996.[50] States are requested to address the matters of concern raised by the Committee on the previous report and the action taken on the Committee's suggestions and recommendations together with any difficulties arising from them, and including changes in legislation, policy, mechanisms, structures and the allocation of resources. The report should also specify the steps taken to publicise the previous report and concluding observations of the Committee. All changes relevant to the remit of the Committee should be reported, as well as future plans. These Guidelines are very detailed, covering information relevant to all articles in the Convention. Two years later, in January 1998, the Committee began the task of drawing up General Comments on the interpretation of the Convention in the light of its experience in monitoring initial reports.[51]

Conclusion

The part played by Professor Lopatka, the Chairperson, and the stability in the representation of States, contributed greatly to the success of drafting the Convention. Individuals do make a difference. The openness and flexibility of the procedures of the Working Group made possible the resolution of difficulties and the contribution of many committed NGOs. The Convention's provisions became more radical and included more rights as a result of the NGOs' participation. Children have been recognised as persons in international law and indirectly in the law of many States, a development of enormous importance. In addition, the Committee has shown itself committed to improving the lot of children, informing itself on issues and conditions throughout the world, and building on the experience of other human rights bodies. It is setting international standards through its scrutiny of the practices of national governments and pressing for their implementation.

Pornography, prostitution and trafficking remain among the most serious abuses of children. They are international as well as national problems, but must be dealt with by national governments since there is no adequate international enforcement body. The Committee's work assists co-operation between governments, international bodies and NGOs in overcoming these abuses.

Notes

[1] GA res. 44/22, annex 44 UN GAOR Supp. (No. 49) at 167, UN Doc. A/44/49 (1989) (*entered into force*, 2 Sept. 1990). Article 12 continues, in para. 2,
'For this purpose, the child shall in particular be provided the opportunity to be heard in any judicial and administrative proceedings affecting the child, either

directly, or through a representative or an appropriate body, in a manner consistent with the procedural rules of national law.'

[2] Records of Fifth Assembly, LNOJ Supp. 23 (1924).

[3] Revision of the 1924 Declaration adopted by the International Union for Child Welfare. See *The World's Children* 398 (1948).

[4] GA res. 1386 (XIV), 14 UN GAOR Supp. (No. 16) at 19, UN Doc. A/4354 (1959).

[5] 226 UNTS 3 (*entered into force*, 30 Apr. 1957), art. 1(c).

[6] See Official Records of ECOSOC 1978, Supp. No. 4, UN Doc. E/1978/34, ch. XXVI, sec. A, res. 20.   See also M. Longford, 'NGOs and the Rights of the Child in the Conscience of the World,' in *The Conscience of the World: The Influence of Non-Governmental Organisations in the UN System* ch. 8 (P. Willetts, ed., 1996); N. Cantwell, 'Origins, Development and Significance of Rights of the Child,' in *The UN Convention on the Rights of the Child — A Guide to the Travaux Préparatoires* 19, 21 (S. Detrick, ed., 1992).

[7] Cantwell, note 6 *supra,* at 20-21.

[8] See *note verbale* of 5 Oct. 1979 from the Permanent Representative of Poland to the UN to the Division of Human Rights, UN Doc. E/CN.4/1349* (1980).

[9] 1249 UNTS 13 (*entered into force*, 3 Sept. 1981).

[10] Cantwell, note 6 *supra,* at 21-24.

[11] *Id.* at 23; Longford, note 6 *supra,* at 214, 220-221.

[12] Cantwell, note 6 *supra,* at 23.

[13] G. Van Bueren, 'The UN Convention on the Rights of the Child,' 3 JCL 63 (1991).

[14] Y. Kubota, 'The Protection of Children's Rights and the UN,' 58 NJIL 7, 22 (1989).

[15] See also art. 13 (concerning freedom of expression, including freedom to seek, receive and impart information).

[16] UN Doc. E/CN.4/1324/Add.1, 8 (France (c)) (1978).

[17] Van Bueren, note 13 *supra,* at 64.

[18] M.-F. Lücker-Babel, 'The Right of the Child to Express Views and to Be Heard: An Attempt to Interpret Article 12 of the UN Convention on the Rights of the Child,' 3 IJCR 391, 394 (1995).

[19] UN Doc. E/CN.4/1989/48, at 42-45.

[20] Articles 32 and 33 provide, respectively, for economic exploitation and abuse of drugs.

[21] UN Doc. E/CN.4/1324, at 35.

[22] UN Doc. E/CN.4/1324 at 42.

[23] UN Doc. E/CN.4/1324, at 43.

[24] UN Doc. E/CN.4/1324/Add.1, 8 (France (b)).

[25] UN Doc. E/1979/36, ch. XI, at 64.

[26] UN Doc. E/CN.4/1983/62, Annex II (E/CN.4/WG.1/WP.3).

[27] UN Doc. E/CN.4/1984/71, 8-11 (the words 'wherein the child's interests will be fully represented' were ultimately deleted).

[28] UN Doc. E/CN.4/1986/39, at 10-11.

[29] UN Doc. E/CN.4/1987/25, at 8-10.

[30] UN Doc. E/CN.4/1987/25, at 16.

[31] UN Doc. E/CN.4/1987/25, at 15-24.

[32] UN Doc. E/CN.4 1987/25, at 16.

[33] UN Doc. E/CN.4/1987/25, 15, at 22-24.

[34] UN Doc. E/CN.4/1987/25, 40-41.

[35] UN Doc. E/CN.4/1989/48, 93-94.

[36] See M. Rendel, *Whose Human Rights?* 96-97 (1997).

[37] Cantwell, note 6 *supra*, at 28.

[38] Kiribati, Poland and Singapore entered reservations to article 12 to the effect that children's rights should be exercised having regard to parental authority and local customs.

[39] R. Brett, 'The Role and Limits of Human Rights NGOs at the United Nations,' 43 *Political Studies* 96, 99 (1995) (quoting the General Review of Arrangements for Consultations with Non-Governmental Organisations, para. 33).

[40] L. Theytaz-Bergman, 'NGO Group for the Convention on the Rights of the Child,' 3 IJCR 452 (1995).

[41] Council of Europe, ETS 160. As of 16 July 1999, this Convention not yet in force, had been ratified by Greece and Poland, and signed by 16 other States <http://www.coe.fr/tablconv/160t.htm> (visited 1 Oct. 1999).

[42] UN Doc., GAOR, Supplement 41, A/47/41, General Guidelines, Annex III, 14-19; Rules of Procedure, Annex IV, 20, rules 32, 34 at 26, 27 (1993).

[43] See Rendel, note 36 *supra*.

[44] G. Van Bueren, *The International Law of the Rights of the Child* 26 (1995).

[45] T. Hammarberg, Preface, in *The Handbook of Children's Rights: Comparative Policy and Practice,* ix, x (B. Franklin ed., 1995).

[46] L. Theytaz-Bergman, 'Committee on the Rights of the Child: Eighth Day of General Discussion on the Girl-Child,' 3 IJCR 270, 271 (1995).

[47] N. Williams, 'Committee on the Rights of the Child,' 5 IJCR 262, 263-266 (1997).

[48] UN Doc. CRC/C/SR.443, at 3 (1998).

[49] 'Children's Rights Committee: Visit to South Asia,' 4 IJCR 85, 85-87 (1996) (no author).

[50] General Guidelines Regarding the Form and Contents of Periodic Reports to be Submitted by States Parties under Article 44, Paragraph 1(b) of the Convention, UN Doc. CRC/C/58 (1996).

[51] UN Doc. CRC/C/73, 27 (1998).

4 The United Nations Convention on the Rights of the Child and British Legislation on Child Abuse and Sexuality

MARGHERITA RENDEL

Introduction

That the effectiveness of international law depends on national law and practice was noted in the preceding chapter. In this chapter, the ways in which the United Kingdom has responded to the Convention on the Rights of the Child ('the Convention')[1] is examined together with the impact of domestic scandals on legislation and practice concerning child abuse and children's rights.

The United Kingdom's First Report

The United Kingdom's first report[2] was presented on time in February 1994. It reviews the United Kingdom's obligation under the Convention in formal, largely legal and administrative terms, stating what had been done and summarising changes in the law. Despite the recommendation in the Guidelines of the Committee on the Rights of the Child,[3] the UK Government did not consult with children or the public in preparing its first report, and non-governmental organisations (NGOs) were invited to contribute only very late.[4] There is no assessment of the effectiveness of these measures or even evidence of monitoring their results in the report. The prosecution of sex tourists was discussed with the Committee: the United Kingdom, believing it was better for prosecutions to take place in the country where offences were committed, expressed a willingness to extradite, as shown by the extradition treaty with Thailand. It offered to assist criminal investigations abroad, for example by the service of legal documents, by taking statements from witnesses and, in some cases, by searching premises and seizing documents and other evidence under the Criminal Justice (International Co-operation) Act 1990.

Stress was laid on the provisions of the Children Act 1989 which *inter alia* enabled children for the first time, with the leave of the Court, to apply for certain orders in relation to their upbringing, to refuse medical or psychiatric examination and, as an exception, to attend Child Protection Conferences under the *Working Together*[5] arrangements for co-operation between different agencies. Children could use the complaints procedures of local authorities and voluntary bodies, and the guidance on the management of children's homes provided that children's views must be taken into account. The Sex Offences Act 1993 removed the assumption that boys under the age of 14 were incapable of sexual intercourse.

The report prompted 48 questions from the Committee, which were answered promptly but uninformatively. The British team, the Committee found, did not enter into a dialogue, but rather defended the Government's position, presumably in accordance with instructions from ministers. The Committee noted that the Report lacked sufficient information on difficulties facing the Government and was uncertain whether the Government had thought enough about methods of co-ordination and monitoring, and whether enough resources were made available in what is a rich country for the social rights of children in the most vulnerable groups in society. They noted that local authorities, responsible for much, were deprived of adequate resources. They were disturbed about reports of sexual and other abuse. The measures to implement the basic functions of the Convention were inadequate; for example there was no right for children to express views on access to sex education (some aspects are compulsory in the National Curriculum), from which parents could withdraw them.[6] It is clear from the Committee's report that the members were well informed.

The Committee made 21 recommendations. For our purposes these included the following, which can be grouped as 'machinery,' information specific to sex, the best interests of the child, and article 12. The Government should establish mechanisms for co-ordinating and monitoring implementation of the Convention and the Children Act by Government departments, local authorities and voluntary bodies throughout the United Kingdom. More should be done to inform the public, and to train professionals dealing with children, such as teachers, police, judges, social workers, health workers, and staff in child care homes and detention centres about the Convention; the training of teachers should include the Convention. More needed to be done to include in legislation and administrative practice provision to ensure both the right of children to express their views and to secure the best interests of the child. Children should have an effective right of appeal against expulsion from school and to express a view on the running of the school. More preventative programmes were needed to reduce the number of teenage pregnancies. More measures were needed urgently to prevent sexual exploitation and drug abuse. More thought was needed to develop strategies for the rehabilitation and recovery of victimised children. The problems of sexual exploitation are, as we know, closely related to questions of poverty. The Committee noted 'the importance of additional efforts to overcome the problems of growing social and economic inequality and increased poverty.'

The Committee's observations were reported in the British press. Predictably, the tabloids were furious that a team from 'Third-World countries' could accuse Britain of ill-treating its children. The broadsheets gave good coverage, but, like the Government, saw the process as an adversarial one. The then Conservative Government took no action on the recommendations.[7]

Other governments have taken the process in a very different spirit. The Russian Federation, for example, was complimented by the Committee on its self-critical approach.[8]   The Committee noted that the Swedish Government had followed the Guidelines closely and that a constructive dialogue had been possible.[9]   A scanning of the Committee's responses to the reports of other governments shows that the British Government's report was inadequate. Worse is the record of the Yugoslav Government. Its initial report was submitted in November 1994.[10]   It is an extensive document covering Serbia and Montenegro, which draws attention to difficulties caused by sanctions. Sanctions are also used as a reason for not appearing before the Committee either in 1994 or 1996. However, in 1996, the Committee considered the report in the light of information received from other sources and reached very critical conclusions, in particular relating to inadequate provision for reducing sex abuse and educating the public on this topic, the lack of freedom of expression and tolerance for minorities, and the situation in Kosovo.[11]   In contrast, Rwanda's Report consisted of seven pages and was referred back very courteously with a reminder about the technical assistance available.[12]

Assessment

The concept of a dialogue based on these reports and comments which reach deep into the internal administration of States Parties shows a far-reaching departure from the concept of 'sealed' sovereign States immune from any external scrutiny. It presupposes instead a concept which can be put something like this: "We have agreed on the principles and rules set out in this Convention to deal with these problems. How are we dealing with them? What difficulties are there? What ways are there of overcoming the difficulties? of making things better? How can we learn from each other? Can international agencies help?' This is a co-operative philosophy, which can be found in other systems of human rights.

Children's Rights in Britain

From the mid-1980s and through the 1990s, there are two groups of developments which occurred and interweave. One consists of policy documents, legislation and case-law. The other is the formation and work of pressure groups for and of children.

Working Together

The British Government, in its Report to the Committee on the Rights of the Child, drew attention to *Working Together*. This is a guide addressed to local authorities, health authorities, and voluntary and other bodies, on dealing with cases of child abuse.[13] It predates the Children Act, but phrases from it are used in the Act. It stresses the importance of co-operation between agencies and sets out procedures for reporting on cases of the various forms of child abuse, whether neglect, physical abuse, sexual abuse, emotional abuse or circumstances giving rise to grave concern. It emphasises the primacy of children's interests and the importance of the child's views being presented at case conferences, and of the child being informed of decisions, their implications and the reasons for them. Equally important, the rights of parents to be heard, of their receiving information and being invited to attend case conferences is also stressed[14] — these rights of parents can be important to the child also. The guide notes that the European Court of Human Rights had found the United Kingdom in breach of articles 6 and 8 of the European Convention on Human Rights, because the authorities failed to involve parents in making decisions about their children, and the parents lacked the means to challenge the local authorities' decisions.[15]   The new Labour Government is consulting on a revised version of the document.

The Children Act 1989

The Children Act 1989 is a major reforming Act which repeals and replaces provisions concerning children scattered in a wide range of enactments.   The Act was being drafted and went through Parliament at the same time as the Convention was in its final stages of drafting.   The immediate impetus for the legislation lay in the scandals associated with a series of cases of child abuse and the objections to and questions about the action taken by social workers.   Other factors and changes in attitudes are discussed by Lyon and Parton.[16]   It is unlikely that these developments in the United Kingdom had any impact on the drafting of the Convention, and what was happening in Geneva almost certainly did not have a major impact on the UK; but there was no clear line between the two developments.   Tim Eggar, Minister of State at the Foreign and Commonwealth Office, declared that, while the Government had no objections to the principles of the draft Convention, they were seeking amendments to 21 articles and paragraphs, including those concerned with non-discrimination, the best interests of the child and the right of the child to express her or his views, to try 'to ensure that they are consistent with UK legal and administrative provisions.'[17]   The most important stages in the Bill were taken in the House of Lords where there was cross-party agreement on the principles.   More interesting than Tim Eggar's answer, and perhaps equally surprising, was the statement by Baroness David that there had been much consultation and that the Lord Chancellor and the Department of Health had listened to those consulted and made changes as a result.[18]

The Children Act does not apply as widely as the Convention in giving priority to the best interests of the child or in giving the child a right for her or his views to be heard and considered seriously. This is not the place to set out all the provisions of the Act; I shall merely indicate its limited provisions relevant to our concerns. The Act provides that the best interests of the child are paramount in relation to action by the Courts.[19]   Local authorities have a duty to safeguard and promote the welfare of the child (Section 22(3)(a)).   What this means is spelt out in the seven paragraphs of Section 1(3) and includes the 'ascertainable wishes and feelings' of the child in the light of her or his age and understanding, physical, emotional and educational needs, the likely effect of a change in circumstances, any harm he or she is actually, or is at risk of, suffering and so on. No such duty is imposed on parents or schools.

The duty to ascertain the child's wishes and feelings is a new express duty applying to Courts and also to local authorities to a limited extent. Local authorities are required to provide and publicise independent procedures open to children, whether in or not in care, or any other person with a sufficient interest in the child's welfare, to make representations and complaints. This provision could enable any child to complain to the local authority of treatment he or she is receiving from parents or others responsible for her or his care. Eekelaar and Dingwall suggest that it could enable a mature girl of south Asian origin to challenge the decision of her parents to send her to the sub-Continent.[20] It could also be used to challenge an arranged marriage or the decision of parent(s) to prevent a girl from continuing her education after the age of 16.

The Act also provides that a sufficiently mature child may apply to the Court for one of the Orders under Section 8, concerning residence and contacts with parents and others. However a child has to apply for leave from the High Court for such an Order.[21] Many children are not aware of this possibility.[22] There is a range of Orders open to the Court such that the child is protected from inappropriate 'protection.' The Act is a beginning towards the recognition of children as subjects rather than merely objects of law, but it is unevenly provided and appears almost more as an afterthought than as a principle underlying the whole Act.

Children's Rights Officers

The provisions requiring local authorities to provide procedures for representations and complaints may be based not only on the need for such procedures, but also on the successful development of Children's Rights Officers (CROs) by some local authorities. Such an officer was first proposed in 1984 at the Children's Congress and was a response to scandals arising out of the maltreatment and abuse of some children by some foster parents and in some children's homes, for example the 'pindown' affair.[23] The first CRO was appointed by Leicestershire Social Services in 1987. Leeds City Social Services Department in conjunction with SCF appointed their CRO slightly later. The Department believed that an officer employed by a voluntary body would have and be seen to have the independence necessary to be effective. In addition to dealing with complaints, the Leeds CRO monitors the policy of the Social Services Department and raises awareness of children's rights under law and the Convention both among children and among councillors and local government staff.   CROs have taken up a range of issues, from abuse, bullying, juvenile justice, religion, special needs (that is disability), to ending bulk buying for children's homes so as to enable children to go shopping to buy, for example, their own clothes and toothpaste. The Children Act has given an impetus to the appointment of such officers, who usually have an independent telephone number and, wherever possible, offices separate from those of the local authority. The Children's Rights Officers Association meets quarterly to provide a network for mutual support and to counteract the isolation that many feel.[24]

The *Gillick Case*

The autonomy of children in relation to sexual activity was considered extensively in *Gillick v. West Norfolk and Wisbech Health Authority and Department of Health and Social Security* in the early 1980s.[25] Mrs Gillick, the mother of five young daughters, challenged guidance given by the Department of Health and Social Security (DHSS) that doctors should, but only in exceptional circumstances, give contraceptive advice and treatment to girls under 16 without their parents' knowledge or consent. In response to her enquiry, her local health authority refused to give an undertaking that her daughters would not be given such advice. The legal issues centred on parental rights, whether such advice would be unlawful since it is a crime for a man to have sexual intercourse with a girl under 16, and whether a girl under 16 could give valid consent to contraceptive treatment. Concern about sexual intercourse without contraception was also discussed. All parties agreed that such advice could be given in an emergency.

In the House of Lords, the majority held that the DHSS advice was lawful, was concerned with clinical medical advice and treatment, that the need to prevent undesired early pregnancies and sexually transmitted diseases justified the advice, and that the confidentiality of the doctor-patient relationship justified not informing a parent. The recognition of the DHSS's advice as lawful was hedged with provisos: that the girl would understand the doctor's advice, that he could not persuade her to or let him inform her parents, that she was likely to have sexual intercourse in any case, that her physical and/or mental health were likely to suffer without advice and that her best interest required that she receive contraceptive advice and/or treatment without parental consent.[26] Lord Scarman traced the somewhat erratic history of the notion that children had increasing capacity: parental authority was a dwindling right. 'A minor's capacity to make h s or her own decision . . . depends upon the minor having sufficient understanding and intelligence' to make the decision.[27] This is known as '*Gillick-competence*'. The Court was less concerned with children's autonomy than with policy.

The majority was narrow: 3-2 in the House of Lords. Lyon and Parton see the autonomy ostensibly given to children as following from this judgment.[28] However, they also show that the Courts, in a series of cases under the Children Act, have drawn back from the principle of *Gillick-competence*, or, more exactly, they tend to respect a child's views when these accord with their own.[29]

Sexual Activity, Prostitution and Pornography

Children's right to engage in sexual activity is restricted. Consenting heterosexual acts are permitted from the age of 16, but consenting homosexual acts from the age of 18 only. There is no regulation of lesbian acts. The Government is trying to equalise the age of consent at 16.

Children cannot legally consent to unlawful sexual acts.[30] Nonetheless, although prostitution is not a crime, girls under 16 are prosecuted for soliciting for prostitution. The men who use girls, or boys, commonly escape prosecution. The Children's Society and the police have complained that these children should be seen as victims and should not be criminalised.[31] Indeed such prosecutions must surely be contrary to article 34 of the Convention. Van Bueren has argued that prostitution is a hazardous occupation from which children should be excluded.[32]

Child prostitution has been shown to be prompted by adults who persuade children, again both boys and girls, to pose for pornographic photographs; the children are usually unaware of the significance of what they are doing. From salacious poses, they are inveigled into sexual activity and prostitution.[33] Pornography is a highly profitable industry for those who organise and sell it, but not for those who work in it. Most of those working in prostitution are in it owing to poverty and this is especially true of children.

Traditional Practices

Female genital mutilation is illegal under the Prohibition of Female Circumcision Act 1985. There have been no prosecutions under the Act, although it is known that it is practised to a limited extent. One doctor was struck off for performing such an operation.

The Children's Rights Development Unit

Of the pressure groups acting for children, some are long established, such as the National Society for the Protection of Children and SCF. Others are of recent origin. The Children's Rights Development Unit (CRDU) began work in March 1993, funded for three years by the Gulbenkian Foundation, to monitor compliance with the Convention by the UK Government. The Unit is bound by three principles: to see whether the Convention is complied with equally in the four jurisdictions of England, Wales, Scotland and Northern Ireland, to become fully conversant with the views of children and young people, and to work in consultation with professionals, academics and others interested in children and their welfare. A Youth Development Worker was appointed to maintain contact with children and young people.

The Unit began by reviewing legislation and practice to find where there was no conformity with the Convention and to locate gaps in their own information. The Unit circulated more than 1,000 questionnaires to bodies concerned for children. Several hundred questionnaires were returned. Papers based on these results were prepared on 15 aspects of the Convention including personal freedoms and physical and personal integrity. Three basic principles of the Convention, non-discrimination, the best interests of the child and the rights of the child to express her or his views, were included in each. These were reduced to summaries of two pages, with questions added, for discussion with some 30 to 40 groups of young people aged from eight to 16 from all parts of the United Kingdom and from all kinds of background. The 15 reports were then redrafted to take account of the views expressed by young people, circulated to all those consulted, and were revised and published.[34]   The result, *UK Agenda for Children*, is a thorough and comprehensive review of how far the United Kingdom fails to comply with the Convention together with recommendations for action.

UK Agenda for Children shows that the United Kingdom fails on every article to comply fully with the Convention. In particular, the United Kingdom fails to comply with the requirements of article 12. The Unit found that *every* group of young people complained that their views were not taken seriously by parents, schools, foster parents or in residential care; nor were they taken seriously by the media, politicians or policy-makers. Children had low status, little power and almost no control over their lives. The CRDU submitted the *Agenda* to the Committee on the Rights of the Child together with a critique of the UK Report. Lansdown notes that there is no culture in Britain of listening to children; persuasion is not enough and legislation is needed to require parents to listen, as local authorities are now required to do. Children should be listened to seriously, and given serious answers and explanations if their wishes cannot be met. Furthermore they should have access to genuine and effective means of complaint.[35]

ARTICLE 12

A member of ARTICLE 12, nine-year-old Alexander Nurnberg, translated article 12 into plain English as: 'Whenever adults make a decision that will affect you in any way, you have the right to give your opinion and the adults have to take that seriously.'[36]

ARTICLE 12 is an organisation run by and for children and young people under the age of 18. It was founded in November 1996 and has two aims: first, to ensure that children have a right to express their views and have their views taken seriously, and second, to try to ensure that the rights set out in the Children's Convention are implemented. Only children may be members of ARTICLE 12 which is managed by a Steering Committee of between 15 and 25 elected members who meet eight times a year. At the annual general meeting one-third of members stand down, so as to ensure a turnover of members. Members are asked to vote for at least one candidate under 11, at least one between 11 and 14 and one between 14 and 17. Members with particular interests or from particular parts of the country may be invited to join the Committee so as to ensure a wide and representative membership.

In 1998 ARTICLE 12 had just over 300 members, aged from six to 17 in all parts of the United Kingdom. Members receive a newsletter three times a year, which gives examples of what young people are doing to ensure their voice is heard, and an Annual Report Card, which sets out how children's views are, or are not, being listened to about law, policy and practice in the United Kingdom. ARTICLE 12 organises special projects and events, and provides guidelines on how to take action. Members are encouraged to share their experiences at the AGM and other meetings and to write about them in the newsletter. They can also set up local groups and meetings. ARTICLE 12 has received many requests for speakers and to run workshops about children's rights.[37]

The Children's Express

Children's Express (CE) looks like a news agency, but is a programme of learning through journalism for children aged eight to 18. It organises training in aspects of journalism, sends out teams of children as reporters, places their work in the media, and provides interviewers. CE began work in this country in London in May 1995 and in 1998 had 114 members. A second bureau was opened in Newcastle-upon-Tyne with 50 members in 1998. Thirty children have been trained in Kent and further expansion throughout the United Kingdom is planned.

In the programme, adults act as facilitators, whilst the children work in teams, deciding which stories to explore. The younger children, from eight to 13, are the reporters. The older children, 14 to 18, train them, undertake responsibility for editing, and initiate research and interviews. The children's work has been published in a range of media. Their investigative reporting has shown, for example, how easy it is for under-age children to buy lottery tickets, and has reported on teenage suicide, bullying, lesbian parents and mothers with pressured City jobs.

During the election campaign, children from CE interviewed all the party education spokespersons for the *Times Educational Supplement* and all the party spokespersons on the family for *Ceefax*. 'More testing than a Westminster press conference' was the comment of Chris Smith (now Secretary of State for Culture, Media and Sport) in April 1997. In 1998, CE held a public seminar on 'stereotypes of children in the media,' and made a presentation on life on estates to the Government's Social Exclusion Unit, which was enthusiastically received. All those interviewed by CE or involved in their broadcast work have commented on the children's professionalism and co-operative way of working.

The children's work is not merely published or broadcast. It does have effect: in March 1997, CE recorded interviews for *The Observer*, also broadcast on BBC1, on the proposed closure of Blakelaw School in Newcastle-upon-Tyne, prompting protests from more than 250 children, whose local secondary school it was. As a result, the Council reconsidered its decision and the school is still open. In four years, the work of CE journalists has reached more than 50,000,000 people through newspapers, both broadsheets and local papers, radio and TV and more than 100 articles have been placed. In March 1996, CE won a special Chairman's Award at the annual British Press Awards. Demand for CE's work is increasing.[38]

Conclusion

The impact of the Convention on the United Kingdom is hard to assess. It seems that the Convention exercised little direct influence on the Children Act. Nevertheless, there was important consultation between the Government and NGOs on the Act. The Convention may in future have more influence on policy. The Convention is also used in the classroom by those teachers interested in human rights and may contribute to the development of a human rights culture in Britain. The activities of children's organisations fully justify the confidence of the drafters of the Convention in requiring that children be consulted and their views be taken seriously.

Notes

[1] GA res. 44/22, annex 44 UN GAOR Supp. (No. 49) at 167, UN Doc. A/44/49 (1989) (*entered into force*, 2 Sept. 1990).

[2] *The United Kingdom's First Report to the Committee on the Rights of the Child*, (Her Majesty's Stationery Office [HMSO], Feb. 1994).

[3] See chapter 3 in this collection.

[4] See U. Kilkelly, 'The UN Committee on the Rights of the Child — An Evaluation in the Light of Recent UK Experience,' 8 CFLQ 105, 110 (1996).

[5] Department of Health and Social Security and Welsh Office, *Working Together* (1988).

[6] UN Doc. GAOR, 51st Session, Supplement No. 1, A/51/41 (1996).

[7] See Kilkelly, *supra* note 4, at 118-119.

[8] UN Doc. CRC/C/15/Add.4, at 1-4 (1993); cf. B. Bowring, 'Russian Children: The Obscenity of Political Fantasy, chapter 5 in this collection.

[9] UN Doc. GAOR, 49th Session, Supplement 41, A/49/41, ch. III B, at 24 (1994).

[10] UN Doc. CRC/C/8/Add.16 (1994).

[11] UN Doc. CRC/C/50, at 17-23 (1993).

[12] See UN Doc. CRC/C/8, Add.1 (1992); CRC/C/15/Add.12 (1993)

[13] See note 5 *supra*.

[14] See note 5 *supra,* at part 5.

[15] See *O v. United Kingdom*, 120 Eur. Ct. H.R. (ser. A) at 4 (1987); *H v. United Kingdom*, 120 Eur. Ct. H.R. 45 (ser. A) at 45 (1987); *W v. United Kingdom*, 121 Eur. Ct. H.R. (ser. A) at 4 (1987); *B v. United Kingdom*, 121 Eur. Ct. H.R. 61 (ser. A) at 61 (1987); *R v. United Kingdom*, 121 Eur. Ct. H.R. 105 (ser. A) at 105 (1987).

[16] C. Lyon & N. Parton, 'Children's Rights and the 1989 Children Act,' in *The Handbook of Children's Rights*, 40, 44 (B. Franklin ed., 1995) [hereinafter *Handbook*].

[17] Hansard, House of Commons Debates, Vol.136, Written Answers, Col. 376, 1 Jul. 1998.

[18] Hansard, House of Lords Debates, Vol. 502, Col. 509, 2 Dec. 1988. The Lord Chancellor was Lord Mackay of Clashfern, the Secretary of State for Health Kenneth Clarke, M.P. and the Minister of State David Mellor, M.P.

[19] Section 1. See also M. Freeman, 'Children's Rights in a Land of Rites,' in *Handbook, supra* note 16, at 70, 71.

[20] J. Eekelaar & R. Dingwall, *The Reform of Child Care Law* 26 (1990).

[21] Practice Direction, High Court, Family Division, 22 Feb. 1993.

[22] G. Lansdown & P. Newell, *UK Agenda for Children,* para. 3.10.3 (1994).

[23] The 'pindown' affair concerned the practice in the children's home of one local authority by which misbehaving children were locked in solitary confinement in pyjamas with nothing to read in an almost bare room for from one to ten days. A. Levy & B. Kahan, *The Pindown Experience and the Protection of Children: Report of the Staffordshire Child Care Inquiry 1990* (1991).

[24] S. Ellis & A. Franklin, 'Children's Rights Officers: Righting Wrongs and Promoting Rights,' in *Handbook, supra* note 16, at 89.

[25] AC 112 (1986).

[26] *Id.* at 162 (Fraser, LJ).

[27] *Id.* at 176 (Scarman, LJ).

[28] Lyon & Parton, note 16 *supra,* at 43.

[29] *Id.* at 49.

[30] J. Hall, 'Can Children Consent to Indecent Assault?' 1996 CLR 184; *Regina* v. *Pickford* 3 WLR 1022 (CA) (1994).

[31] 'Child Prostitutes — Victims or Criminals?' 141 *Childright* 15 (1997); L. Ravenscroft, 'The Need to Decriminalise Child Prostitution,' *id.* at 16.

[32] G. Van Bueren, *The International Law of the Rights of the Child* 277 (1995).

[33] L. Kelly, 'Pornography and Child Sexual Abuse,' in *Pornography* 113-123 (C. Itzin, ed., 1992).

[34] G. Lansdown, 'The Children's Rights Development Unit,' in *Handbook, supra* note 16, at 107.

[35] *Id.* at 104.

[36] Information received from ARTICLE 12 (on file with author).

[37] *Id.*

[38] All information received from CE (on file with author).

5 Russian Children: The Obscenity of Political Fantasy

BILL BOWRING

Introduction

Russia's children have faced a succession of horrors. Despite genuine legal reforms in recent years, child welfare has too often been sacrificed to myths of nationhood. Discourses of national honour and conspiracy have displaced genuine investigations into, and remedies for, child abuse. This chapter begins with a terrifying narrative illustrating the tragedy of Russian children. Yet there is a happy ending, of sorts, which may warrant hope for a brighter future.[1]

A Purely Russian History

The following story appeared under the title 'A Purely Russian History' in 1997, in a special issue of the long-established, and always critical, Russian news magazine *Ogonyok* (Little Flame). This issue was specifically concerned with problems of children. An *Ogonyok* journalist was telephoned by a friend who, 10 years earlier, had gone to live in the United States. The friend explained that with the help of an agency based in New York, an American family had adopted an eight-year-old girl from Omsk, in Siberia. The first evening in her new home, to the family's horror, the girl went to the parents' bedroom and tried to render 'specific oral services.' The girl said that this was what she always had done with the director of her children's home in Russia, and that this was also the case with the other children at the home. The director of the home had told the children that if they loved and respected their elders, this is what they should do. In return, when they were older, he would drive them in his car to his acquaintances' homes. The older children had said that this was not so terrible, since they would then be treated as if they were grown up. This story was investigated by another journalist, based in Siberia, and the facts were confirmed. The director had even been receiving money in advance from his friends. However, no one was prosecuted, and the local press refused to publish the story. The story was not an attempt to shock or titillate. It appeared as part of a serious contribution to a widespread discussion, in 1997, of one of the more controversial problems of Russian politics: inter-country adoption.[2]

The Russian Crisis and the 'Russian Idea'

Russia is suffering an unprecedented economic and demographic crisis. The Soviet Union was not brought down by a mass revolt or even by external pressure. Nor did it simply rot away, consumed by its own corruption. Instead, in December 1991, the leaders of Russia, Ukraine, and Belarus effectively carried out a coup. The leaders of the other components of the former USSR acquiesced, as it was clearly in their personal interest to do so. This transformation did not open the way to a democratic and prosperous 'normality.' Instead, the most memorable events since then have included the shelling and storming of Russia's Parliament in the autumn of 1993; the war in Chechnya, one of the Russian Federation's 89 subjects, in 1994-95; and the collapse of both the rouble and the reforming government of Kiryenko in August 1998. The frenzied prosperity of Moscow is the façade behind which lie countless outrages, including thousands of homeless and destitute children.

While there is a substantial body of 'liberal' opinion which blames the stagnation, corruption, and repression of the Soviet period for what has happened, the self-styled 'national patriots,' led by Gennadii Zyuganov and his Communist Party of the Russian Federation, have, as Wendy Slater points out, 'formulated their own version of Russian and Soviet history which, in turn, has shaped their concepts of Russian national identity and the "Russian idea." They have tried consciously to amalgamate the most "attractive" elements of Soviet history with their nostalgia-fuelled image of Tsarist Russia.'[3] This effort focuses largely on the alleged greater spirituality, humanity, and collectivism of traditional Russian culture. In a recent two-volume work entitled *Russia's Ideological Reference Points,* a section entitled 'Russia's National Interests in the Spiritual Sphere' thus declares that these interests consist in 'the affirmation of the high morality, humanism and culture of the Russian citizen, and the defence and maintenance of the centuries-old spiritual tradition of the Fatherland.'[4]

This high-sounding rhetoric is not to be taken at face value. We can turn for assistance to one of the best-known scholars to emerge from the former communist world, the prolific Slovenian analyst Slavoj Zizek. He has made a special study of the 'gradual retreat of the liberal-democratic tendency' in Eastern Europe 'in the face of the growth of corporate national populism which includes all its usual elements, from xenophobia to anti-Semitism.'[5] He observes that 'the national cause is ultimately nothing but the way subjects of a given ethnic community organise their enjoyment through national myths,'[6] and argues that '[e]very nationality has built its own mythology narrating how other nations deprive it of the vital part of enjoyment the possession of which would allow it to live fully.'[7] Zizek illustrates this, in his own, Lacanian terms, 'imaginary castration,' by reference to a special feature of American ideology in the 1980s:

> [T]he obsessive idea that there might still be some American POWs alive in Vietnam, leading a miserable existence, forgotten by their own country. This obsession articulated itself in a series of macho-adventures in which a hero undertakes a solitary rescue mission (*Rambo II, Missing in Action*). The underlying fantasy-scenario is far more interesting. It is as if down there, far away in the Vietnam jungle, America had lost a precious part of its very life substance, the essence of its potency; and because this loss became the ultimate cause of America's decline and impotence in the post-Vietnam Carter years, recapturing this strong, forgotten past became an element of the Reaganesque reaffirmation of a strong America.[8]

Something very much like this was being enacted in the fetid circles of the Russian communist-nationalist right in 1997, as discussed below. The difference is that for the Russians concerned, it is not their fighters, trapped in Chechnya (although there is a powerful recent film, *Prisoner of the Caucasus*, on just such a theme), but their children, their genetic fund, the future of the nation, who are being kidnapped for purposes of abuse or even killing by the arch-enemy, the United States of America. First, however, it must be noted that there is something of a rational foundation for paranoia in Russia.

Could Russia Cease to Exist?

The existence of Russia as a distinctive culture and State is now in peril. The scale of the demographic catastrophe facing Russia is breathtaking. According to the Russian Government's own State Committee for Statistics, the population of the Russian Federation is likely to fall by one-half by the middle of the next century, and has already declined by over 1.5 million people since 1992 (from 148.7 million to 147.2 million).[9] The average life expectancy fell by six years from 1990 to 1996, and is currently 59.6 years for men and 72.7 years for women, placing Russia somewhere between Egypt and Brazil in terms of its average.[10]

The most striking factor, and the most disturbing for nationalists intent on the preservation of a Russian nation, is the reluctance of Russians to have children at all. From 1989 to 1997, while the death rate grew by 3.5 per cent, as high a rate, it is said, as a country engaged in war, the Russian birth rate fell by 6 per cent. Seven out of ten pregnancies in Russia are terminated by abortion and 2.5 million abortions were performed in 1997, although this represented a decline of 25 per cent since 1992.[11]

According to Russia's 1992 First Report to the UN Committee on the Rights of the Child,[12] the population of the Russian Federation was then 148.7 million people. Of these, **26.9 per cent, 40 million were children, 17** years old or less. The scale of what has happened to the birth rate is demonstrated by the fact that an authoritative 1997 publication put the number of children at about 37 million.[13] This was probably the case, given that between 1987 and 1991 the birth rate in Russia declined by 30 per cent to 12.1 live births per 1,000 population.[14]

Children suffer higher mortality than would be acceptable in Western Europe. The infant mortality rate (death before first birthday) in 1992 was 17.8 per 1,000 live births, according to the government figures presented to the United Nations, primarily the result of the social and economic crisis. Since November 1991 the mortality rate has been higher than the birth rate. Although infant mortality has begun to diminish in the last few years, there is rising teenage mortality, especially suicides — 2,000 in 1997.[15]

In response to this potential disaster, Valentina Matvienko, the Deputy Prime Minister with responsibility for social affairs, used the first official Mother's Day in Russia, on 28 November 1998, to announce that the Government was seriously concerned at the recent decline in the status of motherhood and the numbers of women wanting children. She urged a 10 per cent drop in the abortion rate by the year 2000.[16] The question, of course, is whether this alone will be enough to save Russia as a nation.

The Nightmare of Sick Children

There is a further factor of great relevance to the question of inter-country adoption — another trend which serves to fuel nationalist hysteria. Even the children who survive birth and early childhood are unhealthy. For example, according to the Scientific Research Centre for the Health of Children and Adolescents, Russian children are shorter than they were in the 1970s, chest measurements have shrunk by five to six centimetres, and an ever-greater number of children are underweight. Recent Government surveys show that rickets, hypotrophy, and diathesis are found in 60 per cent of young children, and anaemia in more than 10 per cent. It is believed that 15 to 20 per cent of school-age children suffer from chronic ailments. Only 11 to 14 per cent of schoolchildren are in good health.[17]

There has also been a rapid spread of diseases that were not known, or at any rate not reported, under the Soviet regime. Infectious, especially venereal, diseases are now rampant. In the five years to 1994 the rate of diphtheria among children rose 25-fold in Russia. In big cities such as Moscow and St Petersburg the rate is 2.5 times the average. According to the same reliable source, there was a 12.7 per cent increase in the number of children suffering from active tuberculosis in 1993.[18] This crisis in children's health has not been matched by State spending. In fact, from 1995 to 1997, 50 children's hospitals were closed, and the number of paediatric doctors declined by 7,000.[19]

The nationalist and communist right find clear evidence of the loss of Soviet (or Russian) standards of morality and ethical conduct in the extraordinary rise in sexual promiscuity and the incidence of venereal disease. It is reported that during the five years to 1998 the number of young people suffering from syphilis in Russia as a whole rose by 20 times. In 1993 alone, the rate of gonorrhoea among children increased by 45 per cent, as opposed to a twofold rise for the general population. There are also significant rates of HIV-infection, primarily associated with drug abuse. Sexual abuse and exploitation of children has also shown a sharp increase. In 1997, the moderate Communist deputy, Alevtina Aparina informed the State Duma's Committee on the Affairs of Women, the Family, and Youth, which she chairs, that in the five years to 1997, the number of crimes connected with abuse of adolescents rose by 165 per cent. During the same period crimes connected with child pornography rose by 12 times, while in 1996 alone some 1,500 crimes against minors were committed for sexual reasons, mostly concerning children aged between eight and 12. According to researchers in St Petersburg, she said, 80 per cent of prostitutes are aged under 18.[20]

If the young people are so unhealthy, then how can Russia possibly defend itself? This problem is most graphically illustrated by the crisis of conscription to the Russian army. One-third of the young men called up for national service in 1996 were too unhealthy to serve: they were underweight and had a variety of medical and psychological problems. This compares with five per cent of the total in 1985, and 20 per cent in 1991. The numbers rejected because they had syphilis grew by 11 per cent in the 10 years prior to 1996, while the numbers of young alcoholics and drugs addicts doubled. The situation had worsened by 1997, when 407,000 of those called up were released by reason of ill-health, while only 403,000 were accepted for service.[21] This is a not only a health problem, but a horrifying geopolitical nightmare for Russia. So dangerous is the present situation that, in Rybinsky's view, around 18 million children, of the 37 million in Russia, were, in 1994, found to be in the 'zone of social risk,' that is, about half the child population in the country.[22] This proportion has, without doubt, increased.

Russia and International Children's Rights

The right wing of the communists and nationalists do not cease to remind their audience that the Soviet Union, in its propaganda, prided itself on the care and concern lavished upon children. As Judith Harwin points out, 'in many respects the Revolution was in the name of, and for, children.'[23] But given the ideology of Soviet 'communism,' the prime purpose of this attention was the socialisation of children into Soviet society, to take their place as unquestioning model citizens. The Party was anxious that all children, including those living within families, should participate in mass organisations and activities. For the majority of orphans and displaced children dispossessed by the civil war which followed the 1917 Revolution (at the peak of this *besprizornye*, in 1922, there were estimated to be some seven million homeless children wandering Russia[24]), as well as those who became orphans and homeless as a result of the liquidation of the peasantry by Stalin, and then following the Second World War, there seemed to be no alternative to very large State institutions.

The collapse of the Soviet Union, together with the Party and the values it purported to represent, and of the ideology of collective upbringing, have been accompanied by a revolution in attitudes towards children and childhood. The discourse of this revolution has been the discourse of international obligations, of international human rights — the discourse which for a period supplanted Marxism-Leninism as the official discourse of the Russian State[25] (there has now been a reversion by Russia's leaders to the language of Russian traditions of the strong State).

Thus, the Russian Federation, on paper at least, takes its international obligations concerning the rights of the child seriously. Some of these it inherited from its Communist predecessor State. The USSR was always a model State when it came to ratifying treaties, but rarely implemented them at home. It was one of the first parties to the 1966 International Covenant on Civil and Political Rights as well as the 1966 International Covenant on Economic, Social and Cultural Rights. On 13 July 1990, the USSR ratified the 1989 UN Convention on the Rights of the Child, which came into force for it on 15 September 1990. Following the dissolution of the USSR in December 1991, the Russian Federation as its successor became a party to the Convention, as well as to the other treaties.

Russia has been reasonably punctilious in meeting its formal treaty requirements. On 22 October 1992 it submitted its Initial Report under the 1989 Convention.[26] The Report was considered by the Committee on the Rights of the Child (the UN body of experts set up under the Convention to review the periodic reports submitted by States) on 21 and 22 January 1993, and it adopted concluding observations which were published on 18 February 1993.[27] The Committee praised Russia's timely submission of this report, and the 'frank, self-critical and comprehensive manner in which it was prepared.' It is noteworthy that the report is an invaluable source of reliable information. However, the Committee was gravely concerned at a number of matters, including 'the practice of the institutionalisation in boarding schools of children who are deprived of a family environment, particularly in cases of abandonment or where children are orphaned' as well as 'the occurrence of maltreatment and cruelty towards children in and outside the family.'

The Russian Government has now prepared its First Periodic Report for the Committee on the Rights of the Child, describing how it has realised its obligations under the Convention. This was submitted on 12 January 1998, and is due to be considered by the Committee at its 22nd Session in September to October 1999. This time, however, the Committee will also receive an Alternative Report, prepared by a number of Russian NGOs.[28] This report was presented at a press conference held in February 1999 by State Duma Deputy Valerii Borshchov, a leading human rights activist.[29] These official and alternative reports throw into sharp relief the existence in contemporary Russia of two wholly incompatible accounts of the cause of the tragedy of Russia's children. The Government's report takes a typically post-Soviet line, laying the blame on the rapid transformation of the social system combined with economic crisis, together with new social and economic phenomena associated with greater openness and the shift from authoritarian to democratic methods of administration. The message is that the communist system cared for children better than is possible under the new ideas and methods.

The alternative report, on the contrary, prepared by anti-communists, names three culprits. These are: first, the division of responsibility for the future of children among various ministries and departments, none of which can co-operate with the others; second, the monopolisation by State institutions of the care and rehabilitation of orphans, especially the 'social orphans' discussed below; and third, the absence of effective mechanisms of control with the ability to ensure that the staff at all levels fulfil their clear obligation to protect children's rights. The Government, of course, insists that no 'social control' is necessary. But the NGOs call for the UN to intervene to urge Russia to create an Ombudsman for Children's Rights, as exists in some 30 countries already, and independent social inspectors with power of access to institutions, documents, and the children themselves. There is much more of a consensus, as to the scale of the problem. Alevtina Aparina told the State Duma in February 1999 that the condition of Russia's children means that at least 13 of Russia's obligations under the Convention are violated.[30]

Domestic Legislation — Implementation in Fact?

It is only fair to point out that ratification of the 1989 Convention was not the only step taken by the new Russia on behalf of children. Children were given, at least on paper, special priority by President Yeltsin. In 1992 a new federal programme, 'Children of Russia', was launched, and took effect in 1993.[31] It is a programme with a number of components;[32] its aim is to increase the extent and effectiveness of State action at the central and regional levels. Moreover, the new Russian Constitution adopted in December 1993 provides (Article 38) that 'Motherhood and childhood, and the family are under the protection of the State.' Marat Baglai, Chairman of the Constitutional Court, has explained that this provision signifies constitutional recognition of the fact that childbirth and marriage are not only private affairs, but have great social significance and demand State support.[33] This Constitutional provision was concretised by the policy document entitled Fundamental Directions of State Social Policy for Improving the Position of Children in the Russian

Federation to the Year 2000, which was launched in 1995.[34] It stresses the contradiction between the necessity of guaranteeing the normal life and development of each child, and the inadequate economic possibilities of most families.

The Government is committed to a comprehensive strategy for individualised, social approaches to children's needs. This is a break not only from Soviet traditions, but from a legacy of Tsarism indeed, many aspects of Soviet culture and administration had their roots in Russian life as far back as Peter the Great. As Judith Harwin stresses, 'large -scale foundling homes were part of Russia's landscape from the early 18th century, modelled wholly on French experience. In this way, social attitudes today towards State care, and in particular to large-scale institutions, can be seen as a continuation of a long-standing historical tradition.'[35]   Such institutions helped the Soviet Union to cope with the aftermath of the Civil War and the Second World War (for Russia, the 'Great Patriotic War'), both of which left millions of orphaned children. At the same time, the Soviet Party-State provided a comprehensive set of benefits and subsidies, which brought the State into the life of every child at home.

This Government's new strategy was fully concretised when, on 1 March 1996, the new Family Code of the Russian Federation came into force.[36] The new Code is expressly intended to implement Russia's obligations under the 1989 Convention, and many of its provisions are modelled on the Convention.[37] As a sign of good faith, Article 6 of the Code states that 'If the international treaties of the Russian Federation contain rules other than those contained in family legislation, then the rules of the international treaty are to be applied.' An authoritative commentary to the Code[38] points out that these treaties include the 1948 Universal Declaration of Human Rights, the 1959 Declaration of Rights of the Child, the two International Covenants of 1966, and the 1989 Convention on the Rights of the Child. The formulation in Article 6 follows point 4 of Article 15 of the 1993 Russian Constitution, to the effect that international treaties and generally recognised principles of international law are part of the legal system of the Russian Federation, and there have already been many decisions of the Russian Constitutional Court striking down legislation and executive decisions because of non-compliance with international standards. As a result, a number of laws have been amended, for the better.[39]

There is one serious flaw. The Family Code does not contain the key principle of the 1989 Convention, namely that '[i]n all actions concerning children, whether undertaken by public or private social welfare institutions, courts of law, administrative authorities or legislative bodies, the best interests of the child shall be a primary consideration.' (Article 3.1) Nevertheless, the primacy and direct effect of international law in Russian law means that the 'best interests' principle must be a key aid to interpretation and decision. The Code is in many ways genuinely progressive and contemporary. Its drafters made extensive studies of international experience, including and especially the United Kingdom's 1989 Children Act, as the most up-to-date codification of private and public law relating to children then available. The provisions on fostering and adoption are very much in line with British and other international practice.

The Scandal of 'Social Orphans'

These provisions ought to be a proper response to the most pressing and disturbing contemporary problem of Russian children and the greatest challenge to the new legislation and orientation to international standards. This is exemplified by another set of shocking statistics, which are also reminiscent of wartime conditions. According to the official report[40] on the situation of children in Russia in 1996 produced by the Ministry of Labour and Social Development, there are now, as after the previous disasters described, more than 600,000 children defined as being without parental care (*beznadzorni*). During each of 1995 and 1996, more than 113,000 children were abandoned by their parents, an extraordinary rise from the total of 67,286 in 1992. Another 30,000 run away from home each year.

Other authors suggest that the total number of neglected (*besprizorni*) children in Russia, that is those beyond parental influence and social control, is 2.5 million, or as many as eight per cent of the total number of children. These figures cannot be said to be wholly reliable, and there is at least as much wild exaggeration in the Russian press as in its Western counterparts. However, a UNICEF report published in 1997 put the number of Russian children 'without parental care' at 611,034, of whom 337,527 were housed in a variety of institutions: 'baby houses,' children's homes, and homes for children with disabilities.[41] Another expert considers that the last figure includes children living part-time at home, and that the number of children in full-time institutions is about 200,000, some 30,000 of whom are locked away in psychoneurological *internaty* (boarding establishments) for 'ineducable' children.[42]

The most devastating blow to Russians' pride in their nation's treatment of children fell in December 1998, when the leading international human rights NGO, Human Rights Watch, published a special report,

Abandoned to the State: Cruelty and Neglect in Russian Orphanages.[43] This thorough research, which contains many heart-rending indiv dual cases, identifies two main problems. The first is the veritable 'archipelago of closed institutions' through which Russian orphans are herded, a maze of State structures operated by a number of ministries. Thus, the Ministry of Health is responsible for the care of some 18,000 to 20,000 children aged between birth and four years, in some 252 'baby houses.' Then the Ministry of Education looks after children with no disability or light disability (*debil*), while the Ministry of Labour and Social Development takes charge of those who have been diagnosed as severely disabled — '*imbetsil*' or '*idiot.*' All these institutions are severely under-funded, and have few or no facilities for rehabilitation or socialisation. There are few possibilities for children or their parents, if they have any, to complain or ever to leave the system.

The second problem is a feature and product of the first Children are effectively stigmatised at an early age. The label '*debil*' or '*idiot*' is practically impossible to lose, and ruins the life chances of the person to whom it is attached. This process of stigmatisation has immensely worsened even since Soviet times. The consequences of this segregation on the individual are appalling, wrecking the life chances of the individuals concerned. According to the Russian Procuracy (the institution in Russia which acts both as public prosecutor and ombudsman), some 15,000 children leave State children's homes every year. Within several years 5,000 of these will be unemployed; 6,000 will be homeless; 3,000 will have acquired criminal records; and 1,500 will attempt suicide.[44] The conclusion reached by Human Rights Watch is that there is a 'cycle of discrimiration, violence and impunity that endangers children in Russia.'[45]

NGOs did not and could not exist in Soviet Russia, where all 'social' organisations were under the control of the Party. It is therefore significant that Russian NGOs are now highlighting Russia's non-compliance with its obligations. They have been active in tackling the issue of 'social orphans.' For example, the Moscow-based NGO 'Rights of the Child,' founded in 1997 by the veteran dissident and human rights activist Boris Altshuler, the teacher Lyubov Kushnir, and others, has opened an advice centre for victims of ill-treatment in State institutions. On the basis of the information gained and its own research, it has campaigned for the system of 'social control' of children's homes and hostels at all levels — independent inspection with full investigative powers — which is one of the main demands of the Alternative Report. Their research was primarily responsible for the prosecution, in September 1995, of the Director of the Alpha orphanage in Moscow for the rape of at least five girls aged between 12 and 13 in his care, and the beating of at least three boys with iron rods.[46]

The Problems of Adoption in Russia

In the context of the disaster of State institutions described by Human Rights Watch, it might be thought that fostering and adoption would be preferable to abandonment to the State. According to reports, however, only a small proportion of children are adopted by Russians. In 1997, 30,000 children were adopted by Russians, of whom 18,000 were adopted by relatives and 12,000 by other citizens. The number of children available for adoption are a small proportion of those living in institutions (at least 533,000 inmates of various *priyutskikh* (hostel-type) institutions). About one-third of them could be adopted. The central register of children needing new families, however, contains only 40,000 names. The remaining 'social orphans' have not yet found their way onto the register.[47] The ill-health of Russian children means that even fewer children are now being adopted by Russians. This is principally because most of the children are disabled, have chronic illnesses, or are children of alcoholics and mentally ill parents. It is not surprising that the number of children adopted by foreigners, while still tiny in absolute terms, has risen steadily, from 678 in 1992 to 3,197 in 1996.[48]

It is ironic that, despite its insignificance in comparison to the size of the problem, inter-country adoption has become a dominant issue in present-day discussion of the problems of children.[49] It is itself of recent origin. The first international adoption of a Russian child took place in 1991 through the participation of the 'Lenin Children's Fund' and the personal intervention of Raisa Gorbachev, wife of the then President of the USSR. By the end of 1991, 576 Russian children had found new homes in America, Canada, Sweden, and France.[50] However, as Harwin points out, policy formulation and preparation of legislation did not begin until 1992, following the collapse of the USSR, and for three reasons. First, instructions issued by the new Government had made it harder for children with disabilities to be adopted by Russians. Second, both the Ministries of Education and Health were anxious to find new possibilities for those children Russians did not wish to adopt. Third, Russia was by then receiving many requests from international adoption agencies. In January 1992 the two Ministries issued instructions, setting out four categories of children who could be adopted abroad. These included children with disabilities; those with developmental delays and abnormalities; those from mentally ill, alcoholic, or drug-abusing parents; and those with venereal disease.[51]

These instructions came under heavy criticism, and towards the end of 1992, a new decree, On Urgent Measures Regarding Adoption by Citizens of Other Countries, was issued by the USSR Supreme Soviet (which continued in existence until shelled into submission in late 1993). This was known as the 'Khasbulatov Verdict,' after the then Speaker, and remained in force until 1995.[52] It simply stated that international adoption was possible, but only in 'exceptional, urgent situations in the interests of the child's health.' This vague formulation was thoroughly unsatisfactory and left the way open to profiteering by unregulated agencies.

The Struggle for Decent Legislation on Adoption

Very quickly a conflict emerged between Russian pride and nationalism, and Russia's international obligations, a conflict in which the welfare of the children concerned did not win until late in the day. By the end of 1994 it appeared that there might be a moratorium on all international adoptions, and this was a serious obstacle to enactment of the Family Code, with its progressive provisions for adoption. As Harwin observes, the Ministries had 'failed to appreciate that a well-intentioned child care policy symbolised for many the humiliation of a former superpower.'[53] Whereas before Russia had prided itself in the belief that children were its only privileged class, now it was becoming a mere donor of children to the wealthy West, depleting Russia's 'genetic pool.' The then Procurator-General spoke for many in opposing signature of the Hague Convention:[54] 'The project [of the Convention] is orientated to the Third World. Europe and America don't give away their sons beyond their borders. They prefer to take children from other countries which are trying to cope with problems of survival.' A Duma member, who had previously run children's programmes in St Petersburg said, in debate: 'It's better for them [the children] to stay here and die in Russia and eat cockroaches with us than go and live abroad.'[55]

Nevertheless, the State Duma enacted the Family Code towards the end of 1995. This was not accomplished without difficulties. The President three times refused to sign the Code following approval by both Houses of Parliament, and returned it for reworking. The present legal requirement relating to international adoption is contained in Article 124 point 3 of the Code:

The adoption of children by foreign citizens or persons without citizenship is permitted only in cases where there is no possibility of placing such children to live with families who are citizens of the Russian Federation, permanently resident on the territory of the Russian Federation, or for adoption by relatives of the child irrespective of citizenship and place of residence of those relatives. [...] Children may be transferred for adoption by citizens of the Russian Federation permanently resident outside the territory of the, Russian Federation, or by foreign citizens or persons without citizenship, who are not relatives of the child, on the completion of three months from the day the child was placed on the central register in accordance with point 3 of Article 122 of this Code.

The courts have the final decision in cases of adoption, under procedures which are similar to those operating in the United Kingdom and other Western states. The provisions of the Code set out above appear to comply fully with Article 21 of the 1989 Convention, which provides that 'inter-country adoption may be considered as an alternative means of a child's care, if the child cannot be placed in a foster or an adoptive family or cannot in any suitable manner be cared for in the child's country of origin.' The procedure for adoption by foreigners is appropriately rigorous.

An American Nightmare — And the Nationalist Response

National pride is especially offended by the fact that a primary source of adoptive parents for Russian children has been the United States. In 1996 families in the United States adopted 11,340 children from various countries, 32 per cent of whom came from Russia and Eastern Europe. Recent US immigrant visa statistics show a steady rise in the issuing of visas for orphans. According to the US State Department: 'Adoptions of children from the Russian Federation by American citizens have steadily increased over the past three years and have become increasingly routine. Orphans from nearly every region of Russia are available for adoption by Russian or foreign parents.'[56] The journal *Ogonyok* published a number of moving accounts of sick and disturbed children who have made quite remarkable progress with their American adoptive parents.[57] A sign of the rising numbers of such adoptions is the fact that in September 1997, in Washington DC, the first all-American meeting of families with children adopted from Russia took place. More than 200 families took part, together with their adopted children. Americans adopted more than 3,800 babies from Russia in 1997, according to the US State Department.[58]

In response to this new phenomenon, a sinister return of nationalist sentiment posed a serious threat to Russia's compliance with international law. For a lengthy period during 1997 the State Duma considered a new draft piece of subordinate legislation, the *Postanovleniye* (Decree), 'On Urgent Measures for Strengthening State Control of Adoption.' This decree was based on the premise, according to the authors of the draft, that inter-country adoption demonstrated 'negative tendencies creating a threat to the national security of Russia.' Also under consideration was a draft amendment to the Family Code, which provided that representation of prospective adopters, and indeed the adoption itself, could only be permitted following the conclusion of a bilateral international treaty. As the liberal daily newspaper *Izvestiya*'s commentator Ella Maksimova pointed out at the time, this proposal created the spectre of a new 'iron curtain.'[59] It also contradicted the provisions both of the Constitution and of the Civil Code, which permitted anyone, citizen or foreigner, to be represented by a third party. Prospective adopters could act in accordance with these instruments, only to find themselves in the dock for violation of the Family Code.

It is no surprise that the communist-nationalists' arguments were based on scare-mongering, on nightmarish fears as to the fate of the children adopted by foreigners. One case acquired mythic status for the nationalists and communists. In summer 1997, in the state of Colorado, 42-year-old Renee Paulrays beat her adopted son David-Aleksandr (2 years and 9 months old) to death. All rational commentators recognise that cases such as this are isolated exceptions, in any event much more likely to occur in Russia. However, the nationalists and communists were not to be persuaded. The 'Liberal Democratic Party' leader Vladimir Zhirinovsky, told *Ogonyok* that under the existing law he could not be certain that children taken abroad had really been adopted, or what their conditions were. When it was put to him that the Russian courts required stringent proof of the suitability of potential adopters, his reply demonstrated the extent to which his imagination is coloured by lurid fantasy. According to him, it was well known that children, particularly adolescents, were used for prostitution — 16 year-old girls 'were exported.' He said that he could not be sure that children were really going to live with a family at all.[60] In a similar vein, a Communist deputy, Mikhail Tarantsov, said that, in his view, the lives of Russian children were being placed in danger abroad, and that they were being subjected to aggression. His evidence was once more none other than the Paulrays case. In response, *Ogonyok* noted that every year in Russia at least 10 to 15 children are murdered by their own parents.[61]

There was another point of view. The independent, liberal and anti-communist deputy, Sergei Yushenkov, who voted against the proposed amendments, denounced these colleagues. As he pointed out, their discourse was full of such tropes as the 'export of the nation's genetic inheritance.' This rhetoric was part of general paranoia concerning conspiracies against the nation. It was also, he said, a manifestation of the old communist tendency to hide Russia's internal affairs from the world. Yushenkov declared that 'The logic of the communist is simple: if you were born here, then you must die here too.'[62]

The leading Russian NGOs also came out strongly against these proposals. At a press conference held in early 1998 in the Andrei Sakharov Centre (named after the foremost dissident of Soviet times), a number of leading figures — Anatolii Severniy (Independent Association of Child Psychiatrists and Psychologists), Boris Altshuler (Rights of the Child), Galina Rybchinskaya (editor of the children's journal *Protect Me!*), and Galina Krasnitskaya (Institute of Childhood) — declared that the proposed changes violated the fundamental principle of the Family Code, the protection of the interests of the child. The most vulnerable children, they said, would lose their foremost right — to live and be brought up in a family. On 30 January 1998 they addressed an open letter to two of the leading progressive deputies in the Duma, Ella Pamfilova (a former Minister of Social Protection) and Valerii Borshchov, proposing detailed amendments.[63]

The Triumph of Reason?

The story of the proposed amendments, nevertheless, has something of a happy ending. The combined efforts of journalists and NGOs appeared to influence the majority of deputies on Aparina's Committee, and the amendments which finally passed the Duma on 5 June 1998 (rapidly approved by the Federation Council on 10 June) had the effect of bringing Russia closer to the norms of the 1993 Hague Convention. There was also to be a strengthening of State control over adoption. Foreign citizens who adopt Russian children must now give an undertaking to the Russian adoption court that they will, within a month of arriving home, register with the Russian consul, who is to check the conditions of the adopted child with the same frequency as would be the case for a child adopted in Russia.[64] The conclusion of *Izvestiya*'s Ella Maksimova and Boris Sinyavskii, who had covered the issue throughout, was that the Family Code had been improved, and that the deputies had chosen the correct path.[65]

Another positive sign is that the Deputy Minister of Education, Yelena Chepurnikh, wrote to *Izvestiya*, saying that Russia would now ratify the 1993 Hague Convention. This will permit legislative regulation of the question of intermediaries, by way of accreditation and licensing of all foreign agencies operating on Russian territory.[66] The process of international adoption is now in full swing, and recent reports indicate that the amended Family Code has in no way hampered the adoption process.[67] Nevertheless, the appalling problems of 'social orphanhood', the rising numbers of street children, and the state of health of all children in Russia[68] cannot be resolved by a tiny number of inter-country adoptions, nor by international treaties or legislation alone, however well intentioned. The demographic crisis shows few signs of abating. A Russia shrunk to only 75 millions would represent a disaster of unprecedented magnitude, not only for Russia herself, but for humanity.

Conclusion

Russian children are among the most pathetic and vulnerable victims of Russia's questionable transition to democracy and the market economy. At the same time, their plight symbolises for the nationalist-communists all the loss of pride and honour, all the despair at the loss of great-power status, which must at all costs be blamed on others — in this case, the imagined Americans who seek to steal and abuse Russia's most precious asset, its children. Both sides in the debate recognise the facts: the statistics cited above paint a desperate picture, and in many respects the majority of children are indeed worse off than they were under the previous regime. But this is not simply a debate at the level of ideological discourse. Children could be victims to fantasy and paranoia. Therein lies the obscenity referred to in the title of this chapter.

Notes

[1] See also B. Bowring, 'The Children of Russia: Victims of Crisis Beneficiaries of International Law,' 11 CFLQ 125 (1999).

[2] 'Priyomishi,' *Ogonyok* 3 (13 Oct. 1997).

[3] W. Slater, 'Russia's Imagined History: Visions of the Soviet Past and the New "Russian Idea"' 14 JCSTP 69, 70 (1998).

[4] S. Alekseyev *et al.*, 1 *Ideologicheskiye Orientiry Rossii* 233 (1998).

[5] S. Zizek, *Tarrying with the Negative* 200 (1993).

[6] *Id.* at 202.

[7] *Id.* at 204.

[8] *Id.* at 205.

[9] *Kommersant-Daily* 2 (3 Dec. 1998).

[10] *Sevodnya* 2 (13 Jul. 1998).

[11] *Kommersant-Daily* 2 (3 Dec. 1998).

[12] UN Doc. No. CRC/C/3/Add.5 (1992).

[13] Y. Azarova, *Posobiya i lgoti grazhdanam s detmi* 12 (1997).

[14] E.M. Rybinskii, 'The Position of Children in Russia,' 37 RSSR 37, 78 (1994).

[15] See note 12 *supra.*

[16] *Interfaks* (29 Nov. 1998).

[17] Cited in Alekseyev *et al.*, note 4 *supra*, at 146.

[18] See Rybinskii, note 14 *supra*, at 82.

[19] See E. Maksimova, 'I chest derzhavi...,' *Izvestiya* 1 (17 Dec. 1997).

[20] Stenographic record, Parliamentary Hearing on the Theme 'On Strengthening State Protection for the Rights of the Child,' 8 Apr. 1997, 15-16 (on file with the author).

[21] Aleksyev, *et al.*, note 4 *supra*, at 147.

[22] Rybinskii, note 14 *supra*, at 82.

[23] J. Harwin, *Children of the Russian State: 1917-1995* 3 (1996).

[24] *Id* at 9.

[25] See B. Bowring, 'Human Rights in Russia: Discourse of Emancipation or Only a Mirage?' in *Human Rights in Eastern Europe* 87 (I. Pogany, ed., 1995).

[26] See note 12 *supra.*

[27] UN Doc. CRC/C/15/Add.4 (1993).

[28] These include the Foundation for the Social and Psychological Health of Families and Children, the Independent Association of Child Psychologists and Psychiatrists, the Independent Psychiatric Association of Russia, and the Moscow Centre for Reform of Criminal Justice.

[29] A. Antonov, 'Dva vzglyada na tragediyu detei,' *Express-Chronicle* 2 (22 Feb. 1999).

[30] T. Podolina, 'Gosduma ideti,' Express-Chronicle 2 (22 Feb. 1999).

[31] Presidential *Ukaz* No. 543, 1992; Government *Postanovleniye* No.909, 1993. The full title of this document is "On Priority Measures to Implement the World Declaration to Secure the Survival, Protection, and Development of Children in the 1990s".

[32] These include 'Handicapped Children,' 'Orphaned Children,' 'Family Planning,' 'The Children of Chernobyl,' 'The Children of the North,' and 'The Development of the Baby-Food Industry.'

[33] M. Baglai, *Konstitutsionnoye Pravo Rossiiskoi Federatsii* 233 (1998).

[34] Presidential *Ukaz* No.942 of 14 Sept. 1995, SZRF 1995 No.38, art 3669.

[35] Harwin, note 23 *supra*, at 179.

[36] Signed by President Yeltsin on 29 Dec. 1995.

[37] P. Krashennikova & P. Sedugina, *Kommentarii k Semeinomu kodeksu Rossiiskoi Federatsii* v (1997).

[38] *Id.* at 19-20.

[39] T. Morshchakova, *Konstitutsioniy Sud Rossiskoi Federatsii. Postanovleniye. Opredeleniye* 1992-1996 (1997). Morshchakova is Deputy Chairman of the Court. See also T. Morshchakova, *The Chechen War Case and Other Recent Jurisprudence of the Russian Constitutional Court,* 42 SLULR 743 (1998).

[40] *O Polozheniye detei v. Rossiiskoi Federatsii* 107 (1996).

[41] UNICEF, *Children at Risk in Central and Eastern Europe: Perils and Promises* (1997).

[42] Interview with A. Severny, President of the Independent Association of Psychiatrists and Psychologists, in Human Rights Watch, *Abandoned to the State: Cruelty and Neglect in Russian Orphanages* 19 (1998) [hereinafter *Abandoned*].

[43] *Id.*

[44] UNICEF, note 41 *supra*, at 89.

[45] *Abandoned*, note 42 *supra*, at 10.

[46] US Department of State, Country Report on Russia, released on 26 February 1999, at <http://www.state.gov/www/global/human_rights/1998_hrp_report/russia.html> (visited 1 Oct. 1999).

[47] 'Priyomishi,' *Ogonyok* 3, 13 Oct. 1997.

[48] Maksimova, note 19 *supra*.

[49] See *Ogonyok*, supra note 2. See also I. Mastykina, 'Zachem im nashi dety? Amerikantsi schitayut za schastye usynovit rebyonka s patologiei. A my?' *Sovershenno Sekretno* 8 (April 1998).

[50] 'Poyasnitelnaia zapiska k proektu zakona Rossiskoi Federatsii "O Sotsialnom Obsluzhivanii Naselenii,"' (Ministry of Labour and Social Development [MLSO], 30 June 1994).

[51] Harwin, note 23 *supra*, at 143.

[52] *Id.*

[53] *Id.* at 145.

[54] The Hague Convention on the Protection of Children and Co-operation in Respect of Intercountry Adoption, Convention #33 of the Hague Conference on Private International Law (*adopted*, 29 May 1993; *entered into force*, 1 May 1995). By 29 Sept. 1999, 27 states had ratified, nine had acceded, and 12 signed but not ratified. See <http://www.hcch.net/e/status/adoshte.html> (visited 1 Oct. 1999).

[55] Quoted in Harwin, note 23 *supra*, at 145.

[56] According to USIR-3/4, Immigrant Visas issued to Russian orphans were as follows: 1992 - 324; 1993 - 746; 1994 - 1087; 1995 - 2178; 1996 - 2454.

[57] *Ogonyok*, note 2, *supra*.

[58] Associated Press, 9 January 1999.

[59] Maksimova, note 48 *supra*.

[60] *Ogonyok*, note 2, *supra*.

[61] *Id.*

[62] *Id.*

[63] See <http://www.openweb.ru/p_z/Ku/main.htm> (visited 1 Oct. 99).

[64] See 'Russian Law Would OK More Foreign Adoption,' *Baltimore Sun* 3 (14 June 1998).

[65] E. Maksimova & B. Sinyavskii, 'Deputaty uluchshaiyut Semeiniy kodeks strany,' *Izvestiya*, 1 (16 June 1998).

[66] *Id.*

[67] N. Wadhams, 'Russian Beckons Childless Americans,' Associated Press (9 Jan. 1999).

[68] See S. Sidorenko-Stephenson & G. Chalikova, 'Prichini i posledstviye detskii beznadzornosti,' in *Kuda Idyot Rossiya?* 296 (T. Zaslavskaya, ed., 1998).

Part III

Abusing Childhood:
Critical Dimensions and
Practical Consequences

6   Punishing Children and Pleasuring Adults: One, Both or Neither?

CHRIS BARTON

Introduction

If a generation of children went unsmacked, would a sexual taste die? Would either result be desirable? Must approval of, or participation in, the one practice necessarily mean rejection of the other? Is spanking[1] between or among adults 'privately,' for pleasure, subject to the same sort of ignorance and hostility once reserved for homosexuality? This chapter compares the spanking of children by adults for punishment with the spanking of adults by adults for pleasure. It examines the irony that the same act may be acceptable when imposed on a protesting child, yet criminal when requested by an enthusiastic adult.

The Link Denied

In the United Kingdom, 'coming out' as an adult who desires to engage in spanking is almost unknown. Some have probably gone through life without ever finding a partner. Yet it has been suggested that 10 per cent of the adult population find erotic pleasure in spanking.[2] Is spanking more, or less, related to children's upbringing than are other sexual longings — whether experienced in adulthood or before? What is the place within sex education (still struggling, at least in schools, with 'mere' homosexuality[3]) of these carnal sub-strands, given that they are to be found in males and females, straights and gays alike?

      The relationship between the age-old practices of hitting children for — hopefully — punishment, but adults for pleasure has received suspiciously little attention. The former is applauded, the latter is disdained.

English law permits a level of assault on a protesting child which may be criminal when practised on a consenting, and perhaps even paying, adult. The latter is a matter of sex; in practice, it does not generally attract attention when performed between (or among) consenting adults. Sadly, however, the former may also be about sex.

Even the most studious analyses of the rights and wrongs of the corporal punishment of children have tended to overlook the possibility that it might excite the adult,[4] or might mould the child's sexuality. Proponents of spanking *qua* adult foreplay may — ought it to be 'should,' so far as their own involvement is concerned? — disapprove of physical punishment of children. Following its earlier Consultation Paper, 'Consent and Offences Against the Person,'[5] the English Law Commission, in 'Consent in the Criminal Law,' notes the comment of a practising sado-masochist that 'from a sado-masochistic perspective the caning of children can only be regarded as rape.'[6]

The Law Commission's incomplete forays into these matters reflect a general unwillingness to grasp, as it were, the nettles. In its second Paper of 1995, the Commission (which has no current plans to proceed from the Consultation Paper phase to final Report stage) maintained a rigid distinction between these two forms of spanking. It classified the adult form under 'consent to criminal injury,' thus lumping it together with such practices as circumcision, consent to medical treatment, pub fights, and Viv Richards's preference for batting without a helmet.[7] Yet it relegated adult punishment of children to mere 'lawful correction.'[8] This distinction was maintained despite the Commissioners' observation that:

> A number of respondents criticised us for failing to include this topic in our study. Feminists Against Censorship were concerned about the uncomfortably casual way in which non-consensual beating was treated in the case of discipline to [*sic*] children. They said that all too many adults treat this as a licence to batter their children, who do not consent, and that it was a mistake to ignore the issue. One academic respondent said that although the issue of consent was buried where the parent administered the harm, because it was the parent who is entitled to consent, this should not obscure the consent basis of the defence. Another on the other hand, suggested that consent is irrelevant in the case of lawful correction because the defence derives from the legal right to use reasonable chastisement and not from the acquiescence of the victim [also *sic*].[9]

Even those who criticised the Commission's omission of 'lawful correction' thus failed to draw attention to its more direct links with sexual play.

In *R v. Donovan,* the only reported English criminal case on adult spanking (in that instance, caning), the Court manages, with appropriate paradox, both to deny (indignantly) and to affirm the link:

> It appeared that the appellant was addicted to a form of sexual perversion . . .'. It is not necessary to deal in this judgment with other [examples] which are wholly remote from the present case, such as the reasonable chastisement of a child by a parent or by a person in loco parentis. In the present case . . . the motive of the appellant was to gratify his own perverted desires . . . his corrupt motive.[10]

The Court found that '[t]he act complained of is not illegal in itself and the injuries are only the marks of a cane which would appear in administering ordinary corporal punishment.'[11] Despite its disapproval of the appellant's sexuality, his appeal was allowed on the basis that only if the jury had first been directed to decide whether he had committed actual bodily harm would it have been necessary for them to consider whether the prosecution had negated the role of consent. Had the jury so decided, then his guilt would have been assured, as (in perhaps the earliest judicial venture into policy on the matter) '[n]o person can license another to commit a crime.'[12]

Conversely, and yet similarly, the Scottish Law Commission's consideration[13] of the corporal punishment of children made no cross-reference to the other side of the coin. It would seem that these official law reform bodies are doing no more than to echo the judges in their ingenuousness. In *R v. Donovan,* where the appellant was convicted at first instance of indecent assault and common assault after caning his 17-year-old girlfriend for (at least his) sexual enjoyment,[14] the Court of Criminal Appeal held, as we have seen, that the reasonable chastisement of children was 'wholly remote' from the facts of the case. More recently, in *R v. Brown* (the 'spanner' case, more famously dealing with the 'heavier' end of sado-masochism), Lord Mustill mentioned the 'lawful correction' exception to assault, but saw its significance to *Brown* as being no more than another example of an exempt situation which also involves an upper limit of tolerable harm.[15] Neither, finally, do the cases on parental nor (more significantly) school beatings (see below) evince any recognition of the sexual dimension, either as an abuse of child beating or otherwise. Incidentally, if it is disingenuous to dissociate the physical correction of children from the softer end of adult sado-masochism it is downright astonishing to dissociate the latter from sex — as did Lord Templeman in *Brown:* 'In my opinion sado-masochism is not concerned with sex.'[16] The truth, of course, is that such actions generally lead to sexual release, perhaps involving coitus.

Yet by any appraisal other than that of black-letter law, the two matters are irrevocably connected. Many will see the various links as points on a continuum of disagreeability from the absolutely disagreeable downwards. At the most unpleasant end, there is the potential for child abuse — a particularly well-hidden form of child abuse, at least when beating was allowed in all schools (as will be discussed below) — on the part of adults indulging in what might be called specialist pederasm under the cloak of apparent legitimacy. 'This is going to hurt me more than it hurts you' was always an odious piety, but both children and society are entitled to assume that teachers ('sadists found an easy outlet for their perversions in the education system'[17]) and others are not deriving sexual pleasure from their task, if only to ensure that punishment is not being unjustly administered (if corporal punishment can ever be said to be just).

This article will only be read by adults, mainly liberally minded ones. Yet, moving down the continuum, some would feel only slightly less badly about a child's confused enjoyment of corporal punishment (then or later) than they would about the — less confused — enjoyment of the person who administered it. (Such readers are fairly unlikely to feel such horror at, say, a child's awakening homosexuality.) Ironically, it is this very disapproval, when translated into a failure to ensure a homogenous sexual education in schools and homes, which may ensure and extend the child's confusion, perhaps even into his or her own adulthood.

A 'Politically Incorrect' Sexuality

We now move from the possibly ambivalent chastisement of children to unambiguous sexual play between adults. Why is it variously perceived as wrong or ignominious, or — further along the continuum — funny? Of course, the thought of anyone (else) performing the most conventional of libidinous acts, including even one's own preferences, may also produce the last two reactions in many of us. But these latter reactions do not extend to the activities *per se*, nor to any disapproval of the actors. At first thought, the explanation for these differences might appear to lie in the comparative popularity of the respective practices. Yet what is the incidence of, say, cunnilingus as compared to that of spanking? We do not know. The real reason for the different responses inspired is not that the latter is (more of?) a minority taste but that, as with all such diversions, spanking is borrowed from one of life's other, apparently non-sexual, activities. It has an existence — a longer-standing existence? — incongruous with its present role. In the original — proper? — place, it involves pain *not* pleasure, it occurs unhappily between an adult and a child, *not* joyously between adults, and its roles are co-relative, *not* reciprocal and exchangeable. It is an antithetical, irrelevant, and illogical activity: one of nature's crueller jokes at humanity's expense, and a demeaning one at that. (Other animals' sexuality tends not to stray beyond what is necessary for procreation.)

It is the 'demeaning' nature of the practice which fuels the accusations of wrongness and ignominy, or the sound of laughter. If the woman is the 'top' then the latter two are particularly prevalent; if it is the man then the former are. Beating children (at least by such as parents) has a mixed press, but sexual (if not religious) flagellation by consenting adults in private remains broadly disapproved of (or at least laughed at) by people — straight people — who would faint right away at any slight to homosexuality. (Indeed the former may trump the latter: see Francis Wheen's periodic blasts in *The Guardian* at both lesbian[18] and heterosexual spanking.[19]) It is again *The Guardian,* this time in its Saturday comic, which encourages gays to use its Lonely Hearts column and chat lines but does not allow spankers ('We will not accept ads of a sado-masochistic nature or implication'), a group surely more in need of contact assistance, to do so. It is at times like this when my vow never to use 'politically correct' in the pejorative is put to its greatest test. I fear that poor *Guardian* sub-editors and their readers would faint dead away at the preferences of one or two even lonelier hearts.

In order to examine law and policy in England and Wales, the first question that arises is: what constitutes consent? The second is: what degree of punishment vitiates consent? Before examining each of these matters individually, we should note their differing degrees of relevance to the spanking of children. The second issue is of considerable relevance: whoever the actors and whatever the motive, even a legal spanking can only be so hard. We will compare the criteria applicable to willing adults and to dolorous children, respectively. The consent issue, on the other hand, seems to have no relevance whatsoever to children (but see below).

Consent

The derision and disapproval described above ignores the consensual, or at least accepting, nature of adult play. The problem arises where a claimed lack of consent is, in reality, mere acquiescence. As Birks points out:

> As social animals we are systematically committed to the use of pressure. At the worst it comes to bombs and bullets: when they have done their work we expect the treaty which follows to be respected: *pacta sunt servanda*. Within the community the same exploitation of pressures goes on all the time, though so familiarly as to become almost unobtrusive. The market works in this way. If your need is great you will have to pay more . . . . In politics the same happens. One withholds until the other gives some *quid pro quo*. The same between men and women, sexually. And all without discredit. It is part of life.[20]

Birks's final point about pressured sex is particularly relevant here. Not necessarily for the reason he gives: it may well be that the greater the 'bottom's' display of reluctance and dislike, and the greater the 'top's' apparent sternness, the more they are both enjoying it[21] (even to the point of an exchange of roles). But in view of the difficulty of finding a soul-mate for such arcane activities — the more so for heterosexual men? — the *aficionado* may well encounter a genuine reluctance to participate. The law has erected a two-tier barrier to the relief of such frustration, the first being a cautious attitude to what constitutes consent and the second being a limit on what is acceptable even if validly consented to (as discussed below).

The initial, consent, issue may arise either as a 'personnel' issue — does it make any difference whether they are emotional strangers or domestic partners? Or it may concern the degree of diffidence — is a 'mere' lack of interest (as with the so-called 'vanilla' spouse) sufficient, or must there have been a non-coital equivalent of rape? The problem is, therefore, where on these two continua should pressure be seen as sufficient to negate the appearance of consent.

Metaphor and Reality — Consenting to Sex or Violence?

The consent issue is familiar in law (where it has probably attracted most attention in the field of commercial contracts[22]). However, as adult spanking is a sexual matter, a comparison with rape may prove instructive (although, as we shall see, the English judges see it purely as a question cf consent to criminal injury, as if the event were, say, a football match).

Applying the rape criterion to the first of the continua, the nature of the parties' relationship has been irrelevant to criminal liability for rape since the 1991 decision in *R v. R*, where the House of Lords excised the long-standing exception of husbandly immunity.[23] Indeed, far from a marital (or other supposedly loving) relationship excusing or even mitigating such behaviour, it is arguably an exacerbation in its abuse of trust and duty: surely a person is entitled to look for better, not worse, behaviour from her partner than she does from a stranger? Finally, it must be remembered that, in one vital particular, rape is an inadequate metaphor for the law's attitude to other expressions of unwanted sexual attention within marriage. *R v. R* only established that a husband may not use the remedy of self-help to enforce what is, and remains, a *right to copulate* with one's spouse: a right which does not extend to foreplay, such as fellatio.[24] Marriage does not confer a right to non-coital, non-consummatory sex. Thus, in civil law, a refusal to participate in anything else would not breach the 'duty of consortium.' Unlike a denial of sexual intercourse, it would normally[25] be the refused, and not the refuser, who would have 'behaved in such a way that [the other] cannot reasonably be expected to live with [him or her]' for the purposes of demonstrating irretrievable breakdown of marriage as the ground for divorce under the Matrimonial Causes Act 1973.[26]

As regards the required degree of diffidence, sections 142(a), (b) of the Criminal Justice and Public Order Act 1994 holds that rape is 'sexual intercourse . . . with a person who at the time of the intercourse does not consent to it; and . . . at the time [the other] knows that the person does not consent to the intercourse.' Beyond that flat statement, as the English Law Commission has since pointed out, 'English criminal law has never concerned itself with subtle analyses of the extent to which consent was voluntary or free in situations in which there is no question of threats or intimidation.'[27]

This approach is illustrated in the spanking context by the Rhodesian case *R v. McCoy*, in which a rare example of this milder end of sado-masochism attracted the Court's attention. A female air stewardess, who had failed to secure her seatbelt when landing, agreed to a caning from her manager in lieu of disciplinary action involving loss of pay. He was nonetheless convicted of assault, on the premise that her consent was unreal.[28] What many would see as an unpleasantly opportunistic gratifying of an illicit sexual taste, achieved by an abuse of authority and a hypocritical pretence at legitimacy (not to mention a failure to save his employer's money), can become, on further examination, less morally clear. First, as seen above, the manager would not, in English law, have been guilty of rape had he exploited his colleague by penetrating, rather than by spanking, her. Second, his conduct involved neither force nor the threat of force. Third, *insofar as* he could be said to have threatened her, the consequence of her non-compliance was a legitimate one. Fourth, insofar as he offered to improve her position[29] — to add to her options — rather than to worsen it, could he be said to have threatened her? Even if his conduct was wrong, did it wrong her?

What moral and legal difference would it have made in *Donovan* and *McCoy* had the accused been women and their victims men? None, legally at least. But what if Donovan's and McCoy's sexual inclinations — and such people are often 'switches' — had led them to persuade the women to beat them? In criminal law terms, there would have been crimes without victims, or at least without complainants. The women might have experienced revulsion and distaste, but not pain or humiliation. The degree of sado-masochism (and its homosexual element) apart, the matter would then have been on a par with *Brown*, were it not that the beaters, enjoying their role, needed no urging in that case.

In further elaboration of Birks's thoughts, E. Griew explains (purportedly) the reasons behind the lack of concern as to what constitutes consent:

> In what circumstances does a wife (or any other woman) who has sexual intercourse *not* consent to do so? [. . .]We are not talking about the (surely very common) case of disgruntled capitulation to persistent opportunity. The circumstances may well constrain the wife's choice — because of her need for sleep and for freedom from stress in the quotidian relationship, because of her dependence on her husband's affection and his purse, because of the balance between their competing personalities and the sheer unremitting pressure of cohabitation with him, she may feel she has no real alternative. Yet when she gives in, it cannot be doubted that she does consent within the meaning of the Act.[30]

Finally, is consent the factor which most distances adult sex beatings from the corporal punishment of children? Subject to its severity and other components of so-called 'reasonableness,' it would seem that the latter is a right of the inflicter. Yet Hohfeldian analysis would therefore involve the child in a co-relative duty to submit to it,[31] and old cases on school beatings say that physical force should not be used to force a child to submit to chastisement. On the other hand, Blackstone flatly states (albeit generally) that children owe 'subjection and obedience to their procreators.'[32]

Consent Irrelevant: Upper Limits on Beating Between Adults

Turning to the upper limit of consent-excused 'violence,' it is clear in English law that it must fall short of death: suicide is no longer a crime but assisting it remains murder or manslaughter. Similarly, self-wounding is not criminal, but when do obliging, if enthusiastic, suppliers cross the threshold? Where the motive, whether it be on one or both sides, is sexual, then the domestic and European authority is *R v. Brown and other appeals*.[33] Or at least it is when it involves groups of gay men indulging themselves at the extremes of consensual sexual violence. It is one of the ironies of our difficulties with sexuality that, just as some people might want to criminalise 'the many more heterosexual people quietly having SM sex in the suburbs than there are gay leather men in London clubs,'[34] so might some of those same 'quiet suburbians' take the same attitude to the men in *Brown*. The 'exemplary' charges against the latter mainly involved ill-treatment of the genitalia with, for example, hot wax, sandpaper, fishhooks, and needles, plus beatings with, for example, nettles, spiked belts, and a cat-o'-nine tails. Violence was also done to the buttocks, anus and nipples. The recipients had a codeword to stop the attacks. The resulting injuries included the drawing of blood and scarring, although there were no instances of (the need for) medical attention, infection, or permanent injury. It seems that pleasure was given both to the attackers and the attacked. The victims were young men and the accused were middle-aged. These events took place over a 10-year period in a number of private locations, some equipped as torture chambers. Nearly 50 men were involved in all. They were 'caught' because they videotaped their torture sessions for distribution to group members and some of the films fell, by chance, into the hands of the police.

If the domestic and European decisions in *Brown* are synthesised sequentially, the outcome is that consensual, private, sado-masochistic activities causing injuries (however impermanent) beyond the transient and trifling, thereby contravene section 47 of the Offences Against the Person Act 1861 as being actual bodily harm and section 20 (unlawful wounding). This result is consistent with article 8 of the European Convention of Human Rights, 'respect for private life,' because of the exception for restrictions 'necessary in a democratic society.' These include the protection of health. Given the degree of injury, it was not necessary to determine whether the interference could also be justified on the basis of the protection of morals.

Members of the two courts attacked the *a priori* rights and wrongs of the matter much in the same varied ways as any other similarly sized group of inappropriately-qualified citizens. As Lord Templeman said in the House of Lords, 'The question of whether the defence of consent [applies] can only be decided by consideration of policy and public interest. Parliament can call on the advice of doctors, psychiatrists, criminologists, sociologists and other experts.'[35]

Let us examine the arguments advanced to and by the judges, from the minority permissive through to the majority authoritarian-paternalistic. The activities lack true hostility and aggression; the risk of infection from what the accused did has been greatly reduced by modern science; no expense was caused to the public purse; the participants should not be penalised because of the possibility that their conduct might have lead to more serious injury, or because it might have spread AIDS (buggery itself is legal); and the anti-proselytising argument is circuitous in that if the activity itself is not criminal then the risk that others will participate cannot be a ground for making it so. The risk of escalation is already met by the law in that either consent would cease or undeniably criminal serious harm would result. Boxers have died without ensuing criminal proceedings. There is no evidence that this form of sexual activity poses any greater risk of involvement of the young and vulnerable than does any other form of homosexual or heterosexual activity.

In an area where moral and social factors are so important, and changeable, it is a matter of policy for the legislature to decide. Yet a court must rule on such matters in the interim in order to deal with the cases before it. There is no evidence that the activities are essential to anyone's happiness. Such practices are degrading to body and mind. Pleasure derived from the infliction of pain is evil. It is not comparable to boxing, a manly diversion, which is subject to strict controls, including medical supervision. The conduct in question is not conducive to the enjoyment of family life. Given the number of places and people involved, and the making of videos intended for dissemination, it cannot be said to be a State intrusion into private bedroom activities. There is no discrimination against homosexuals given that the principle is of equal application to heterosexuals.

How is this law, and how are these policy arguments, to be applied to 'mere' spanking, perhaps in the marital bedroom at that? If *Donovan* gets the closest to reflecting the behaviour we are examining, then *R v. Wilson (Alan)* does the same for the *dramatis personae* and the circumstances. Mr Wilson had been convicted of actual bodily harm in the Crown Court, having branded his initials on his wife's buttocks: 'she wanted my name tattooing on her bum . . . . I didn't know how to do it; so I burned it on with a hot knife . . . it was done for love . . . . I think her exact words were summat like, "I'm not scared of anyone knowing that I love you enough to have your name on my body."'[36]

The trial judge decided that *Brown* and *Donovan* constrained him to direct the jury to convict Wilson. Mr Wilson's appeal was allowed by the Court of Appeal on the ground that his conduct merely amounted to adorning his wife at her instigation, and that the closest existing parallel was tattooing, which, as allowed in *Brown*, is entirely legal upon a consenting adult. If public policy is the yardstick (*Brown* again), then:

> Consensual activity between husband and wife, in the privacy of the matrimonial home, is not . . . normally a matter for criminal investigation let alone criminal prosecution . . . the law should develop upon a case by case basis rather than upon general propositions to which, in the changing times in which we live, exceptions may arise from time to time not expressly covered by authority.[37]

Adult spanking, as many a 19th century Victorian brothel (the *vice anglaise*) demonstrated, is not a product of our 'changing times,' but its growing image is. When is it illegal, whether between husband or wife, between cohabitants male and female, lovers male and female or amongst emotional strangers at a theme party? One knowledgeable English Law Commission respondent answered the question thus:

> I am a very active and independent woman. But I have also enjoyed taking a very submissive role during sex. To me an essential part of taking a submissive role is that my partner punishes me. This punishment would typically involve him spanking me very hard or using a cane or whip on my behind. *It is often likely that this punishment would leave more than transient and trifling harm.*[38]

It is unavoidably inferable from *Brown* that such conduct is the crime of actual bodily harm under section 47 of the Offences Against the Person Act 1861. This obtains irrespective of the absence of organised groups of male homosexuals, blood-letting, the danger of AIDS or video taping. This criminality is similarly unaffected not only by the presence of 'mere' consent, but by the absolute, long-standing control of the recipient, the disinclination of the supplier to act unless the other is enjoying it, and the love (marital or not, heterosexual or not) which the parties may have for one another. It is the likely existence of these factors, particularly the penultimate one, which make a nonsense of Lord Templeman's gratuitous explanation in *Brown* of a sadist as being one 'who draws pleasure from inflicting . . . cruelty.'[39] In truth, these people are obligingly giving the pleasure on which their own, if any, is absolutely dependent: perhaps they need to re-categorise themselves, as pederasts have managed to do with the egregious 'paedophile.' It is both brave and right of the English Law Commission to suggest that their activities should only be criminal in the event of a 'seriously disabling injury,' i.e. one which causes serious distress, and which 'involve[s] the loss of a bodily member or organ or permanent bodily injury or permanent functional impairment, or serious or permanent disfigurement, or severe and prolonged pain, or serious impairment of mental health, or prolonged unconsciousness.'[40] No spanking could approach illegality under that criterion.

Adult and Child

We will now identify the relevant actors, the domestic and European legal limits, the incidence of such conduct, its value, and the proposals for reform.[41] We will first borrow Murray Strauss's definition of the conduct in question: 'Corporal punishment is the use of physical force with the intention of causing a child to experience pain, but not injury, for the purpose of correction or control of the child's behaviour.'[42] Note its careful distinction from other actions which (may) also cause pain, but which have other purposes, such as medical treatment.

Who Qualifies?

So far as the somatic punishment of children is concerned, Parliament and the Courts have enthusiastically created exceptions to the normal prohibitions (both civil and criminal) on assault. English Law, of course, has yet to go down the road taken by Sweden (1979), Finland (1984), Denmark (1986),

Norway (1987), Austria (1989), and Cyprus (1994), all of which have either restricted or eliminated corporal punishment in the home. Yet it is equally well-known that Parliament effectively ended it in most schools, the Education (No 2) Act 1986 having been extended by the Education Reform Act 1988 to grant maintained schools and to some independent schools.[43] (In September 1999, section 131 of the School Standards and Framework Act 1998 will come into force, thus liberating even privately funded pupils in independent schools from the threat of corporal punishment.) It is banned in community homes by the Children's Homes Regulations[44] although it seems that registered child-minders may not be required to sign a declaration that they will not hit their charges.[45] Children are generally safe from legitimate chastisement from their elder siblings.[46]

But with regard to parents[47] we still follow the Testaments both Old ('He that spareth his rod hateth his son; but he that loveth him chasteneth him betimes'[48]) and New ('For whom the Lord loveth he chasteneth, and scourgeth every son whom he receiveth'[49]). Not that the right to hit is restricted just to those *prima facie* imbued with legal 'parental responsibility' — who, by sections 2(1) and 2(2)(a) of the Children Act 1989, are the mother and father of the marital child but only the mother of the non-marital child.[50] The long-standing right of such parents to delegate the chastisement of their children would now seem to be covered by section 2(9) of the 1989 Act whereby a person 'who has parental responsibility . . . may arrange for some or all of it . . . to be met . . . on his behalf.' Presumably this is the only way in which a man can lawfully hit his cohabitant's children from a previous relationship, unless he is named with her in a residence order under section 10, probably following her divorce from the father. Permission under section 2(9) would even be needed by a putative father cohabitant, in the absence of a s 4 parental responsibility agreement with the mother. Finally, *any* person who has been granted a residence order 'over' a child thereby obtains parental responsibility — and thus hitting powers — even if, under section 12(2), that person is neither parent nor guardian.

It is these people who are covered by the tattered remnants of the flag of section 1(7) of the Children and Young Persons Act 1933, which refers to 'the right of any parent, teacher, or other person having the lawful control or charge of a child or young person to administer punishment to him.' What of the recipient? Since *Gillick v. West Norfolk and Wisbech Area Health Authority*,[51] it seems unlikely that such 'punishment' could be justified at all in the case of a child over 16. Yet surely the younger the child, the less the Court would sanction hitting, at least in terms of severity.

How Hard?

During the passage of the Children Bill (now the Children Act 1989) through the House of Lords there was an unsuccessful attempt to render physical punishment by parents unlawful. The position therefore remains that laid down in *R v. Hopley*, where it was held that 'moderate and reasonable' parental chastisement does not attract the attention of the criminal law. Hopefully, it now takes rather less to exceed the limit than it did in *Hopley* itself, where a school teacher wrote to a boy's father asking whether he could chastise him severely, and 'that if necessary he should do it again and again' and 'continue it at intervals even if he held out for hours'. The father did not 'wish to interfere with [the] plan' and when the 'thirteen or fourteen-year-old' later died as a result of the ensuing assault — a secret two-hour night-time flogging with a thick stick which led to a conviction for manslaughter — Cockburn CJ held that the parental authority actually granted had not been excessive.[52]   Incidentally, it appears that the modern Scottish courts have not lowered the level of permitted violence as much as some might prefer. In *B v. Harris*, a mother who (literally) belted her nine-year-old daughter hard enough to leave bruising visible on her thigh four days later was subsequently acquitted of assault,[53] a decision which was communicated to other parents by a banner headline in one newspaper which read 'IT'S OK TO BELT YOUR KIDS.' Whatever view one takes about abolition, it would seem desirable for the law to be more precise about when chastisement becomes unreasonable.

It seems clear that article 37 of the United Nations Convention on the Rights of the Child (which has been ratified by the United Kingdom) would now outlaw at least some of the sorts of parental beatings which were seen as legitimate in the past: 'No child shall be subjected to . . . cruel, inhuman or degrading treatment or punishment.'[54]   In their 1985 Paper, the Committee of Ministers of the Council of Europe merely *hoped* that member States would 'review their legislation on the power to punish children in order to limit or indeed prohibit corporal punishment.'[55] But the important point is that all these criteria — domestic, European, international — would seem to permit that degree of punishment, beyond the 'trifling and transient,' which would render it criminal between consenting adults.

The European Convention on Human Rights

There have been a number of Strasbourg cases involving school beatings in the United Kingdom,[56] but only recently has the European Court had to deal with its first case of 'parental' corporal punishment. In *A and B v. UK,* the European Commission of Human Rights decided that the issues raised by the caning of a nine-year-old boy in his home should be decided on their merits.[57] In 1990, the applicant, then aged six, was placed on the local Child Protection Register. After his mother's cohabitant had been given a police caution for caning him, the boy was removed from the Register. Three years later, further canings culminated in the boy's stepfather — as he had since become — being acquitted of assault causing actual bodily harm. The facts were that during the course of about a week the boy (who was 'difficult to handle ... would not respond to school discipline ... could not be controlled at home') had received more than one caning, causing bruises and marks on his bottom, thigh, and calf. The acquittal followed a summing-up which stated, 'It is a perfectly good defence that the alleged assault was merely the correcting of a child ... provided that correction be moderate in the manner, the instrument and the quantity. Or put another way, reasonable . . . . It is for the prosecution to prove it was not.'

Counsel representing the boy, headed by Alan Levy QC, claimed that the canings violated, *inter alia*, articles 3 and 8 of the European Convention of Human Rights. This contention was disputed by the Government, led by David Pannick QC, who argued as follows. First, in contrast with corporal punishment in schools, the United Kingdom was not responsible for the stepfather's behaviour. Second, a civil action for assault, with its lighter burden of proof, would have provided the effective remedy required by articles 13 and 14. Third, as *Costello-Roberts v. United Kingdom* indicates that corporal punishment is not prohibited in schools,[58] higher standards should not obtain in the home, where the punishment is not at the hands of a relative stranger and is unlikely to be public. Fourth, the domestic law, in requiring that chastisement be reasonable, complies with article 3 in prohibiting torture and inhuman or degrading punishment. Finally, it was established in *Costello-Roberts* that school punishments which do not breach article 3 are unlikely to breach article 8 (respect for private life): the same principle should therefore apply to home punishments.

In rebuttal, counsel representing the boy first pointed out that article 1 of the Convention requires Contracting Parties to secure 'to everyone within their jurisdiction' the rights defined in, amongst others, article 3. Second, once the criminal prosecution had failed, legal aid would have been unavailable for civil proceedings. Third the beatings here were worse than in *Costello-Roberts* (three strokes of a gym shoe) which was itself regarded as borderline by the Court. Fourth, there is nothing less inherently inhuman or degrading in home punishments: no one would argue that, for example, a woman should have less legal protection against domestic assault than in the workplace. Finally, *Costello-Roberts* left open the question of whether a punishment not proscribed by article 3 is nonetheless prohibited under article 8.

In concluding that there was a case to be admitted to the Court, the Commission observed that it had not been referred to any cases which indicate that the civil courts interpret 'reasonable chastisement' differently from the criminal courts. Further, the case raised 'complex issues of law and fact' under the Convention. Its conclusion thus required an examination of its merits. The application was not, therefore, 'manifestly ill-founded' under article 27, paragraph 2 of the Convention.

Ultimately, the European Court of Human Rights recalled that 'ill-treatment must attain a minimum level of severity if it is to fall within the scope of article 3 of the Convention. The assessment of this minimum is relative: it depends on all the circumstances of the case, such as the nature and context of the treatment, its duration, its physical and mental effects and, in some cases, the sex, age and state of health of the victim.'[59] The Court found that the treatment meted out to the applicant had reached that degree of severity.[60]

Two matters here. The first is the surprisingly little-known case of *Re H (minors) (Wardship: Cultural Background)*, in which Callman J disapproved (admittedly with regard to blows to the head and face) the use of 'a stick or other implements.'[61] Second, was the assailant acting *in loco parentis* for this purpose? Neither as the boy's mother's cohabitant, nor subsequently as his stepfather, did he have 'parental responsibility' for him under section 3 of the Children Act 1989. Is the punishment of children outside school restricted to those who possess such 'responsibility'? Whilst section 2(9) of the Children Act 1989 permits those who do have parental responsibility to 'arrange for some or all of it to be met by one or more persons acting on his behalf', it is clear from the report that the mother neither knew nor approved of the canings. This leaves the Government with s 3(5) of the 1989 Act, whereby a person who does not have parental responsibility, but who does have care of a child, may 'do what is reasonable . . . for the purpose of promoting . . . the child's welfare'. Failing that, there is always section 1(7) of the Children and Young Persons Act 1933, which refers to the right of any 'person having the lawful control or charge of a child or young person to administer punishment to him.'

Incidence

How much, or how often, are children hit by their parents in the United Kingdom? The most significant available information is that produced by John and Elizabeth Newson's long-term study of child-rearing habits in a random sample of 700 'indigenous' Nottingham families.[62] In July 1986, they presented their paper to the Children's Legal Centre. It was reported that 91 per cent of the boys and 59 per cent of the girls (three-quarters of the sample) had been smacked, hit with *or threatened by* an implement by the age of seven. Implements used, or with which children were threatened, were, in order of (parental) preference: belt or strap; cane or stick; slipper; miscellaneous objects — rulers, backs of hairbrushes, etc. By the age of 11, hitting had decreased considerably, involving 60 per cent of children either less than once per month or not at all. Surprisingly perhaps, the study found little significance in class differences. So far as ethnicity is concerned, they reported that parents of Punjabi origin hardly resorted to hitting at all, whereas those of Caribbean origin did so more frequently and more severely than 'indigenous' white parents. A more recent study commissioned by the Department of Health, [63] did discover that families which took part in frequent or severe punishment were more readily identifiable by social variables — but that 91 per cent of the mothers interviewed said that they had hit their children. From the United States, there is recent evidence to challenge the assumption that Corporal Punishment ends at puberty: 40 per cent of 13-year-olds are said to be hit regularly, [64] as are more than 25 per cent of boys in their 15th year. [65]

Is it Right?

It is not right, the adult lawmakers would seem to believe, for (non-consenting) adults, for whom the gradual elimination of corporal punishment began in the United Kingdom in the 19th Century: army floggings were abolished in 1906; birching and flogging as judicial punishment in 1948; naval floggings in 1957; and corporal punishment in prison and borstals in 1957. If legal prohibition is any indication, neither is it right if inflicted in schools by teachers. The abolitionists claim that it is basically unjust, on the assumption that 'it is acceptable to hit children, but . . . it is quite unacceptable for them to hit others, or for adults to hit anyone else.'[66] It is said to be ineffective in that young children do not remember what they are being smacked *for*. Links have been drawn with child abuse, 'accidental' injury, the learning of aggressive behaviour, delinquency, and even extreme pathological behaviour. As early as 1886, Krafft-Ebing felt able to condemn it as being sexually dangerous — 'On account of the dangers to which this form of punishment gives rise, it would be better if parents, teachers and nurses were to avoid it entirely.'[67] A more contemporary view may be found in the submission of the British Psychological Society to the Scottish Law Commission:

> an inefficient method of modifying behaviour, being situation-specific and of short-term effect, and with a possibility of providing undesirable side-effects of both fear and learned imitative behaviour. More socially desirable attitudes would be encouraged by alternative methods of managing behaviour, such as the withdrawing of privileges and the rewarding of more desirable alternatives.[68]

It is not for an academic family lawyer to write with other than vicarious confidence about the deleterious effects of the physical punishment of children; but he can note the submitted evidence:[69] that, for example, children subject to Corporal Punishment are more likely to experience more marital conflict as adults than are others;[70] are more likely to become violent adults with criminal records;[71] and are more disposed to become child and substance abusers.[72]

Reform: The Scottish Proposals

A public opinion survey conducted in 1991 showed that the Scottish public drew a clear distinction between a smack with the open hand and the use of belts and other objects. For example, in relation to a nine-year-old child only 11 per cent thought that smacking should be unlawful but 91 per cent thought that hitting with a belt, etc., should be unlawful. In broad terms this represents the eventual recommendation of the Scottish Law Commission, which is that it should become civilly and criminally illegal for a parent to hit a child with an implement *or* to cause, or risk causing, a) injury, or b) pain or discomfort lasting more than a very short time.[73] The net effect is that the use of implements would always be illegal as would hitting by hand other than a light smack. The Commission rejected the suggestion that corporal punishment become only a civil wrong as that would be to give the impression that it was simply a private matter between parent and child in which the State had no interest.

Even had Parliament followed this recommendation — it was in fact omitted from the Children (Scotland) Act 1995 — the United Kingdom would still be less liberal than Scandinavia in matters of parental discipline. The

Swedish reform of 1979, in amending the 1949 Parenthood and Guardianship Code, also de-legalised 'other injurious or humiliating treatment.' This includes 'threatening, scaring, ridiculing or ostracising, including not speaking to a child for several days, or locking a child up.'

Conclusion

Even mild sado-masochism brings together the law of violence, sex and domestic partnership. When the same treatment is administered to children, we gain the law of education, parenthood and children's rights, but, unpleasantly, we do not necessarily lose the sex and violence angles. We have seen that what has been held to be criminal in genitalia torture amongst large groups of organised, video-taping, homosexual men, is potentially so between, for example, a respectable, long-married couple, whose love and compatibility for one another are cemented by a common enthusiasm for not wholly dissimilar behaviour. In yet a third context, it may be legal if applied to protesting children, whose chances of experiencing such treatment are entirely dependent, even within our one legal system, upon who their parents are and (now to much a lesser extent, and due for extinction in 1999) where they go to school. The generic activity is, we know, a commonplace experience in the home — much more so for unwilling children than for, at least, compliant adults.

This disparity of incidence may well explain why adult spanking has attracted far less attention, both in law and elsewhere, than the corporal punishment of children. Yet the numbers involved in the former may well be as large as, say, the numbers of practising homosexuals (some of whom are in both camps) and the history of all three activities is long, perhaps even of equal length in each case. Does this mean that there is little (if anything) left to say about the one but a lot left to say about the other? There is certainly much to say about each in the light of the other. First, the fear of escalation, which has led courts to outlaw adult practice at an appropriately vigorous level, is more pertinent when children are involved, as the latter are less able to resist. There are no codewords for them, and unambiguous physical child abuse often originates in lawful hitting, as well as from the idea that the law permits, and society encourages, corporal 'discipline.' Second, such punishment may well have that element of hostility and aggression about it that apologists for consensual adult sex play claim (unsuccessfully, so far as the law is concerned) is vitally absent from their activities. Third, the need for, and the desirability of, family privacy is advanced as necessarily justifying (or at least not precluding) the one, yet it is not thought sufficiently vital to deny the other: perhaps the past role of family privacy in permitting non-sexual, non-consensual domestic violence, is too recent. Fourth, it may well be that the imposed beatings of childhood fuel the search for them in adulthood, and not merely in the extreme case of Old School Ties frequenting flagellation brothels. (There is obviously no automatic co-relation here: given the probable respective numbers involved, it is clear that many, indeed most, smacked children do not have their subsequent sexuality influenced by the experience. Conversely, the anecdotal evidence is that some unsmacked children desire such experiences as adults — when, ironically, they may be included amongst those who remain 'virginal' in this respect, balked by the rarity and risibility of their wishes!)

One, both, or neither? Whether it permits or precludes beating, law surely has more influence upon reluctant children than it does upon willing adults. Because it is illegal in Sweden, it seems likely that fewer children are smacked there than would otherwise be the case, yet can the same be said of masochists in England and Wales since *Brown*? It is not realistic to attempt to deny like-minded adults reciprocal sexual satisfaction, particularly, some might think, when it is merely foreplay to coitus on the right side of the blanket. (Bondage, potentially much more dangerous, is not illegal in the absence of bruising.) This is not to say that just because a crime is popular, long-standing and ineradicable, it should cease to be a crime, merely that where it is also victimless and consensual, the threshold should be beyond actual bodily harm. Yet, at the time of writing, the paradox is being affirmed, or at least not disaffirmed: whilst the Law Commission has slept for four years on its liberalising Consultation Paper proposals on 'pain for sexual pleasure,'[74] the Government 'does not consider that the right way [to protect children better] is to ban all physical punishment.'[75] The entry into force of the Human Rights Act 1998 may break both these silences. In the latter case, the second visit of the UN Committee on the Rights of the Child to the United Kingdom, in 2000, will surely do so.[76]

Notes

[1] In this chapter, the term 'spanking' refers to caning and other forms of moderate beating, generally on the buttocks. 'Heavier' sado-masochistic activity has no dual significance, and has already attracted scholarly and other attention, and is thus introduced only to the extent that it provides insights relevant to the broader analysis.

[2] See <http://members.aol.com/stevert302/private/homeotk.htm#Top> (visited 1 Oct. 99). The internet, with some 72,091 pages on the subject as of 17 Feb. 1999, has facilitated contact rather than openness. More important, for the purposes of this chapter, is the punctilious way in which many of these websites disclaim approval of corporal punishment of children.

[3] See D. Monk, 'Health and Education: Conflicting Programmes for Sex Education,' in this collection.

[4] There are some honourable exceptions. See, e.g., P. Newell, *Children are People Too. the Case Against Physical Punishment* 48-49, 119-120 (1989).

[5] Consultation Paper No. 134 (1994).

[6] Consultation Paper No. 139, para. 11.4 (1995).

[7] Earlier, in *R v. Donovan*, the court, in dealing with a case of adult sex play, had averred: 'Nothing could be more absurd or more repellent to the ordinary intelligence than to regard his conduct as comparable with that of a participant in one of [the] manly "diversions."' 2 KB 498, 509 (1934) (Swift, J.).

[8] All of these are subject to different criteria. See, e.g., W. Wilson, *Criminal Law* 328-344 (1998).

[9] See note 6 *supra* (footnotes omitted).

[10] 2 KB at 502-509.

[11] *Id.* at 500.

[12] *Id.* at 507.

[13] Report on Family Law, SLC No. 135, para. 2.67 *et seq.* (1992) (hereinafter SLC No. 135).

[14] 2 KB at 509. There was 'no doubt that she had expressed her willingness to submit herself to the kind of conduct to which he was addicted.' *Id.* at 503 (Swift, J.). There is nothing in the law report to sustain the suggestion made by Wilson that the woman was a prostitute (nor, indeed, for the claim that '[s]he suffered cuts and bruises'). See Wilson, note 8 *supra*, at 333.

[15] 1 AC 212, 266-267 (1994).

[16] *Id.* at 235.

[17] Newell, note 4 *supra*, at 121.

[18] See, e.g., Wheen's half-page attack on the publicity given to one enthusiast ('London's duckie divas get too carried away by their enthusiasm for this spanking new media star'), in 'Who's a Naughty Boy?' *The Guardian* 5 (18 Mar. 1988).

[19] *Id.* (mocking the alleged sexual inclinations of Paul Johnson, a right-wing public figure).

[20] P. Birks, *An Introduction to the Law of Restitution* 173 (1985).

[21] This may seem unconvincing in the light of the 'No means No' anti-rape argument. However, mock reluctance may be part of the pleasure for the masochist.

[22] See, e.g, *Pau On v. Lau Yiu Long* AC 614, 635 (1980) (Scarman, L.J.) (finding that 'a coercion of the will so as to vitiate . . . consent' is required).

[23] 1 AC 599 (1992). Sec. 142 of the Criminal Justice and Public Order Act 1994 has since been changed to confirm that the accused's marriage to the victim is no longer a defence to the charge of rape.

[24] See *R v. Kowalski*, 1 FLR 447 (1988).

[25] A history of consent, particularly prior to the marriage, might yield a different result.

[26] Secs. 1(2)(b), 1(1). When the Family Law Act 1996 is activated, there will be no matrimonial offence element in divorce, and thus little, if any, place for consortium in family law.

[27] Consent in the Criminal Law, Law Commission No. 139 (1995).

[28] (2) SA4 (1953).

[29] Such moves are known in philosophy as 'coercive offers.' See, e.g., J. Feinburg, 3 *The Moral Limits of the Criminal Law* 199 (1986).

[30] 11 *Archbold News* 5 (1992).

[31] See, e.g., J. Caldwell, 'Parental Physical Punishment and the Law,' 13 NZULR 370 (1989).

[32] 1 William Blackstone, *Commentaries* *453.

[33] 2 AER 75 (1993); *Laskey v. United Kingdom*, 1997 Eur. Ct. H. R. (ser. A) 120.

[34] Consent in the Criminal Law, Law Com No. 139, para. 10.17 (1995).

[35] 2 AER at 82.

[36] 3 WLR 125 (1996).

[37] *Id.* at 128 (Russell, L.J.).

[38] Law Commission No. 139 (emphasis added).

[39] 2 AER at 82.

[40] Law Commission, note 38 *supra*, at 198.

[41] See, e.g., C. Barton, '*A v. United Kingdom*: The Thirty Thousand Pound Caning — An English Vice in Europe,' 11 CFLQ 63-74 (1999).

[42] M. Strauss, 'Corporal Punishment of Adolescents by American Parents,' 24 *Society* 419, 420 (1993).

[43] By SI 1989/1233 and 1825.

[44] SI 1991/1506.

[45] *London Borough of Sutton v. Davis*, 1 FLR 737 (1994).

[46] *R v. Woods* 85 JP 272 (1921) (Parental responsibility could, however, be "delegated" for this purpose under sec. 2(9) of the Children Act 1989).

[47] In X and Y v Sweden, 29 Eur. Comm'n H. R. DR 104 (1982), the European Commission on Human Rights held inadmissible an application by members of a religious group under art. 8 (respect for private and family life) that their children were more likely to be taken into care because of their belief that biblical authority necessitated the beating of their children.

[48] Proverbs 13:24 (King James).

[49] Hebrews 12:6 (King James).

[50] In March 1998, the Lord Chancellor's Department issued a Consultation Paper, asking for views on (amongst other things) whether 'unmarried' fathers should have automatic parental responsibility.

[51] AC 112 (1986).

[52] 2 FF 202 (1860).

[53] SLT 208 (1990).

[54] UNGA res. 44/22, annex 44 UN GAOR Supp. (No. 49) at 167, UN Doc. A/44/49 (1989) (*entered into force*, 2 Sep. 1990).

[55] Recommendation No 85(4) para. 12.

[56] See, e.g., *Warwick v. United Kingdom*, 60 Eur. Comm'n H. R. DR 5 (1986) (finding that one stroke of the cane on the hand of a 16-year old schoolgirl leaving mark visible eight days later constituted degrading treatment contrary to ECHR art. 3); *Y v. United Kingdom*, 17 Eur. Comm'n H. R. DR 238 (1992) (wheals caused by caning on buttocks of 15-year old schoolboy found to constitute degrading treatment.)

[57] 22 Eur. Comm'n H. R. DR 190 (1996).

[58] 247 Eur. Ct. H. R. (Ser. A) (1993).

[59] 2 FLR 959, 964 (1998).

[60] *Id.*

[61] 2 FLR 12 (1987).

[62] J. Newson & E. Newson, *The Extent of Parental Physical Punishment in the UK* (1989).

[63] M. Smith, *A Community Study of Physical Violence to Children in the Home, and Associated Variables* (1995).

[64] Disciplining Children in America: A Gallup Poll Report (Survey 765) (1995).

[65] M. Strauss & J. Stewart, *Corporal Punishment by American Parents: National Data on Prevalence, Chronicity, Severity and Duration in Relation to Child and Family Characteristics* (1998).

[66] Newell, note 4 *supra*, at 12.

[67] W. Krafft-Ebing, *Psychopathia Sexualis* (1886).

[68] SLC No. 135, note 13 *supra*, at para. 2.73.

[69] For a helpful literature review, see P. Leach, *The Physical Punishment of Children: Some Input from Recent Research* (NSPCC Policy Practice Research Series, 1999).

[70] 101 *Guidance for Effective Discipline: Pediatrics* 723 (American Academy of Pediatrics, 1988).

[71] See Newson & Newson, note 62 *supra,* at 4.

[72] S. Coopersmith, *The Antecedents of Self Esteem* (1967).

[73] SLC No. 135, note 13 *supra*, at para. 2.105.

[74] See note 6 *supra*.

[75] Supporting Families (1998), para 5.10. A further Government Paper is expected to concentrate on the specific issue of parental corporal punishment.

[76] Subsequent to its first visit, in 1994, the Committee condemned the Government's

failure to comply with art. 19 of the 1989 Convention on the Rights of the Child, which provides that 'States Parties shall take . . . all measures to protect the child from all forms of physical . . . violence . . . .' See UN Doc. CRC/C/SR.205, at para. 63 (1994).

7   *Lolita* at the Interface of Obscenity: Children and the Right to Free Expression*

ELENA LOIZIDOU

> *[B]ut Lolita is a tragedy. Pornography is not an image plucked out of context. Pornography is an attitude and an intuition. The tragic and the obscene exclude each other.*[1]

> *Lolita should be banned if it is proved that even . . . a single little girl was likely to be seduced as a result of its publication.*[2]

Introduction: Imagining Rights

Rights are constantly discussed — in the classroom, in the courtroom, in the newspapers, in bars and in coffee shops. Rights are constantly contested between groups, individuals, women, men, racial minorities, sexual minorities and children. Rights are taken as a truth, as property, possessed by individuals in civic, liberal, democratic society, and which those individuals can repossess if they are taken away. Yet we do not always stop to question the purported truths about these rights: what they are, who possesses them, or how they are possessed. We contest them or claim that we possess them, but do not always examine their foundations. Our attachment to rights reflects a belief that we live in democratic States, that we, as individuals or groups, are responsible for and in control of our political being. We have formed a collective imagination about the nature of rights. In our individual or

---

* The author thanks Clare Gilroy for her suggestions and proof-reading, as well as Julie Wallbank for her support and Michael Salter for his valuable suggestions.

124

collective imagination, rights signify our belief that we breathe and exist in liberal democracies. Yet their actual 'performativity'[3] tells a different story.

The aim of this chapter is to show how the right to free expression, one of the most fundamental rights that democracy offers,[4] allows one to tell a different story about human rights. It seeks to show that the right to free expression is not a right that the individual possesses *par excellence*. It is not a right that we can use to challenge the State when the State infringes upon our right of free expression. Rather, it is a right that the State possesses and uses to regulate and invent public spaces. This is not to say that I am under a misconception that rights should be absolute, but rather to point out who is in possession of rights and how they are used. The 'who' and 'how' indices allow one to re-think what we take for granted (a possessory discourse of rights) and to re-think the politics of the post-modern State.

This chapter offers not a nihilistic reading of human rights, but rather one that re-thinks human rights and their limits, in the light of debates and discourses surrounding children's rights. If one can question whether adults possess the rights that the Enlightenment project promises them,[5] then questions arise about the extent to which rights can be given to a 'subjectivity' (the child) whose voice is restricted, policed and interpreted through adults.[6] The right to free expression and the limitations (censorship or banning of materials due to their indecent or obscene nature) that are imposed on this basic democratic right will allow us to explore these issues.

Lolita

The right to free expression is not absolute. It is limited when free expression violates civic notions of decency, when it threatens to create public disorder, or when it challenges State images of itself. The right to free expression is also limited when what is expressed is deemed obscene or pornographic. In the United Kingdom a variety of statutes set limitations on freedom of expression, and simultaneously set the standards by which free expression can be measured and ultimately judged.[7] The Obscene Publications Act 1959 limits, for example, the right to free expression if the materials in question (books, films etc.) could 'deprave and corrupt' those most likely to come into contact with them, unless the materials can be proven through expert witnesses to be of educational, scientific or literary value.[8] What is of importance is not whether freedom of expression ought to be limited but rather how limitations of freedom of expression come about and what these limitations tell us about the right.

Vladimir Nabokov's *Lolita* has managed to escape censorship, despite the fact that there were cries calling for its banning, on the grounds that it would 'deprave and corrupt' young girls. The book and the discourses surrounding it are important not only because they address the issue of what can be deemed obscene, and what therefore can limit free expression, but also because the discourses construct an understanding and a response to representations of childhood. By focusing on *Lolita*, we can see how our western mythology[9] fails to live up to the possibility of synthesising conflicts or contests of rights through a higher principle.[10]

Nabokov, in the introductory quote of this paper, states that *Lolita*, his most infamous book, cannot be classified as an obscene publication. In distinguishing between the pornographic and the tragic, he simultaneously distinguishes between the surface of the representation and the depth of the representation. He defines pornography in a Baudrillardian way. Baudrillard claims that pornography does not represent a reality about sex, but rather makes sex so overt, so surface-based as to capture the real. But in its attempt to do so, the real becomes something else. It becomes hyperreal: 'The only fantasy in pornography, if there is one, is thus not a fantasy of sex, but of the real, and its absorption into something other than the real, the hyperreal.'[11]

The tragic for Nabokov has a context which plays a significant role in classifying or naming a book. What then makes the tragic tragic? What kind of context is necessary for a book to become a tragedy? In his *Poetics,* Aristotle elaborates on what makes a play a tragedy.[12] He states that 'tragedy is mimesis not of persons but of action and life . . . .'[13] Tragedy is a representation of acts which, in their cumulative effect, can represent the dilemmas and conflicts of life. The mimetic aspect of the tragedy for Aristotle seems not to obscure reality (through a non-actual representation of events) but rather to reveal conflictual acts in life, through the possibility of such events occurring: '[i]t is not the poet's function to relate actual events, but the kinds of things that might occur and are possible in terms of probability or necessity.'[14] The pornographic and the tragic can be distinguished therefore on these grounds: the tragic is a representation of a possible reality, the pornographic represents an attempt to make the real visible. *Lolita* for Nabokov is not pornographic; it is rather tragic, for it does represent a reality, a sombre reality perhaps, but still a possible reality.

These are not the only indices that separate or distinguish the tragic from the pornographic. Nabokov's statement allows us to draw further distinctions between the tragic and the pornographic. Aristotle states that the plot of a tragic work should be unitary and whole.[15] It should provide the audience with emotions of pity and fear, so that the required catharsis[16] may come about. In addition, where a reversal of fortune occurs, the character is punished not because he or she is evil, but because of an error of judgement.[17] Aristotle's reference to unity is important here. Wholeness and unity allow the audience to know what has happened, to know the outcome of fate. Tragedy, then, can be defined as a literary representation that provides, through mimesis, knowledge about the possible or necessary events in life.

Pornography cannot have the same effect. Consider Baudrillard's discussion of Japanese pornography:

> Pornography is the quadraphonic of sex. It adds a fourth track to the sexual act. It is the hallucination of detail that rules. Science has already habituated us to these microscopics, this excess of the real in its microscopic detail, this voyeurism of exactitude — a close-up of the invisible structures of the cell — to this notion of an inexorable truth that can no longer be measured with reference to the play of appearances, and that can only be revealed by a sophisticated technical apparatus . . . .[18]

He writes, further,

> Something else fascinates (but no longer seduces) you: technical perfection, "high fidelity," which is just as obsessive and puritanical as the other, conjugal fidelity. This time, however, one no longer knows what object it is faithful to, for one knows neither where the real begins or ends, nor understands, therefore, the fever of perfectibility that persists in the real's reproduction.'[19]

The context of the pornographic for Baudrillard is one that is obsessed with the detail that will unveil the truth about sex. Yet this obsession with detail fails either to capture the illusion of a holistic 'truth' or to provide knowledge about the object of representation. In Baudrillard's terms, the subject no longer knows where the real is Tragedy and pornography are different insofar as the former provides the audience with a knowledge of possible events in life, while the latter, because of it is failed attempt to capture the real, fails to provide the audience with a knowledge about life, or about a possible life. One could say that tragedy is under no illusion that it is representing the real. Rather it represents a possible real, while pornography, with its overt or naked representation of the body as the real, always fails to capture the real. It always finds itself in a hyperreal position. Surface and depth, absence of context and presence of context, and the content of the context distinguish the tragic from the pornographic. Can this explain why Nabokov's *Lolita* has never really ever been banned? Let us return to both the history of the publication and its context and to the indices discussed above to see whether abstract theories can explain why *Lolita* was never banned.

Lolita faced a myriad of problems until it was finally published. Nabokov was living and working in the United States when he wrote *Lolita*. He was at the time a professor of Russian literature at Cornell University. When he finished writing the book he looked for a publisher in the United States,[20] but no American publisher was willing to take the risk of publishing it and facing litigation (despite evidence that the Supreme Court was taking a liberal approach to publications that might be deemed obscene[21]). Nabokov was forced to seek a publisher in Europe, and successfully found one in France. The book was first issued in 1955 by the French publishing house Olympia. Olympia was not 'respectable.' It was known for publishing books deemed pornographic and obscene. Despite Olympia's bad reputation, *Lolita's* first years were unproblematic.

In 1958, however, Olympia faced a legal action concerning a ban on several of its publications, including *Lolita*. The French government was forced to lift the ban, after Olympia sued for damages, as the prestigious French publishing house Gallimard had subsequently published and distributed *Lolita*. It could be suggested that the lifting of the ban was due to the cunning strategy employed by Olympia, but that does not explain how *Lolita* was unproblematically allowed to be published and distributed by Gallimard. Nor does it explain how a book that had difficulties being published in the United States could be published and distributed in France. More specifically, it does not explain how the controversial issue of paedophilia raised in *Lolita* does not render the book obscene, or why the book has not been classified as pornographic. Similarly, cunning publishing strategies cannot explain how a book that was deemed so immoral managed to escape the apprehension or paranoia it had inspired in the United States.

Despite the fact that there is something objectionable about the novel, there seems to be something that prevents it from being obscene. Attempts to characterise *Lolita* as obscene, harmful, and seductive have always failed. *Lolita* always makes it: she always receives a certificate.[22] Perhaps the answer lies in Nabokov's description of the book as a tragedy: a mimeses of action, a representation of possible acts or life events. Let us, then, examine the sequence of events in the book, and consider some of the episodes that suggest that the book belongs to a tradition that could be called tragedy.

'*Lolita*, light of my life, fire of my loins. My sin, my soul. Lo-lee-ta: the tip of the tongue taking a trip of three steps down the palate to tap, at three, on the teeth. Lo. Lee. Ta.'[23] That is how Nabokov introduces his controversial book. In the first three lines, he playfully tells us that this is a book about passion as sin. What is this passion as sin about? *Lolita* represents events surrounding the life of 37-year-old Humbert Humbert, whose life is painted or stained by his fascination with a 12-year-old girl, who will play a significant role in his life. *Lolita* and Humbert meet under uneventful circumstances, when Humbert becomes *Lolita*'s mother's lodger. Humbert, though just a lodger in this insignificant New Haven residence, develops a passion, and will do anything to be in proximity to his passion, or as he calls it, his 'sin': 'Loleeta.' This longing to be close to *Lolita* prompts Humbert to marry her mother, Mrs Haze. But the marriage comes to an end when Mrs Haze is hit by a car.

Humbert now finds the perfect opportunity to be with *Lolita*. He 'kidnaps' her from her boarding school and takes her for a road trip around America. The trip turns Humbert's fantasies into reality. He and *Lolita* become lovers. Yet the trip is not the perfect honeymoon. Things turn sour when *Lolita* escapes and runs away with another man, Quilty. Humbert is devastated. His perfectly imagined affair has come to an end. In desperation he begins another trip in search of *Lolita*. His attempts to find her prove unsuccessful, until she eventually contacts him. It is then that he finds out that *Lolita* has left him for Quilty. Betrayed by his imagined love, he tracks down Quilty and kills him. Humbert is arrested and sentenced to death. It is from his prison cell that he narrates his story.

The context and the events that make up *Lolita* fall within a category of plays or literature that Aristotle would call tragedy. There is a context, a depth that mimics acts which could be real. Humbert would have been nothing without the passion that drives him to be close to the little girl. *Lolita* and Humbert never would have never been lovers if Mrs Haze had not accidentally died. Humbert still would have been enjoying his fantasy honeymoon if *Lolita* had not left him for Quilty. This turn of events brings about Humbert's fall, his final act of passion (murdering Quilty), which leads to a death sentence. Like King Creon in Sophocles's *Antigone*, Humbert is blinded by his passion, which brings about an error in his judgement along with Quilty's physical death, and his own metaphorical and actual death: his metaphorical death comes about when the prison eternally separates him from *Lolita*; his actual death will come about when he faces his execution.

Does the story meet Aristotle's further criteria of wholeness and unity? If so, it becomes clearer why attempts to ban the book have failed, and why the book was never deemed pornographic. The novel is written mostly in the first person, from Humbert's perspective. From the beginning of the book, we know what is going through Humbert's mind. We know why he is fascinated with young girls (his whole life is structured around his eternal mourning for his childhood sweetheart, Annabel, who died of typhus in Corfu). Humbert tells us what kind of girls attract him — 'nymphets':

> Now I wish to introduce the following idea. Between the age limits of nine and fourteen there occur maidens who, to certain bewitched travellers, twice or many times older than they, reveal their true nature, which is not human, but nymphic (that is demoniac); and these chosen creatures I propose to designate as "nymphets".
>
> 'It will be marked that I substitute time terms for spatial ones. In fact, I would have the reader see "nine" and "fourteen" as the boundaries — the mirrory beaches and rosy rocks — of an enchanted island haunted by those nymphets of mine and surrounded by a vast, misty sea. Between those age limits, are all girl-children nymphets? Of course not. Otherwise, we who are in the know, we lone voyagers, we nympholepts, would have long gone insane. Neither are good looks a criterion; and vulgarity, or at least what a given community terms so, does not necessarily impair certain mysterious characteristics, the fey grace, the elusive, shifty, soul-shattering, insidious charm that separates the nymphet from such coevals of hers as are incomparably more dependent on the spatial world of synchronous phenomena than on that intangible island of entranced time where *Lolita* plays with her likes . . . *she* stands unrecognised by them and unconscious herself of her fantastic power.[24]

Humbert tells us how 'nympholepts,' whom the current discourse would call 'paedophiles,' construct and imagine the object of their desires as boundaries, or rather landscapes, where they can rest their tired travelling bodies or their tired travelling imagination. At least that is how Humbert's description allows us to see it. The criteria for qualifying as a nymphet are elusiveness and seductive smiles that lead the traveller, the voyager or voyeur, on a journey with no answers, with no knowledge as to where he is going; and thus he relaxes in the endless dream. These descriptions give the reader a unitary understanding not only of Humbert but also of the events to come, thus placing the story into the category of tragedy.

We know all the time what goes through Humbert's mind, but also that what goes through his mind produces suffering. This suffering inspires feelings of fear and pity for Humbert, characteristics that are essential to tragedy or to the creation of a tragic character. We know what his passion for nymphets does to him; it drives him mad, it causes him to kill a man, it sends him to prison, it gives him a death sentence. *Lolita* thus becomes the tragedy of a 37-year-old man, where the reader knows the destiny of the 'anti-hero,' Humbert. It is this knowledge of what happens, of the revelation of a truth and destiny through tragedy, that saves *Lolita* from the censor, and allows the author, the producer, the film director, the distributor and finally the reader to enjoy a freedom of expression. The book could not have corrupted an audience or threatened the public because the regulator knows what happens and can interpret *Lolita* as a story we can learn from.

The Invention of the Public

Lolita is not pornographic when placed in context. It conveys a knowledge about possible life events which can produce a catharsis, a release of fear and pity through punishment. Because the one who has erred, the tragic 'anti-hero', is punished, the book reveals how knowledge of effects regulates what can be deemed obscene. The right to free expression, and the public space that is created out of this right, is subject to how 'knowledge' is used. Our rights are not our possessions. They are not items without a context. They are not shields by which we can protect ourselves as adults or can protect our children. They are rather signifiers that can be granted by the State when the State possesses a knowledge as to how the context (book, film, etc.) of these rights can affect our lives. Inevitably, what becomes a public space is subject to this arbitrary use and application of knowledge by the State. What is a public space is never fixed but rather is invented through this performativity of knowledge allegedly possessed by the State. The formal structure of the Obscene Publications Act 1959 provides an example. What follows is a structural analysis of the Obscene Publications Act 1959 and how it invents, controls and regulates the public space.

The history of prosecutions against publications and articles that are deemed obscene has been long.[25] Section 1(1) of the Obscene Publications Act 1959 provides the legal reason as to why not all publications or articles, or authors, filmmakers, and artists enjoy the right to free expression: such publications could 'deprave and corrupt persons who are likely, having regard to all relevant circumstances, to read, see or hear the matter contained or embodied in it,'[26] unless they can be proven to be for educational or other value.[27] The limit to the right of free expression is therefore the possibility that literary and other materials can 'deprave and corrupt' a likely audience. Nevertheless, as Beverley Brown rightly argues, the 'deprave and corrupt' criterion is not concerned in reality with protecting the civic individual from harm. It is rather concerned with controlling the civic individual's character and psyche.[28] Brown's differentiation between protection and control enables us to see that the right to 'free expression' is not a right that we possess, but rather a right that the State possesses and uses to form our civic character.

Nevertheless, Brown's important distinction fails to stress that the 'deprave and corrupt' criterion does not only control the moral and psychic constitution of the 'the likely audience'[29] but also effectively invents public spaces. One can see how this comes about if S1(2) and S1(3) are considered in conjunction with S1(1). S1(2) defines what is an article within the Act,[30] while S1(3) defines who is a person that publishes an article.[31] Both sections, while concerned with defining, are also concerned with inventing and regulating the public space. The way in which a publication is defined creates spaces as public that otherwise would not have been considered as public. The home, for example, is generally understood as a private space. However, if a distributed material that is deemed obscene is found in someone's home, then the home, the private space, is immediately transformed into a public space: a space that can be regulated and controlled by the State. The film, the book or the photograph that could be deemed obscene becomes a signifier of morality, a projector of how the State wants the public space to be. The Act in its entirety is interested not in protecting civic individuals from being harmed through an abuse of the right to 'free expression' but rather to invent and regulate the public space.

One can argue that the fundamental reasons behind any regulatory attempt implicating publications that can be deemed obscene is not the possible harm (whether physical or moral) that the possible audience might incur, but rather an inherent concern of the State that public disorder might break out. The regulation of obscenity becomes a regulation of public space. The 'deprave and corrupt' test, along with the definitions of the words 'articles' and 'publications,' are utilised to control what is permissible in public. The statutory terms 'deprave and corrupt' allow the State to invent new public spaces (such as, the Internet or the home) and not only to regulate existent public spaces.

While the limitation of the right to freedom of expression is presented by legal discourse as protecting the subject, we can see that the effect of this concern is to control and to regulate what can go on in a public space and what can be a public space. In Foucauldian[32] terms one could say then that the phrase 'deprave and corrupt' and its satellites (articles and publications) form part of an economy of power that enables the State, through law, to repress certain representations of sex and violence. This repression not only dictates what is obscene, but also defines the public space.

This public space is never fixed. It is constantly constructed through the term 'deprave and corrupt' and the satellite words 'article' and 'publication.' Does this mean then that these terms comport a set of norms that enable the State to regulate and invent the public space? Lauren Berlant and Michael Warner argue that the public space is controlled and defined by a set of norms that they coin 'heteronormativity.' By the term heteronormativity they mean:

> The institutions, structures of understanding, and practical orientations that make heterosexuality seem not only coherent — that is, organised as a sexuality — but also privileged. Its coherence is always provisional, and its privilege can take several (sometimes contradictory) forms: unmarked, as the basic idiom of the personal and the social; or marked as a natural state; or projected as an ideal or moral accomplishment. It consists less of norms that could be summarised as a body of doctrine than of a sense of rightness produced in contradictory manifestations — often unconscious, immanent to practice or to institutions. Contexts that have little visible relation to sex practice, such as life narrative and generation identity, can be heteronormative in this sense, while in other contexts forms of sex between men and women might not be heteronormative. Heteronormativity is thus a concept distinct from heterosexuality. One of the most conspicuous differences is that it has no parallel, unlike heterosexuality, which organises homosexuality as its opposite. Because homosexuality can never have the invisible, tacit, society-founding rightness that heterosexuality has, it would not be possible to speak of "homonormativity" in the same sense.[33]

For Berlant and Warner, therefore, the public space and what is permissible to be exhibited in public is pre-ordered by heteronormative trajectories. One such trajectory is 'intimacy.' 'Intimacy' (sex being one expression of intimacy) is an idiom that heteronormativity positions in the private domain. This positioning, they argue, creates a differentiation between the personal and the public,[34] which privileges 'institutions of social reproduction'[35] and 'block(s) the building of . . . explicit public sexual cultures.'[36] The heteronormative trajectories control and invent the public space through this process of differentiation (invention coming about through what is prohibited in public spaces). These processes 'conjure a mirage: a home base of pre-political humanity from which citizens are thought to come into political discourse and to which they are expected to return in the (always imaginary) future after political conflict.'[37] The differentiation that 'intimacy' brings is to locate the 'sexual' outside the public political discourse. Following this argument, the terms 'deprave and corrupt,' 'article' and 'publication' can be seen as part of the heteronormative trajectory that regulates what is obscene and should be banned or censored and what can be made public.

Still, this reading of regulation, definition and invention of public spaces leaves unanswered a vital question: how could heteronormative trajectories such as the terms 'deprave and corrupt,' 'article' and 'publication' produce spaces so different that they can all be called public spaces (galleries, book shops, the home, the internet)? How can the combination of these three words have produced over time so many different public spaces? Are' these heteronormative trajectories so inflexible, so ahistorical? Are the criteria of what can 'deprave and corrupt,' for example, constantly the same? Berlant and Warner would argue that they are the same but they disguise themselves in different masks, reflecting political and cultural changes. The essence remains the same while the form changes.[38] Nevertheless, the problem with this argument is that it understands regulations to be determined through a particular set of preconditions (heteronormative) that are highly visible and tangible. While this framework can explain how certain materials are deemed obscene and therefore censored, it cannot explain how some articles might be deemed as being obscene or having the possibility to 'deprave and corrupt,' but still be given a film certificate or be published without successful litigation being brought against them.

What, then, makes such books as *Lolita* not obscene? There is always something that remains outside the heteronormative trajectory. What becomes a public space is unpredictable and intangible, beyond legal or State knowledge.   Similarly, what becomes obscene, what, in other words, 'depraves and corrupts,' is not what we know will 'deprave and corrupt,' but what we don't know whether it will 'deprave and corrupt.'   What is regulated, what should not be allowed to be publicised (depraving and corrupting a public space) is the unknown, which carries an element of risk.[39]

Purifying the Obscene: 'Innocence' as a Right of Childhood

In law and political ideology . . . for example, the fetus and the child have been spectacularly elevated to the place of sanctified nationality. The state now sponsors stings and legislation to purify the Internet on behalf of children. New welfare and tax 'reforms' passed under the co-operation between the Contract with America and Clintonian familialism seek to increase the legal and economic privileges of married couples and parents. Vouchers and privatisation rezone education of parents rather than citizens. Meanwhile, senators such as Ted Kennedy and Jesse Helms support amendments that refuse federal funds to organizations that 'promote, disseminate, or produce materials that are obscene or that depict or describe, in a patently offensive way, sexual or excretory activities or organs, including but not limited to obscene depictions of sadomasochism, homoeroticism, the sexual exploitation of children, or individuals engaged in sexual intercourse.[40]

This quote suggests that the foetus and the child are used as rhetorical tropes to continue the regulation of obscene publications. Current obscenity legislation in the United Kingdom is also concerned with regulating pornography for the sake of children.[41] The child, becomes the site that ought to be protected from obscene or pornographic material. Public spaces such as the Internet, legislators suggest, should be purified in order to protect children from sexual harm, whether it is the harm of potential sexual abuse or representational harm. This reference to purification suggests that the legislator's discourse represents children as being pure and innocent. The political and legal crusade becomes a crusade to maintain and protect the 'innocence' of children.[42] 'Innocence' is represented as a right of children.

This political and legal crusade echoes some feminist antipornography arguments. Catherine Mackinnon and Andrea Dworkin have repeatedly attacked pornography on the grounds that it is discriminatory against women because it denigrates them to the position of sexual objectification and causes actual sexual harm to women (accepting the causal link between pornography and rape).[43] The legal and political discourse concerning child pornography and material deemed obscene or harmful to children simulates the feminist anti-pornography stance. This legal and political discourse disguises under the terms 'harm,' 'innocence' and 'children' the true object of obscenity regulations: the control, definition and invention of public spaces. The right to freedom of expression is not actually limited because some 'expressions' are harmful, but rather because the State, through legal and political arenas, wants to regulate what is and becomes public. The Mackinnon and Dworkin anti-pornography stance fails to recognise that the harm principle is only a rhetorical device.

The harm principle is translated as 'deprave and corrupt' in the Obscene Publications Act 1959. It is a rhetorical device used to accumulate information and the damage that material might inflict on the psychic world of those who come in contact with it. The State, through child psychologists, child councillors, teachers and other experts, accumulates information as to what could damage, harm or corrupt the essence of childhood, what in other words will harm 'innocence.' This expertise assumes that what it produces is truthful when its object of study, the child, does not possess the language, articulation and cognitive skills that the experts possess. The truth about children derives not from the child but rather from the interpreter of the child (parents, psychologists, teachers etc.). The knowledge of what it is to be a child derives from non-knowledge. What is deemed obscene for a child is based on a non-understanding of the child. It is lack of knowledge as to whether the material that is deemed obscene will harm the child that regulates the publication of obscene material.

Conclusion

What is deemed obscene, what violates our common right to freedom of expression is not the obscene *per se*, but that which we cannot classify, that as to which we have no knowledge whether it is obscene. Limits on rights like freedom of expression do not come about because the State and its institutions want to protect the audience, whether an adult audience or a child audience, but because the State wants to control, regulate and invent its public spaces. Knowledge of the possible 'harm' or the term 'deprave and corrupt' become the masks that the State deploys to justify limitations to a right. These common harms manage to exclude our ability to choose the materials that we want to see. Before discussing the rights of children and regulating obscenity on behalf of the child, we need to question why and how we regulate, for whom we regulate, and the rhetorical devices we use to achieve our aims.

Notes

[1] Letter written to publisher Pat Covici by Vladimir Nabokov (cited in Edward de Grazia, *Girls Lean Back Everywhere: The Law of Obscenity and the Assault on Genius* 255 (1992)).

[2] *Id.* at 268.

[3] See J. Butler, *Bodies that Matter* 225 (1993). Butler argues that legal pronouncements gain binding power through a ritual (performativity) followed by judges, including citing statutes, previous cases, and declarations of rights. In other words, law gains its power through acts. It will be argued in this chapter that the performativity of human rights allows us to ask who possesses human rights and how they can be interpreted.

[4] R. Gaete, *Human Rights and the limits of Critical Reason* 82 (1993).

[5] *Id.* at 1.

[6] From the early 18th century the child was thought of and constructed differently from adults. The child was not any more an early reflection of adulthood but rather a subject that was vulnerable and needed protection. These constructions of childhood that are still with us are not just mere constructions. They carry, like every construction, a series of repercussions. The child is restricted in its mode of expression: the child, for example, is not allowed to enter such adult spaces as the pub. For a discussion of child restriction and construction, see R. Sennet, *The Fall of the Public Man* 91-97 (1978).

[7] See, e.g., in the United Kingdom, Obscene Publications Act 1959, Obscene Publications Act 1964, Criminal and Public Order Act 1994.

[8] Obscene Publications Act 1959, S.4.

[9] Like Gaete, I use the term mythology to criticise the totalising myth about human rights. See Gaete, note 4 *supra*, at 167-172.

[10] *Id.* at 170.

[11] J. Baudrillard, *Seduction* 29 (B. Singer, trans. 1989).

[12] Aristotle, *Poetics* 41-141 (S. Halliwell trans. 1995).

[13] *Id.* at 51.

[14] *Id.* at 59.

[15] *Id.*

[16] *Id.* at 47, 49.

[17] *Id.* at 71.

[18] Baudrillard, note 11 *supra*, at 31.

[19] *Id.* at 30.

[20] Nabokov began writing *Lolita* in 1949 and he finished in 1954. Among the American Publishers rejecting the book where Pascal Covici from Viking Press and Wallace Brockway of Simon and Schuster Press.

[21] See, e.g., *Roth v. United States*, 354 U.S. 476 (1957).

[22] This refers to the attempts that have been made to censor cinematic representations of *Lolita*. Recently there has been debate about Adrian Lyne's cinematic adaptation. The film has been described as 'a paedophiliac's, bible.' which could lead to the seduction of little girls. Nevertheless, the film has been given a certificate, even in the United States. Stanley Kubrick's *Lolita* (1962) also stirred debate (even in an era where paedophilia was not a culturally visible term) and there were calls for banning the film. It was given an X-rating in 1962.

[23] V. Nabokov, *Lolita* 9 (Penguin ed. 1995).

[24] *Id.* at 16-17.

[25] For a history of obscenity laws and prosecutions, see S. Heath *et al. On Pornography* (1993).

[26] The 'deprave and corrupt' test is a test that has been instituted in the Act from the common law case of *R v. Hicklin*, LR 3 QB 360 (1868).

[27] Obscene Publications Act 1959, S4.

[28] B. Brown, 'Troubled Vision: Legal Understandings of Obscenity,' 19 NF 29, 35 (1993).

[29] *Id.* at 37.

[30] 'In this Act "article" means any description of article containing or embodying matter to be read or looked at or both, any sound record, and any film or other record of a picture or pictures.'

[31] 'For the purposes of this Act a person publishes an article who — (a) distributes, circulates, sells, lets on hire, gives or lends it, or who offers it for sale or for letting on hire; or (b) in the case of an article containing or embodying matter to be looked at or a record, shows, plays or projects it . . . .'

[32] M. Foucault, 1 *History of Sexuality* (R. Hurley, trans. 1990).

[33] L. Berlant & M. Warner, *Sex in Public Critical Inquiry* 547, 548 n. 2 (1998).

[34] *Id.* at 553.

[35] *Id.*

[36] *Id.*

[37] *Id.*

[38] See Brown, note 28 *supra*, at 37.

[39] *Id.* at 36.

[40] Berlant & Warner, note 33 *supra*, at 550.

[41] See, e.g., Criminal Justice and Public Order Act 1994, S. 84.

42 I use here the word 'innocent' not to signify any natural essence to children, but rather to focus on the discourse of innocence. The dominant discourse constructs children as innocent. See Foucault, note 32 *supra*, at xx. See also C. Piper, 'Historical Constructions of Childhood Innocence: Removing Sexuality,' chapter 2 in this collection.

43 A. Dworkin & C. Mackinnon, *Pornography and Civil Rights: A New Day for Women's Equality* (1998). For a critique, see D. Cornell, *The Imaginary Domain* ch. 3 (1995).

8 Childhood Sexual Abuse as a Predictor of Substance Use and HIV/AIDS Risk Behaviour among Women at Admission to Prison

JANET L. MULLINGS, VICTORIA E. BREWER & JAMES W. MARQUART

Introduction

Between December 1980 and June 1996, the number of women incarcerated in federal and state prisons in the United States grew by 451 per cent. The female jail population has grown 10.2 per cent annually since 1985.[1] The incarceration rate for women in the United States is increasing at over twice that of men. Roughly 80,000 women now imprisoned nationally account for over six per cent of all inmates.[2] Rising female prison populations have prompted scholars to examine the psychological and physical health needs of women prisoners.[3] The lives of female prisoners before incarceration are characterised by poverty, unemployment, under-education, lack of access to health care services, violence, substance abuse, and high-risk behaviours (intravenous drug use and unsafe sexual practices).[4] Growing prison populations now display an array of health problems associated with such histories, particularly prior drug use.[5] Studies also continue to find that childhood abuse is prevalent among prison populations.[6] Lifetime victimisation is common to many women in prison. Yet little is known about the impact of such experiences in shaping prisoners' lives. Some research suggests an association between child abuse and later criminal offending.[7] Little research to date, however, has examined the relationships between child sexual abuse, offending, and HIV drug and sex risk behaviours among women in prison.

This chapter explores the relationship between childhood sexual abuse, substance use, criminal behaviour, and high-risk behaviour among a sample of 488 women entering Texas prisons in 1994. First we examine current research regarding the relationship between child abuse and drug use, criminality, and high-risk behaviours among both incarcerated women and women within the population at large. We then present analyses of 488 female inmates at admission to prison to ascertain the role of childhood sexual victimisation in patterns of offending, drug use, and high-risk HIV/AIDS-related behaviours. We conclude by discussing some of the policy implications of these findings.

General Findings from the Relevant Literature

Before examining the findings from the present study, it is useful to review the literature on physical and sexual abuse among incarcerated women in the United States.

Physical/Sexual Abuse among Female Prisoners

A survey of women in prison conducted by the American Correctional Association in 1990 found that one-half (50 per cent) of the inmates reported prior physical abuse and more than one-third (35 per cent) reported prior sexual abuse.[8] Pollack-Byrne, in a review of research examining the extent of abuse among female inmates, estimates sexual abuse rates from 35 per cent to 63 per cent and physical abuse rates from 35 per cent to 53 per cent.[9] Other studies have since confirmed high rates of prior victimisation among women entering prison.[10] These high rates of past physical and sexual victimisation have exacerbated the problems of an increasing number of female inmates with drug-using histories. Successful intervention and treatment programmes for female prisoners, therefore, require an understanding of the effects of child sexual abuse on women prisoners.

Childhood Abuse and HIV Risk Behaviour

Whether problems in adulthood are a consequence of 1) having been a teen-aged runaway,[11] 2) substance abuse,[12] 3) suicidal tendencies,[13] 4) being adult victims of abuse[14] or other factors, the adverse effects of child sexual abuse are well documented. An emerging body of literature strongly suggests that early experiences of sexual abuse may also lead to HIV/AIDS-related high-risk behaviours. These behaviours include involvement in the sex trade industry,[15] sexual compulsivity,[16] and greater-than-average numbers of sexual partners.[17]

One study of childhood sexual abuse and high-risk HIV-related behaviours examined 51 juvenile runaways. This study reports three important reasons why sexually abused teenagers are at greater risk of becoming infected with HIV. These young people had gaps in their HIV knowledge, were temporally more concerned about the present than the future, and exhibited classic survivor characteristics of chronic depression. Chronic depression, manifested as passively suicidal behaviour, served to impede self-protection behaviours.[18] Another study examined the incidence of childhood sexual abuse among 567 male and female college students and their high-risk sexual behaviours, drug use, and the prevalence of HIV infection. Males with histories of childhood sexual abuse had twice the prevalence of HIV infection of non-abused men. Though this same relationship was not found among the abused women in their study, they emphasised the importance of this factor when considering management of HIV risk.[19]

In their study of the incidence of childhood sexual/physical abuse among 52 HIV-symptomatic patients, Allers and Benjack observed adult survivor characteristics of sexual compulsivity, re-victimisation, chronic depression, and alcohol/drug abuse in both abused and non-abused subjects. Sixty-five per cent of these HIV-infected persons had been sexually or physically abused in childhood. Likewise, these researchers noted that abused subjects were significantly more likely to have a greater number of adult survivor characteristics than their non-abused counterparts. Among other observations, Allers and Benjack assert that educational efforts alone may prove insufficient with these victims of previous abuse trauma.[20]

In an even more detailed analysis, Klein and Chao examined the relationships between specific types of childhood and adolescent sexual abuse and HIV-related sexual risk behaviours during adulthood. Examining a sample of approximately 2,800 women in the United States, Puerto Rico, and Mexico, all of whom had been intravenous drugs users (IDUs) and had been sexual partners of IDUs, these researchers found a strong correlation between sexual abuse early in life and HIV higher-risk behaviour later in life. Among these women, over one-third had been sexually abused as children and over one-third had experienced sexual abuse as adolescents. Nearly one in five (18.4 per cent) had been abused in both stages of childhood. Among the additional findings in this extensive study were that certain *types* of sexual risk-taking behaviours (e.g., having sexual relations while high, trading sex for drugs or money) were found to be related more closely than were other types of sexual risk-taking behaviours to women's sexual abuse histories. For both measures of risk-taking, every childhood sexual abuse item studied was found to differ significantly for abused and non-abused women, with women who had been abused engaging in higher-risk sexual behaviours than the non-abused women. For example, the mean number of times for having sex while high on alcohol or drugs was 75 per cent higher among women who reported having been forced to show their sexual parts or to view someone else's during childhood. Klein and Chao also reported a 66 per cent higher incidence of higher-risk sexual behaviour among women who said they had been forced to fondle someone else genitally, or to be fondled, than the women who had not had this experience. Furthermore, when comparing those subjects who had experienced sexual abuse as children (ages 11 or younger) with those for whom this abuse had occurred in adolescence (ages 12 to 18), abuse experienced during adolescence was not found to be associated with the number of times adult women engaged in sexual relations while high; yet this adolescent experience was a significant predictor of the number of IDU sexual partners they reported having.[21]

One study examining the relationships between child maltreatment and later substance abuse and criminality among male and female prisoners found the effects of child abuse to be more severe for women. In addition to finding higher rates of child maltreatment among women prisoners, the researchers also found increased rates of victimisation for women as they moved into adulthood. These female inmates also scored higher on adult depression and substance abuse diagnostic scales than their male counterparts. Finally, this research suggests child maltreatment and substance abuse are stronger predictors of criminal activity for women than men prisoners.[22]

High-Risk Groups for HIV/AIDS among Female Offenders

Female prison populations are also over-represented by groups at high risk of HIV infection, based on their membership in racial/ethnic minorities. Race is associated with the incidence of STD/HIV infection (with disproportionate representation among African-Americans and Hispanics) and race/ethnicity is likewise assumed to be a marker for both sexual and health care-seeking behaviour. What is thought to be potentially more true for women than men is that, because of the higher overall prevalence of infection among African-Americans, Hispanics, and native Americans, the risk to any individual member of these groups, even those with few sexual partners and good health care behaviours, is increased because they tend to have sex within their own racial groups.[23]

Empirical evidence of cultural differences in the relationship between childhood sexual abuse and involvement in sexual risk behaviours in adulthood is yet another important contribution of Klein and Chao's study. With regard to the effects of race/ethnicity, White women's sexual abuse experiences were unrelated to adulthood involvement in sexual risk behaviours. Yet among African-American women, childhood sexual abuse was consistently found to be predictive of the number of times they had sex while high, and of their overall HIV-related sexual risk levels. In addition, while sexually abused women engaged in sexual relations while high anywhere from 78 per cent to 152 per cent more often (on average) than those women who were not abused sexually prior to age 12, levels of HIV-related sexual risk were from 18 per cent to 30 per cent higher for African-American women in this category. Mexican/Mexican American and Puerto Rican women were also consistently more involved in HIV-related sexual risk in adulthood than their non-abused ethnic counterparts. Yet the results for these subgroups of Latina women varied from those of African-Americans in that there was a significant correlation between childhood sexual abuse and increased numbers of sexual partners during adulthood among the former but not among the latter.[24]

Sexually Transmitted Diseases among Substance-Abusing Women

Substance abuse has been strongly associated with high levels of sexually transmitted diseases (STDs).[25] Erickson and Trocki report that women who abuse alcohol are four and one-half times more likely to have STDs than non-alcohol-abusing women.[26] The use of drugs, crack-cocaine in particular, is also highly associated with the risk of contracting STD's, including HIV.[27] Drug use suppresses self-efficacy and constrains women's and men's abilities to protect themselves. It also increases the likelihood of exchanging sex for drugs or money, engaging in sex without a condom, and taking anonymous sex partners.[28] Women crack users are at especially high risk of contracting HIV because they frequently trade sex for drugs or money with men who have relatively high rates of HIV infections.[29]

Methods

The data used for this study were collected by The Texas Commission on Alcohol and Drug Abuse, in conjunction with Texas A&M University's Institute of Public Policy, through face-to-face interviews with a sample of women prisoners at admission in 1994. An interview schedule was administered to a random sample of 500 female prisoners admitted to the Institutional Division of the Texas Department of Criminal Justice in 1994. Respondents consisted of new admissions to the prison system that were interviewed during the intake process at the Central Medical Diagnostic unit for women prisoners in Texas. There were 574 inmates originally selected in the sampling process, with 500 completing the entire interview, yielding an 87 per cent co-operation rate. Each structured interview lasted an average of 90 minutes.

Twelve respondents were excluded from the sample prior to analysis: four who had refused to answer the majority of questions and eight who identified their race/ethnicity as 'other.' As to the current research controls for racial/ethnic differences in child sexual abuse, substance use, and HIV risk behaviour, a racial category consisting of only eight members was considered too small to allow for analysis. The reduced sample for this study included 488 women prisoners (85 per cent of the originally selected sample).

The survey instrument consisted of six major areas: prevalence of licit and illicit substance use, criminal history, physical and mental health, high-risk sexual behaviours, prior physical and sexual abuse, and demographics. Twelve trained female interviewers using a Computer Assisted Interviewing (CAI) system collected the data. Data collection benefits associated with CAI techniques include the automatic branching of interview questions into different or additional sets of questions based on subjects' responses and rejection of responses which are out of range or inconsistent with previous responses.[30]

Sample Characteristics

Descriptive statistics for sociodemographics of 488 female inmates retained for analysis are summarised in Table 1. With few exceptions, this sample closely reflects national level data regarding sociodemographic characteristics of female prison inmates in 1991. The US Department of Justice reports that in 1991 the majority of female prison inmates were over the age of 30, members of a racial/ethnic minority, unmarried, and had children under the age of 18.[31]

Table 1 Descriptive Statistics for Sample: Demographics (n=488)

Demographic Characteristic	Frequency	Percent	Mean	St. Dev.
Mean Age (Range 17-63)			32.4	7.85
Race/Ethnicity				
African-American	236	48.4%		
White	157	32.2		
Hispanic	95	19.5		
Education				
0 through 8th	91	18.6		
9th through 11th	261	53.5		
12th through some college	136	27.9		
Received GED? (n=352)	124	35.2		
Employment week prior to confinement				
Unemployed	273	55.9		
Employed (full or part-time)	215	44.1		
Marital Status				
Not Married (div/sep/widow)	190	39.0		
Never Married	166	34.0		
Married	132	27.0		
Has Children:				
Yes	408	83.6		
No	80	16.4		
Avg. Num. Children (Range 1-9)			2.73	1.59
Current Offence				
Drug	198	40.6		
Property	143	29.3		
Violent	61	12.5		
Probation Parole Violation	86	17.6		
Average Sentence Length			10.6	8.60

The average age of the sample was 32 (32.4), with a range of 17 to 63 years. The majority were African-American (47.4 per cent), while White inmates comprised nearly one-third (32.2 per cent) and Hispanics almost twenty per cent (19.5 per cent). Again, the racial/ethnic composition of this sample closely reflects the national sample; however, these data contain slightly fewer Whites and slightly more Hispanic women. Women in this sample were more likely to report being married at the time of incarceration (27 per cent) than the national sample (17.3 per cent) and less likely to report never married (34 per cent). The remaining 39 per cent reported either divorced, widowed, or separated marital status. Much like the national prison sample, the majority (83.6 per cent) of these women were mothers, with a reported average of three (2.7) children (see Table 1).

The Bureau of Justice statistics reveal that in 1991 over one-third (38.2 per cent) of women in prison reported educational attainment of having graduated from high school or higher. In contrast, less than one-third (27.9 per cent) of this sample reported completing the 12th grade or higher. Thus, it appears that these women were slightly less educated than the national sample. Among those in this sample not completing high school, over one-third (35.2 per cent) reported receiving a Graduate Equivalency Diploma (GED).

Over one-half (55.9 per cent) of the women were unemployed during the week prior to incarceration, and nearly one-half (47.3 per cent) reported receiving some welfare support during that same time period. This unemployment rate closely resembles the national female prison population in 1991 where more than half (53.3 per cent) reported being unemployed prior to incarceration. Much like the national prison population, the majority of these inmates (40.6 per cent) were serving their current prison sentence for drug-related offences. Over one-quarter (29.3 per cent) of these inmates were property offenders and nearly 13 per cent (12.5 per cent) were serving time for violent offences. These data also contain 86 women (17.6 per cent) who reported violation of probation or parole requirements as their current offence. The distribution of sentence length across three categories — one to five years, six to 10 years, and 11 to 50 plus years — was equally distributed, indicating that these inmates were as likely to enter prison with lengthy sentences as shorter ones. The reported average current sentence length was nearly 11 (10.6) years, higher than the 1991 prison sample reported mean of nearly nine (8.75) years.

Analysis and Findings

The following section presents the findings of this research. Specifically, we examine differences between prisoners who reported child sexual abuse and those who did not in relation to later drug use, other criminal activity, and HIV/AIDS-associated high-risk sexual and drug taking behaviours.

Exploring Child Sexual Abuse and Later Life Experiences

The interview instrument used to collect data for this study asked one direct question regarding childhood sexual abuse: 'As you were growing up, how often were you sexually mistreated, abused, or raped?' Table 2 indicates that these prisoners experienced child sexual abuse at similarly high rates as other incarcerated female populations,[32] with over one-quarter (26.2 per cent) reporting having ever been sexually mistreated, abused, or raped as children (see Table 2).

Table 2 Chi-Square Differences for Victimisation by Race/Ethnicity and Age

Race/Ethnicity & Age		Percent (n)	Percent (n)	Percent (n)
	Total	**African-Am**	**White**	**Hispanic**
Any Child Sexual Abuse *By Race/Ethnicity* (n=488)	26.2% (128)	22.0% (52)	35.0% (55)**	22.1% (21)
	Total	**Young**	**Mid Age**	**Older**
Any Child Sexual Abuse *By Age* (n=488)	26.2% (128)	34.0% (34)*	27.9% (65)	18.7% (29)
	Total	**Drug**	**Property**	**Violent**
Any Child Sexual Abuse *By Offence Type* (n=102)	25.4% (102)	22.7% (45)	26.6% (38)	31.1% (19)

X^2 *p.<.05 ** p.<.01

White inmates reported significantly more child sexual abuse (p.<01) than the other racial/ethnic groups. Examining the extent of reported child sexual abuse across age categories reveals some differences. As also demonstrated in Table 2, younger (17 to 25 years) inmates reported significantly more child sexual abuse (p.<05) than their older counterparts while the oldest inmates (36 to 63 years) were significantly less likely to report child sexual abuse (p.<.01). No significant differences were detected among the prisoners with regard to the type of offence for which they were serving their current confinement.

We can not infer causal relationships between measures of child sexual abuse and later negative life events with our cross-sectional data.

Descriptive measures are appropriate, however, to examine whether there is an association between child sexual abuse and other negative life events among the sample. As summarised in Table 3, over one-quarter (26.2 per cent) of the sample reported having experienced child sexual abuse. It is striking to note that women who reported child sexual abuse were significantly more likely to have also experienced *all* of the later negative life events than women who were not sexually abused as children (see Table 3).

Table 3 Negative Life Experiences — Sexually Abused/Not Sexually Abused as Child

Life Experiences	Sexually Abused as Child (n=128/26.2%)	Not Sexually Abused as Child (n=360/73.8%)
Used any drug before age 15	64 (50.0%)*	134 (37.2%)
Ever run away as child	88 (68.8)***	116 (37.3)
Experienced child neglect	114 (89.1)***	129 (35.8)
Experienced child physical abuse	66 (51.6)***	49 (13.6)
Severely depressed (high CES-D score)	95 (74.2)***	192 (53.3)
Used drugs in last year	96 (75.0)***	204 (56.7)
Any sexual risk behaviours	72 (56.3)***	134 (37.2)
Any drug risk behaviours	105 (82.0)**	224 (68.1)
Any adult physical abuse	99 (77.3)***	161 (44.7)
Any adult sexual abuse	74 (57.8)***	74 (20.6)

X^2 *p.<.05 ** p.<.01 ***p.<.001

In this analysis it appears that child abuse, child neglect, and child physical abuse often occur simultaneously, as 89.1 per cent of the women who reported child sexual abuse also reported child neglect and 51.6 per cent also reported child physical abuse. These findings are consistent with the literature suggesting that high rates of child neglect and physical abuse are often found among sexually abused children.[33] Women who had been sexually abused as children reported other measures of negative early life experiences. Nearly 70 per cent (68.8 per cent) reported running away from home as children, compared to 37.3 per cent of the non-abused group. This finding supports results from Widom's longitudinal study, which showed that individuals who had experienced child abuse were more likely to be arrested as runaways during their juvenile years than the non-abused control group.[34]

Three-quarters of the child sexual abuse sample scored as severely depressed (74.2 per cent; p.<001) and reported having used drugs in the past year (75.0 per cent; p.<.001), significantly more than the non-abused group. Furthermore, inmates who reported experiencing child abuse were significantly more likely (82.0 per cent; p.<.01) to report engaging in HIV/AIDS drug risk behaviours (ever injected drugs, smoked crack-cocaine, or shared needles with an AIDS-infected person) and HIV/AIDS (56.3 per cent; p.<.001 per cent) sexual risk behaviours (prostitution, sex without a condom with multiple partners, sex with IV drug users, sex with others who smoke crack, sex while high on drugs or alcohol, trading sex for drugs or money, anal sex, and sex with one who has AIDS). Additionally, early sexual victimisation appears to be associated with later adult physical (77.3 per cent; p.<.001) and sexual (57.8 per cent; p.<.001) abuse. Future research with longitudinal samples is needed to determine the direct or indirect influences that childhood sexual victimisation may have on later risk outcomes.

Linkages between Child Sexual Abuse, Criminal Behaviour and Drug Use

As reported in Table 4, inmates who had been sexually abused as children reported more substance use for each of the categories than the non-abused group. Prisoners who had been sexually abused as children were significantly more likely to have used barbiturates (p.<01), crack (p.<01), inhalants (p.<01), psychedelics (p.<01), heroin (p.<05), and marijuana (p.<05). These findings support other studies reporting greater substance involvement by women who were sexually abused as children[35] (see Table 4).

Similarly, as revealed in Table 5, sexually abused prisoners were more likely to have engaged in various offending behaviours in the past than non-abused prisoners. Specifically, these women were significantly more likely to report having purchased stolen goods (p<.01), engaged in prostitution (p<.01), and involvement in selling drugs (p.<05) than non-abused inmates. The finding that abused inmates were significantly more likely ever to have engaged in prostitution has special relevance for risk of contracting HIV, as the relationship between prostitution and HIV is well documented[36] (see Table 5).

Table 4 Lifetime Prevalence Using Licit and Illicit Substances: Percentage Total Sample, Sexually Abused, Not Abused, and Chi-Square

Substance Use	% Total Sample (n=488)	% Sexually Abused (n=128)	% Not Sexually Abused (n=360)	Chi-Square
Alcohol	93.6%	96.9%	92.5%	3.04
Amphetamines	27.7	31.3	26.4	1.11
Barbiturates	34.2	47.7**	29.4	13.91
Cocaine	64.5	71.1	62.2	3.25
Crack	54.9	66.4**	50.8	9.25
Heroin	35.0	42.2*	32.5	3.89
Inhalants	15.0	24.2**	11.7	11.69
Marijuana	83.4	89.8*	81.1	5.20
Opiates	15.2	20.3	13.3	3.58
Psychedelics	29.9	39.8**	26.4	8.15

*p<.05; **p<.01

Table 5 Lifetime Prevalence of Offending Behaviour: Percentage Total Sample, Sexually Abused, Not Abused, and Chi-Square

Offence Type	% Total Sample (n=488)	% Sexually Abused (n=128)	% Not Sexually Abused (n=360)	Chi-Square
Beating Someone Up	22.7	27.3	21.1	2.09
Buying Stolen Goods	26.8	35.9**	23.6	7.31
Burglary	23.2	24.2	22.8	.11
Prostitution	24.8	38.3**	20.0	16.92
Shoplifting	26.2	50.8	46.1	.82
Selling Drugs	26.2	28.1*	19.7	3.89

*p<.05; **p<.01

The prevalence of substance use and offending behaviours among this sample supports research findings of higher rates of these behaviours among women who experienced child sexual abuse.[37] Our research also reveals that prisoners who had been sexually abused as children typically began substance use and had contact with the criminal justice system at younger ages than non-abused prisoners. Table 6 presents results from independent sample T-tests examining the average age reported for first instance of substance use and other offending behaviours. The analysis reveals that inmates who reported child sexual abuse began using drugs and alcohol earlier than the non-abused group. Specifically, sexually abused inmates were significantly more likely to have begun using alcohol, cocaine, marijuana, and opiates (all at p.<05) at younger ages. While sexually abused prisoners were more likely to report ever having engaged in many of the offending behaviours, they do not appear to have begun their criminal behaviour at younger ages. They were, however, significantly more likely to report first arrest and jail time (both p.<05) earlier than non-abused inmates. Apparently, among sexually abused inmates, early involvement with substance use contributed to early contact with the criminal justice system (see Table 6).

Higher rates of substance use and substance use at younger ages escalates the risk of HIV infection. The risk of contracting HIV/AIDS increases with substance use and increases substantially for injecting drug users. Additionally, other studies have found increased risk of contracting HIV among crack-cocaine users.[38] The use of crack-cocaine has been associated with indiscriminate sexual activity with multiple partners who are also at high risk of HIV.[39] Drug and alcohol use, in general, has been identified as a high-risk marker among certain populations, including incarcerated women.

Table 6 Average Age at First Substance Use, Criminal Behaviour, and Contact with the Criminal Justice System: Mean (Standard Deviation in Parentheses), and T-Test

	X Sexually Abused (n=128)	X Not-Abused (n=360)	T-Test
Mean Age First Substance Use			
Alcohol	15.54 (4.28)	16.47 (4.14)	2.12*
Amphetamines	19.13 (7.16)	20.01 (5.44)	.78
Barbiturates	18.45 (5.93)	19.86 (5.83)	1.60
Cocaine	21.90 (5.68)	23.71 (7.61)	2.04*
Crack	25.63 (6.42)	26.71 (7.62)	1.18
Heroin	23.61 (6.78)	22.81 (5.73)	-.92
Inhalants	16.00 (3.95)	18.12 (4.92)	1.98

Marijuana	15.20 (4.02)	16.78 (5.33)	2.98*
Opiates	19.94 (6.49)	23.02 (6.83)	2.09*
Psychedelics	19.24 (5.70)	18.86 (4.61)	-.43
Mean Number of Drugs			-3.97**
Lifetime Use (range 0-9)	4.30 (2.44)	3.33 (2.36)	
Mean Age First Offending			
Burglary	22.32 (7.61)	23.33 (7.34)	.65
Buying Stolen Goods	24.20 (8.18)	24.42 (6.58)	.17
Prostitution	23.13 (7.08)	24.77 (6.97)	1.32
Beating Someone Up	16.31 (6.99)	16.68 (7.43)	.26
Selling Drugs	22.78 (8.08)	23.18 (7.79)	.27
Shoplifting	17.64 (7.38)	19.78 (8.36)	1.83
Mean Age First Arrest	20.46 (6.26)	22.29 (6.62)	2.72*
Mean Age First Jail Stay	20.84 (6.98)	23.20 (7.12)	3.24*
Mean Age First Prison Stay	27.46 (7.28)	28.89 (7.94)	1.78

*p<.05; **p<.01

Involvement in HIV Risk Behaviours

This study also examined the relationship between child sexual abuse and involvement in HIV risk behaviours. Twelve risk behaviours known to be associated with increased risk of contracting HIV were assessed. These behaviours include injecting drugs, smoking crack-cocaine, engaging in prostitution, and having sex or sharing needles with one known to have AIDS. Additional practices measure HIV/AIDS sexual risk behaviours without a condom within 30 days of confinement, including sex with more than one partner, with a non-regular partner, with an injecting drug user or with a partner who smokes crack-cocaine, while high or with a partner who was high on drugs/alcohol, while trading sex for drugs or money, and anal sex.

Table 7 reveals that women prisoners who reported child sexual abuse were significantly more likely to report having engaged in most of the HIV/AIDS drug and sexual risk behaviours examined in this study (see Table 7).

Table 7 Prevalence of Self-Reported HIV Sex and Drug Risk Behaviours: Percentage Total Sample, Sexually Abused, Not Abused, and Chi-Square

HIV Risk Behaviours	%Total Sample (n=488)	% Sexually Abused (n=128)	% Not-abused (n=360)	Chi-Square
Drug Risk Behaviours				
Ever smoked crack	54.9	66.4**	50.8	9.25
Ever injected drugs	47.3	56.3*	44.2	5.53
Shared needle with HIV infected person	1.4	2.3	1.1	1.01
Sex Risk Behaviours:				
30 days before incarceration, without a condom:				
Sex with an IV drug user	7.8	13.3**	5.8	7.29
Sex with crack user	7.8	14.1**	5.6	9.52
Anal sex	1.2	3.1*	0.6	5.13
Multiple partners	8.8	17.2***	5.8	15.15
Sex with non-regular partner	9.8	14.1	8.3	3.49
Trade sex for drugs/money	3.7	10.2***	1.4	20.43
Sex while high (or partner high) on drugs/alcohol	17.8	26.6**	14.7	9.04
Ever had sex with HIV-infected person	0.4	0	0.6	0.71
Ever engaged in prostitution	24.8	38.3***	20.0	16.92

*p<.05; **p<.01; ***p.<.001

Over half of the total sample reported having smoked crack-cocaine (54.9 per cent) and nearly half reported intravenous drug use (47.3 per cent) in the past. Prisoners reporting child sexual abuse, however, were significantly more likely to have engaged in both drug behaviours with two-thirds (66.4%; p.<01) reporting crack-cocaine use and over one-half reporting injecting drug use (56.3%; p.<05). Few women reported sharing a needle with a person known to have HIV; however, inmates reporting child sexual abuse were twice as likely to report this extremely high-risk behaviour.

Table 7 also summarises nine known high-risk sexual behaviours.[40] Seven sexual behaviours reflect sexual activity without a condom one month prior to incarceration, the remaining two reflect ever having engaged in prostitution or sexual activity with an HIV-infected partner. High-risk sexual behaviours are known to be associated with certain drug taking behaviours and with earlier child sexual abuse experiences. As summarised earlier, child sexual abuse has been linked with multiple sexual partners in adulthood,[41] a lack of efficacy in negotiating condom use, and lowered self-esteem.[42] The current analysis reveals significant differences in sexual risk behaviours between prisoners who were sexually abused as children and those who were not.

Sexually abused inmates were more than twice as likely to have sex without a condom with partners who smoke crack-cocaine (p.<01) or inject drugs (p.<01). Further, the sexually abused group was three times as likely to report unprotected sex with multiple partners one month prior to incarceration (p.<01). They were nearly twice as likely to have ever engaged in prostitution (p<.01) and to have had unprotected sex while high or with a partner high on drugs or alcohol (p.<05) 30 days prior to confinement. Finally, prisoners reporting child sexual abuse were nearly ten times more likely to report trading sex for drugs or money (p.<01) without a condom 30 days before incarceration.

This analysis suggests that women who experienced child sexual abuse also reported significantly higher rates of individual HIV risk behaviours considered in this study. Further, Table 8 reveals significant differences in the average number of sexual and drug risk behaviours reported by the two groups (see Table 8). Inmates who reported child sexual abuse were also more likely to report engaging in more than one kind of risk behaviour (p.<01) than non-abused inmates.

Table 8 Average Number HIV Risk Behaviours Between Sexually Abused and Non-abused Inmates: Mean, (Standard Deviation in Parentheses), and T-Test

Mean Number HIV Risk Behaviours	Sexually Abused (n=128)	Not-abused (n=360)	T-Test
Sex Risk Behaviours (Range 0-9)	1.37 (1.74 SD)	.63 (1.03 SD)	-5.72**
Drug Risk Behaviours (Range 0-3)	1.25 (.77 SD)	.96 (.79 SD)	-3.58**
Total Risk Behaviours (Range 0-12)	2.61 (2.21 SD)	1.59 (1.47 SD)	-5.91**

**p<.01

Conclusion

The number of women offenders entering prison is rapidly expanding and will continue to increase in the near future. Sentencing policies in the United States are punitive and more women will enter prison and stay for longer periods of time. Coupled with the current 'get tough' mood is a politically motivated 'no frills' movement underscored by eliminating prison programmes and amenities which appear to 'soften' the environment.[43] Prison programmes which do not reduce recidivism are being eliminated. Increasing numbers of women prisoners who have unique needs are falling under this collage of conservative offender management policies.

The female prisoner population is not a monolithic group. Women prisoners, like their male counterparts, represent a diverse population. One sizeable population segment are women who have been sexually abused as children. Through self-reported information from 488 female prisoners, 26 per cent of the interviewees reported that they had been sexually abused as children. This inmate subgroup, when compared to women prisoners who reported they were not sexually abused as children, were also more likely to use drugs, engage in drug and sexual risk behaviours, and experience physical and sexual abuse as adults. Women prisoners in the sexually abused group were also much more likely to begin using drugs and to have contact with the criminal justice system at earlier ages. The findings in this chapter support those that have been reported in the literature.[44] Most important, sexual abuse in childhood was associated with HIV/AIDS-related risk behaviour in adulthood. Sexual abuse in childhood thus emerges as a marker for drug abuse, sexual risk taking behaviour, and delinquency in the juvenile and early adult years.

The bulk of prison welfare programmes are aimed at general audiences and are meant for prisoners as a group. However, if society is committed to the long-term welfare of women offenders who were sexually abused as children, specific programmes will have to be developed and implemented in prison settings. Programming must assist women offenders in addressing past victimisation before they can be helped to focus on their current needs. The prison may be the last setting where these women can obtain the necessary skills to enhance their sense of self-efficacy and self-concept. Researchers must examine the relationship between new kinds of programming and offending patterns over the life course as well as assess the relationship between women who report childhood sexual victimisation and their children. Our call for more programming for women prisoners runs contrary to the growing disillusionment with prison programming and the rise of incapacitation as a penal strategy.   95 per cent of all prisoners will eventually be released and failure to invest in any form of treatment, however minimal, only increases the probability of re-offending. Eliminating prison programming related to the risk of HIV only increases the potential for policy-makers to define these women as public health risks worthy of additional control and confinement.

Notes

[1] Bureau of Justice Statistics, National Institute of Justice, *Prison and Jail Inmates 1995* (1996).

[2] Several factors have contributed to the disproportionate increase in women prisoners. The 'war on drugs,' for example, has emphasised incarceration of street-level drug dealers. While women's arrest rates are lower than men's for almost all crimes, their rates for drug and property crimes are much higher than their arrest rates for violent crimes. See Bureau of Justice Statistics, National Institute of Justice, *Sourcebook 1995* 406 (1996). In 1991 nearly one in three female inmates was incarcerated for drug-related offences, up from one in eight in 1986. See B. Owen & B. Bloom, 'Profiling Women Prisoners: Findings from National Surveys and a California Sample,' 75 PJ 165 (1995). In addition, the proliferation of sentencing guidelines has reflected efforts toward gender equality in the certainty and severity of sentencing, resulting in more likely and longer sentences for women in comparison to past practice. Moreover, while women's arrest rates for violent crimes are far below those of men, they have risen faster than men's rates over the past twenty years.

[3] See, Owen & Bloom, note 2 *supra*. See also Bureau of Justice Statistics, US Department of Justice, *Special Report: Women in Prison* (1994) [hereinafter *Special Report*].

[4] See *Special Report*, note 3 *supra*.

[5] Drug use, for example, increases the risk of infectious diseases, such as hepatitis and tuberculosis, as well as sexually transmitted diseases (STDs). See National Center for Health Statistics, *Health, United States, and Healthy People 2000 Review* (1992); Bureau of Justice Statistics, Office of Justice Programs, US Department of Justice, *HIV in Prisons and Jails 1995* (1997).

[6] J.M. Pollack-Byrne, *Women, Prison, and Crime* (1990).

[7] T. Ireland & C.S. Widom, 'Childhood Victimization and Risk for Alcohol and Drug Arrests,' 29 IJA 235 (1994).

[8] American Correctional Association, *The Female Offender: What Does the Future Hold?* (1990).

[9] Pollack-Byrne, note 6 *supra*.

[10] B.R. Fletcher *et al.*, *Women Prisoners: A Forgotten Population* (1993); *Special Report* note 3 *supra*; A. Morris & C. Wilkinson, 'Responding to Female Prisoners' Needs,' 75 PJ 295 (1995).

[11] E. Carmen & P.R. Rieker, 'A Psychosocial Model of the Victim-to-Patient Process,' 12 PCNA 431 (1989).

[12] D. Paone & W. Chavkin, 'From the Private Family Domain to the Public Health Forum: Sexual Abuse, Women and Risk for HIV infection,' 21 *SIECUS Report* 13 (1993); D. J. Rohsenow *et al.*, 'Molested as Children: A Hidden Contribution to Substance Abuse?' 5 JSA 13 (1988).

[13] C. Bagley & R. Ramsay, 'Disrupted Childhood and Vulnerability to Sexual Assault: Long-Term Sequel with Implications for Counseling,' 4 SWHS 33 (1986); C. Briere & M. Runtz, 'Suicidal Thoughts and Behaviors in Former Spousal Abuse Victims,' 18 CJBS 413 (1986).

[14] D.E.H. Russell, *The Secret Trauma: Incest in the Lives of Girls and Women* (1986).

[15] J. James & J. Meyerding, 'Early Sexual Experiences and Prostitution,' 134 AJP 1381 (1977); Paone & Chavkin, note 12 *supra*, at 13-15.

[16] C.T. Allers & K.J. Benjack, 'Connections Between Child Abuse and HIV Infection,' 70 JCD 309 (1991); A. Browne & D. Finkelhor, 'Impact of Child Sexual Abuse: A Review of the Research,' 99 PB 66-77 (1986).

[17] M. DeYoung, *The Sexual Victimization of Children* (1982).

[18] E.M. Kaliski, *et al.*, 'AIDS, Runaways, and Self-Efficacy,' 13 FCH 65 (1990).

[19] S. Zierler *et al.*, 'Adult Survivors of Childhood Sexual Abuse and Subsequent Risk of HIV Infection,' 81 AJPH 572 (1991).

[20] C.T. Allers & K.J. Benjack, 'Barriers to HIV Education and Prevention: The Role of Unresolved Childhood Sexual Abuse,' 1 JCSA 309 (1992).

[21] H. Klein & B.S. Chao, 'Sexual Abuse During Childhood and Adolescence as Predictors of HIV-Related Sexual Risk During Adulthood Among Female Sexual Partners of Injection Drug Users,' 1 VW 55-76 (1995).

[22] D.S. McClellan *et al.*, 'Early Victimization, Drug Use, and Criminality: A Comparison of Male and Female Prisoners,' 24 CJB 455 (1997).

[23] See Division of Health Promotion and Disease Prevention, Institute of Medicine, *The Hidden Epidemic: Confronting Sexually Transmitted Diseases* (T.R. Eng & W.T. Butler, eds., 1996) [hereinafter *Hidden Epidemic*].

[24] Klein & Chao, note 21 *supra*.

[25] G. Weissman & V. Brown, 'Drug-Using Women and HIV: Risk-Reduction and Prevention Issues,' in *Women at Risk: Issues in the Primary Prevention of AIDS* 175 (A. O'Leary & L. Jemmott, eds., 1995).

[26] K.P. Erickson & K.F. Trocki, 'Behavioral Risk Factors for Sexually Transmitted Diseases in American Households,' 34 SSM 843 (1992).

[27] M.T. Fullilove & R.E. Fullilove, 'Intersecting Epidemics: Black teen crack use and sexually transmitted disease, 44 JAMWA 146 (1989).

[28] S. Aral & J.N. Wasserheit, 'Interactions Among HIV, Other Sexually Transmitted Diseases, Socio-Economic Status, and Poverty in Women,' in *Women at Risk*, note 25 *supra*, at 13.

[29] J.A. Inciardi *et al., Women and Crack-Cocaine* (1993).

[30] D. Farabee, *Substance Use Among Female Inmates Entering the Texas Department of Criminal Justice — Institutional Division 1994* (Texas Commission on Alcohol and Drug Abuse, 1995). The Texas Commission on Alcohol and Drug Abuse furnished funds for the activity described in this paper. This does not imply the Commission's endorsement or concurrence with statements or conclusions contained therein. The National Institute of Mental Health also provided research funds for this project, grant 1 R03 MH58082-01.

[31] *Special Report*, note 3 *supra*.

[32] C. Brett, 'The American Correctional Association, from Victim to Victimizer,' in *Female Offenders: Meeting Needs of a Neglected Population* (1993); Pollack-Byrne, note 6 *supra*; E. Sargent *et al.*, 'Abuse and the Woman Prisoner,' in *Women Prisoners: Forgotten Population*, 55 (B. Fletcher *et al.*, eds., 1993); *Special Report*, note 3 *supra*.

[33] National Research Council on Child Abuse and Neglect, *Understanding Child Abuse and Neglect* (1993).

[34] C.S. Widom, *Victims of Childhood Sexual Abuse: Later Criminal Consequences* (U.S. Department of Justice, 1995).

[35] S. Polonsky *et al.*, 'HIV Prevention in Prisons and Jails: Obstacles and Opportunities,' 109 PHR 615 (1994).

[36] M.H. Silbert & A.M. Pines, 'Early Sexual Exploitation as an Influence in Prostitution,' 28 SW 285 (1983).

[37] Polonsky, note 35 *supra*.

[38] *Hidden Epidemic, supra* note 23.

[39] Inciardi, *supra* note 29.

[40] R.R. Robles *et al.*, 'Risk Factors and HIV Infection among Three Different Cultural Groups of Injection Drug Users,' in *Handbook on Risk of AIDS* 256 (B. Brown & G. Beschner, eds., 1993).

[41] Klein & Chao, note 21 *supra*.

[42] A. Browne & D. Finkelhor, 'Impact of Child Sexual Abuse: A Review of the Research,' 99 PB 66-77 (1986).

[43] W. Johnson *et al.*, 'Getting Tough on Prisoners: Results from the National Corrections Executive Survey 1995*, 43 CD 24 (1997).

[44] Owen & Bloom, note 3 *supra*; Ireland & Widom, note 7 *supra*; Klein & Chao, note 21 *supra*.

Part IV

Empowering Childhood: Awareness, Development and Education

9   Sex Education: Child's Right, Parent's Choice or State's Obligation?

CORINNE PACKER

Introduction

Three principal parties are involved in the decision to seek or to make available sex education to children: children, parents, and the State. In the event of conflicts between these parties, a hierarchy for decision-making must be clear. In order to determine that hierarchy, we must ask whether sex education is a child's right, a parent's choice, or a State's obligation. This chapter examines the rights of children to sex education under international human rights law with reference to these three parties.

The Need for Sex Education

While many parents understand the benefits of sex education, the idea of children learning about human reproduction still causes unease. Some parents reject the idea altogether, believing that the more young people know about sexuality and contraception, the more likely they are to become sexually active or even promiscuous. Sex education is seen as the beginning of the end of childhood innocence — a first step to adulthood or, as some believe, to a corrupted or immoral understanding of sex and human relationships. Nevertheless, many States now consider it important to teach children about sex. While increasingly stressing the positive elements of healthy sexual lives,[1] most sex education curricula also address the possibility of negative consequences on the health of young people and the ways in which these can be prevented.

The figures regarding teenage pregnancies and the spread of sexually transmitted diseases (STDs) among young populations worldwide speak volumes. An estimated 40 per cent of all 14-year-old girls alive today will have been pregnant at least once by the time they have reached the age of 20.[2] Adolescent women in Africa fare worst. An average of three out of five give birth at least once between the ages of 15 to 19.[3] Yet the problem is not limited to the developing world. As recently as 1995, an estimated half a million teenagers in the United States had children.[4] The high rates of teenage abortions attest to the fact that these are in large part unplanned and undesired pregnancies.

Preventing the harmful effects of unprotected sex is central to preserving the mental and physical health of young individuals. The risks to young individuals of ill-health owing to unprotected sex is well documented. For the young woman who is pregnant, childbirth generally poses a high risk because her body has not yet fully developed. If she does not die, she may suffer internal damage or permanent physical injury. Social, psychological, and economic problems often follow.[5] The child born to a young woman is also at greater risk of premature delivery, malformation or death. Data from 27 studies demonstrate that approximately 60 per cent of adolescent women suffer from abortion-related complications.[6] Where abortion for adolescents is illegal or inaccessible, horror stories of botched 'home-made' abortions ending in death abound.[7] It is also estimated that at least two million children have already died of AIDS — the equivalent of 40 children an hour. A million more are infected with HIV today.[8] This is to say nothing of the millions of other young individuals who have acquired other, albeit less fatal, STDs. Young women are more susceptible to contracting STDs because their genitalia are not fully mature. Moreover, the risk of lifetime infertility owing to STDs is greater for young women.

The question that logically follows is whether adequate sex education does indeed *prevent* pregnancy, the spread of STD's, or general reproductive ill-health in children. A comparison of conclusions from numerous national studies prior to and following the introduction of sex education for children strongly confirms a positive response. For example, in the 1970s STDs among the young population of Thailand was widespread. Since the introduction of education campaigns on the risks of contracting STDs and the use of modern contraception, this trend has been significantly curbed.[9] A study by the Alan Guttmacher Institute similarly found that countries with the most open-minded sex education have made the best progress in the prevention of unintended teenage pregnancies and abortions.[10] Sex education had increased the adoption of safer sexual practices. This is particularly visible in Nordic countries, where sex education programmes for pupils aged 11 to 15 years have been an integral part of the school curriculum for several decades.

It is equally important to rephrase the question to reflect the concerns of many parents: Does sex education *contribute to* early sexual activity and promiscuity? Here studies firmly conclude in the negative. For example, a study by the WHO Global Program on AIDS, which comprised 35 surveys, found no evidence that sex education leads to earlier or increased sexual activity among teenagers. Indeed, a number found that sex education delayed sexual activity by adolescents and reduced the frequency with which they changed partners because they were made aware of the risks at hand.[11] More recent national studies continue to confirm that access to sex education and contraception does not lead to increased promiscuity in children.[12]

Sex education programmes have traditionally been geared to preventing adolescent sexual activity. While sexual abstinence certainly is an option for adolescents and all well-rounded sex education curricula include this option in discussions, it is not realistic to expect *all* young individuals to choose it. Indeed, the reality in many societies is that most children will not choose abstinence, be it morally right or wrong. As expressed by one social commentator, the economic and social circumstances of modern day living — with working mothers, single-parent families, greater affluence, changes in sexual morals, fewer social constraints — only contribute to the increased liberty of children.[13] Of course, it is false nostalgia to think that young unwed mothers did not exist in the days of 'traditional' families and social restraints.[14] It is also a dangerous fallacy to believe that the absence of pregnancy implies that no sexual intercourse is taking place.

In conclusion, young individuals need sex education to minimise the negative consequences of sexual activity and thereby preserve their physical and psychosocial health. In light of this conclusion, the question which must next be considered is whether children are entitled by right to sex education.

The Rights of Children to Sex Education

There are a number of rights which may be called upon as broadly supporting a child's independent choice to seek and obtain sex education. These can include the rights to life, dignity, privacy, education, and freedom of thought. However, the more specific rights to freedom to information and to health carry the most direct impact and provide the greatest degree of protection.

The Right to Freedom to Information

A number of provisions in international and regional human rights instruments both directly and indirectly guarantee children the right to seek and obtain information. These are listed in Table 1. A number of these provisions refer to the right of individuals to information on family planning specifically. This is particularly so in the Convention on the Elimination of all Forms of Discrimination against Women.[15] Other instruments provide for the right to freedom to seek and obtain information of all kinds in general. These can be interpreted to include the right of children to freedom to education about sex. In the case of the Convention on the Rights of the Child[16] this interpretation appears to be secured on several fronts, most notably because the Committee on the Rights of the Child regularly seeks information from States parties on the status of sex education for adolescents. Assertions made by some commentators that parents are entitled by right to place limitations on this freedom are discussed below.

The Right to Health

In order to preserve our health, we need information on how to do so. The logic therefore easily follows that provisions for the right to health, in particular those which specify the right to access to the means of preventive health care, infer the right to access to sex education. Indeed, a number of provisions clearly illustrate that information and health are two sides of the same coin and cannot be separated one from the other, as evidenced in articles 10(h), 14.2(b), and 16.1(e) of the Women's Convention and article 14.2(f) of the African Charter on the Rights and Welfare of the Child. Access for adolescents specifically to reproductive health and family planning information as a component of the right to health is also stressed in international consensus documents, such as in the Cairo Programme of Action[17] and the Beijing Platform for Action.[18] Interestingly, the Children's Convention provides specifically in article 24 for 'the right of the child to the enjoyment of the highest attainable standard of health . . . . States shall pursue full implementation of this right and, in particular, shall take appropriate measures . . . to develop preventive health care, guidance for parents and family planning education and services.' The phrasing of this provision is somewhat unfortunate as it raises doubt as to the intended beneficiary, i.e., whether it is the child or the parents who should receive family planning education as part of a preventive health care package.[19] However, from the perspective of *preventive* health care, it would seem illogical that family planning education and services be received only *after* one has become a parent.[20] In light of this fact, it is the conclusion of this author that article 24 provides for family planning education to be made available for children.

To conclude, a number provisions on the right to health for children entitle young individuals to sex education, that is to information on how sex can be made safe in order to preserve their health. The sources and texts of provisions for the right to health appear in Table 1.

The Rights of Parents

It is widely understood and accepted that parents have rights and may make choices in matters relating to the education of their child. Sex education is no exception. As a result, parents usually have a say about whether their child is given sex education. Yet a dilemma may arise when parental consent or permission is required for children to attend sex education classes. Should parents not give their consent, their children will not obtain the education offered to them or which they seek. In some cases, this may be in direct opposition to the desires of the child. As a result, a conflict arises between the right of the child to information and health and the right of the parent to provide direction and guidance to their child with regard to education. Thus, the first question to resolve is whether human rights provisions give greater weight to the rights of parents or children in the event of such a conflict.

The answer lies in the Children's Convention, which demonstrates that the rights of parents with regard to the upbringing of their children are not without limits. While recognising the need to respect the responsibilities, rights, and duties of parents in the upbringing of their children,[21] the Convention gives ultimate weight to the child, bearing in mind the principles of the child's best interests and evolving capacities. The first notion is best articulated in article 18.1 which states that while parents have the primary responsibility for the upbringing and development of the child, 'the best interests of the child will be their basic concern.' The evolving capacities of the child must also be considered with 'the views of the child being given due weight in accordance with the age and maturity of the child' (Article 12.1). The supremacy of the child's interests is also recognised in the Women's Convention which, while acknowledging the rights and responsibilities of parents in matters relating to their children, similarly stipulates that the interests of the children 'shall be paramount' in all cases (Article 16.1.(d)).

Table 1   Provisions Supporting Children's Rights to Sex Education

	Right to information	Right to health (including information)
Convention on the Rights of the Child (1989)	*Art. 13.1* 'to seek, receive and impart information and ideas of all kinds.'	*Art. 24.1* 'to the enjoyment of the highest attainable standard of health.' *Art. 24.2(f)* States shall 'develop preventive health care, guidance for parents and family planning education and services.'
Convention on the Elimination of all Forms of Discrimination against Women (1979)	*Art. 10(h)* 'to ensure ... access to specific educational information to help to ensure the health and well-being of families, including information and advice on family planning.'	*Art. 14.2(b)* 'to access to adequate health care facilities, including information, counselling and services in family planning.' *Art. 16.1(e)* 'to decide freely and responsibly on the number and spacing of their children and to have access to the information, education and means to enable them to exercise these rights.'
Covenant on Civil and Political Rights (1966)	*Art. 19.2* 'to freedom of expression; this right shall include freedom to seek, receive and impart information and ideas of all kinds...'	
Covenant on Economic, Social and Cultural Rights (1966)	*Art. 13.1* 'to education... directed to the full development of human personality and the sense of its dignity...'	*Art. 12.1* 'to the highest attainable standard of physical and mental health.'
European Convention of Human Rights (1950)	*Art.10.1* 'to receive and impart information and ideas without the interference by public authority...'	
American Convention on Human Rights (ACHR) 1969	*Art. 13.1* 'freedom to seek, receive and impart information and ideas of all kinds...'	

Table 1 *(continued)*

	Right to information	Right to health (including information)
Additional Protocol to the ACHR (1988)		*Art. 10.1* 'to health, understood to mean the enjoyment of the highest level of physical, mental and social well-being.'
African Charter on the Rights and Welfare of the Child (1990)	*Art. 14.2(f)* States shall 'develop preventive health care and family life education…'	*Art. 14.1* 'to enjoy the best attainable state of physical, mental and spiritual health.'
African Charter on Human and Peoples' Rights (1981)	*Art. 9* 'to receive information.'	*Art. 16* 'to enjoy the best attainable state of physical and mental health.'

In terms of the issue of evolving capacities, the dilemma can be quickly set to rest if one accepts that any young individual seeking information on sex and human reproduction demonstrates *ipso facto* a certain degree of maturity and competency to deal with the subject matter (with the information tailored to his or her level of understanding and needs). Failure to recognise this fact can result in a bitterly ironic situation where the young individual engages in a 'mature' sexual relationship without the 'mature' knowledge of how to protect him or herself.

This brings us to the question of whether sex education is indeed in the best interests of the child. In light of the proven risks to the health of children who lack knowledge of safe sex practices (as established earlier), sex education can be none other than in the best interests of the child. This is true even, and perhaps particularly so, for the child who is not sexually active since *prevention* is the operative word. Following this train of thought, Freeman refers to a test of irrationality, where the parent's right to intervene is justified only in certain truly irrational circumstances. According to this test of irrationality, a child seeking sex education can hardly be construed as irrational since he or she seeks it specifically as a means of protecting health. As Richards similarly proposes, the action of a child should be dismissed only when it is manifestly irrational and when taking the action will lead to major, irreversible impairment of interests, or injury.[22] Here again, the argument of parents against sex education as a means of protecting young persons from possible harm is untenable since sex education is precisely one of the means of *preventing* injury by, for example, preventing possible pregnancy at too early an age, reducing the risk of STD infection, or diminishing the likelihood of mental harm.

In conclusion, young individuals seeking information in order to protect their health should not be restricted from doing so by their parents. Indeed, a strong argument can be made that an adolescent's right to seek and obtain contraceptive information and services cannot be overruled by the right of parents to have a say in matters of their child's education. Coliver arrives at a similar conclusion with regard to prior rights, arguing that 'because of the increased risk to the health of adolescent women posed by unwanted pregnancies . . . the interest of parents or guardians in providing "guidance" should not override the right of adolescents to information necessary for health.'[23]

Two cases in the European context sustain this conclusion. In the first case, that of *Hendriks v. The Netherlands*, the European Commission of Human Rights described the child's best interests as overriding.[24] In *Kjeldsen, Busk, Madsen and Pedersen v. Denmark* the European Court of Human Rights raised the issue of parents as the prior rights-holder and the possibility of conflict with the wishes of the child.[25] In the opinion of the Court, the drafters of the European Convention on Human Rights would not have intended to give parents dictatorial decision-making powers. As a result, the Court ruled that it would be wrong for children who hold different views from their parents to have to abide by their parents' decisions concerning educational matters. Based on this ruling, it could be inferred that a child who wishes to attend sex education classes may attend, despite the expressed choice of parents to refuse their child attendance.

This being resolved, the dilemma remains that children whose wishes differ from those of their parents very often feel powerless to demand otherwise. Effectively, children are in a weak position, unable to exercise their rights. As a result, the question arises whether parental consent for sex education should indeed be required, particularly in light of the recognition that sex education is a key element of preventive health care. The dilemma is a sensitive one as it is not the intention of human rights law to pit one individual's right against another's, nor is it to diminish the responsibilities of parents and interfere in the privacy of the family. A delicate balance must therefore be struck, enabling parents to have a say in matters of their children's education while at the same time guaranteeing children access to the education they seek in a non-confrontational manner. Removing parental consent as a prerequisite to sex education for children may be necessary in some cases.

The Obligations of the State

At a minimum, the rights of children to information and health imply a negative obligation (or obligation of forbearance) on the part of the State. This means that the State cannot interfere with a child's ability to seek and receive information or prevent him or her from taking preventive health care measures, including with regard to sex, human reproduction, and reproductive health.[26] Accordingly, States must not implement legislation, policies, or other measures which violate these rights.

Similarly, human rights provisions entail positive obligations to act (or obligations of performance) on the part of the State. In the case of the child's right to freedom to information, this requires States to take direct affirmative action. On the one hand, a State is required to protect the right against violations by the State itself. The State must therefore fulfil the right via legislation, policies, and judicial decisions. Some advocates, such as Coliver, go beyond this interpretation to suggest an obligation on the part of the State to introduce programmes aimed at ensuring the effective enjoyment of the right.[27] Following this logic, and with particular reference to adolescents, Coliver argues that publicly funded programmes may not discriminate in providing information and education on the basis of age.[28] Indeed, she extends added weight to the right of adolescents, arguing that they 'have an enhanced right to information and counselling tailored to their particular needs.'[29] The obligation to act similarly requires a State to actively repeal any legislation which interferes with a child's right. On the other hand, the horizontal effect of human rights law also implies that a State must not allow one individual within its jurisdiction, acting in a private capacity, to interfere with the ability of another individual to seek and obtain the information he or she desires.[30] In the opinion of this author, this would arguably include interference and possible violations by parents. With respect to a child's right to health, human rights law obligates the State not to interfere with a child's access to health care. Similarly, the State must ensure that health care is made as accessible to children as possible so that they may attain the best possible state of health.

Drawing a Link to the Protection of Public Health

Because of the nature in which HIV/AIDS and other STDs are transmitted, the argument could be made that the State has the obligation to inform the public, including children, of the risks of contracting these diseases and their potentially detrimental impact on health. In other words, if STDs were recognised as a threat to public health, the State would be required to inform its population of their effect. This should not be seen as unusual. States regularly inform young individuals of the harmful effects of alcohol consumption, cigarette smoking, or drug abuse as matters of public health, when in fact these are not in any way publicly transmittable as are STDs. Ironically, no parental consent is required to educate children about these subjects. Following this logic, it seems reasonable to argue that information and education regarding STDs and sex-related risks should also be made available or, indeed, obligatory for children, as a measure of public health.

Interpretations by the Committee on the Rights of the Child

The Committee on the Rights of the Child has strongly supported the interpretation of a duty on the part of the State to educate adolescents about sex. In a recent recommendation to the Government of Uganda, for example, the Committee noted its concern for the high drop-out rate of girls in schools due to early pregnancy and the rapid spread of HIV/AIDS throughout the country.[31] Accordingly, it recommended that Uganda should:

> take all appropriate measures, including through international cooperation, to ... strengthen its information and prevention programmes to combat HIV/AIDS, particularly to prevent the transmission to children of HIV/AIDS and other sexually transmitted diseases (STDs) .... The Committee further recommends that the State party pursue and strengthen its family planning and reproductive health education programmes, including for adolescents.[32]

Recommendations such as these for the inclusion of sex education programmes within school curricula are now made by the Committee with increasing regularity in response to State party reports. Indeed, any interference with access to and availability of this information to adolescents which is permitted by the State is questioned. For example, following the report of Ireland on its implementation of the Convention on the Rights of the

Child, the Committee requested information on 'what steps the Government had taken with regard to those school teachers who had refused to teach sex education, whether they were permitted to keep their posts, and, if so, how the sex education curricula was taught.'[33]

Clearly, the provisions for sex education (or more precisely family planning information and counselling and family life education) in the relevant human rights instruments do not stipulate the precise content of this education. Not surprisingly, the content does vary from country to country and even within countries. However, it is clear that the Committee on the Rights of the Child expects the education offered to cover a wide breadth of issues including the risks to health such as HIV/AIDS infection and pregnancy in an adolescent woman. Indeed, as an indication of the understanding of States Parties of the obligation under the Children's Convention, States regularly report on the content of their sex education programmes,[34] and even the means by which they are carried through.[35] The Committee similarly makes suggestions to States Parties regarding the subjects to be covered in sex and family life education programmes and the means by which they can be most appropriately and effectively taught.[36]

Conclusions

States Parties to the relevant human rights instruments have an obligation to provide or to make available sex education to young individuals in respect of the rights to health and to freedom to information. The argument could even be made that sex education for children is obligatory as a measure of protection of public health. Any interference with access to this education by individuals within its territory must be recognised by the State as a violation of human rights law. Parents interfering in their child's access to sex education where he or she has indicated his/her desire to obtain it represents a violation. Accordingly, States must take action.

The rights of parents to guide and direct the education of their children must be given last consideration in the case of sex education because it is information which is essential to the health and well-being of the child. In other words, the best interests of the child override the rights of the parents in the specific case of sex education. This point accepted, one may go even one step further to question whether consent by the parent for sex education is indeed required or could be deemed a violation of the child's unhindered rights to freedom to information and to health. Again, this can only represent a violation if sex education is accepted as a measure of preventive health care.

The fact remains that, despite the figures and conclusions from studies overwhelmingly supporting sex education for children, many parents and States still refuse sex education for children.[37] While confrontation and interference in parental decision-making is not ideal, the lack of protection of children's rights and effective hindered access of children to preventive health care education should no longer be accepted. States must also be informed of their lack of respect for the provisions of the relevant human rights instruments in this regard and urged to act accordingly.

Notes

[1] See D. Monk, 'Health and Education: Conflicting Programmes for Sex Education,' in this collection.

[2] United Nations Population Fund (UNFPA) *Meeting the Population Challenge* 12 (1992).

[3] World Assembly of Youth and Population Reference Bureau, *The World's Youth Data Sheet 1990* (1990); Findings of the United Nations Sixth Inquiry among Governments, cited in 'Adolescent Reproductive Behaviour: Evidence from Developing Countries,' UN Doc. ST/ESA/SER.A/109/Add.1, 68 (1989).

[4] See *The Economist* 63 (28 Oct. 1995).

[5] See C. Packer, 'Preventing Adolescent Pregnancy: The Protection Offered by International Human Rights Law,' 5 IJCR 47, 49-50 (1997).

[6] J. Hirsch & G. Barker, *Adolescents and Abortion in Developing Countries: A Preventable Tragedy* (1990).

[7] See A.A. Mohamud, 'Adolescent Fertility and Adolescent Reproductive Health,' in Proceedings of the United Nations Experts Group Meeting on Family Planning, Health and Family Well-Being, Bangalore, India, 26-30 Oct. 1992, 152, 154 (1996).

[8] See 'Children and the Plague of AIDS,' *International Herald Tribune* 6 (29-30 Nov. 1997).

[9] Adolescent Reproductive Behaviour: Evidence from Developing Countries II, UN Doc. ST/ESA/SER.A/109/ Add.1 (1989).

[10] See E. Kosunen, *Report on Adolescents and Their Right to Reproductive Health*, in *Guaranteeing Freedom of Choice in Matters of Reproduction, Sexuality and Lifestyles in Europe* 42 (Council of Europe, 1999).

[11] See World Health Organisation, *The Health of Young People: A Challenge and a Promise* (1993).

[12] See, e.g., 'With Lives at Stake, Moralizing is Cruel,' *International Herald Tribune* 7, 3 Oct. 1997; 'Condom Access Shows no Effect on Teen Sex Rate,' *USA Today* 15 (15

Apr. 1998).

[13] See 'A Way to Help Teens Live Through Adolescence,' *International Herald Tribune* 9 (31 Oct. 1997).

[14] See, e.g., 'The Prom Mom Phenomenon Predates Our Libertine Age,' *International Herald Tribune* 8 (18 July 1997).

[15] UNGA res. 34/180, UN GAOR Supp. (No. 46), at 193, 1249 UNTS 13 (*entered into force* 3 Sept. 1981) [hereinafter Women's Convention].

[16] UNGA res. 44/22, annex 44 UN GAOR Supp. (No. 49) at 167, UN Doc. A/44/49 (1989) (*entered into force* 2 Sept. 1990) [hereinafter Children's Convention].

[17] Paragraph 6.15 reads:

> Youth should be actively involved in information, education and communication activities and services concerning reproductive and sexual health, including the prevention of early pregnancies, sex education and the prevention of HIV/AIDS and other sexually transmitted diseases. Access to, as well as confidentiality and privacy of, these services must be ensured with the support, and guidance of their parents and in line with the Convention on the Rights of the Child.

Drawing a closer link between information and health, paragraph 7.41 similarly recommends that 'information and services should be made available to adolescents that can help them to understand their sexuality and protect them from unwanted pregnancies, sexually transmitted diseases and subsequent risk of infertility.' See Report of the International Conference on Population and Development, Cairo, 5-14 September 1994, Programme of Action of the International Conference on Population and Development, UN doc. A/CONF.171/13 (1994).

[18] As illustrated in paragraphs 107(e) and (g). Paragraphs 93-95 of the Platform outline the particular problems of adolescent girls with respect to inadequate sexual and reproductive health information and services and the ensuing consequences of unprotected and premature sexual relations. The Platform calls for States to meet 'the educational and service needs of adolescents to enable them to deal in a positive and responsible way with their sexuality.' Report of the Fourth World Conference on Women, Beijing, 4-15 Sept. 1995, Beijing Declaration and Platform for Action, UN Doc. A/CONF.177/20 (1995).

[19] Neither the *travaux préparatoires* of the Convention on the Rights of the Child nor the Committee on the Rights of the Child shed light on this issue.

[20] For a more detailed discussion of the ambiguity of this provision, see C. Packer, 'Preventing Adolescent Pregnancy: The Protection Offered by International Human Rights Law,' 5 IJCR 47, 60-61 (1997).

[21] As provided in various forms in Articles 5, 12.1, 14.2(b), 18.1.

[22] M. Freeman, 'The Limits of Children's Rights,' in *The Ideologies of Children's Rights* 29, 38 (M. Freeman & P. Veerman, eds., 1992).

[23] S. Coliver, 'The Right to Know: Human Rights and Access to Reproductive Health Information,' in *The Right to Know: Human Rights and Access to Reproductive Health Information* 38, 66 (S. Coliver, ed., 1995).

[24] For a description of the case and the Commission's observations, see G. Van Bueren, *The International Law on the Rights of the Child* 73-76 (1995).

[25] *Kjeldsen, Busk Madsen and Pedersen v. Denmark*, 23 Eur. Ct. H. R. (Ser. A) (1976).

[26] See C. Packer, *The Right to Reproductive Choice: A Study in International Law* 65-69, 93-94, 97 (1996).

[27] See Coliver, *supra* note 23, at 58.

[28] *Id.* at 65.

[29] *Id.* at 66.

[30] For a brief discussion of the horizontal effect with regard to an individual's right to seek and to receive family planning information, see Packer, note 26 *supra*, at 94-96. For a general description of horizontal effects in international human rights law, see M. Nowak, *U.N. Covenant on Civil and Political Rights: CCPR Commentary* 37-38 (1993); P. van Dijk & G.J.H. van Hoof, *Theory and Practice of the European Convention on Human Rights* 22-26 (3rd ed. 1998).

[31] Committee on the Rights of the Child, Report of the Sixteenth Session, CRC/C/69, 26 November 1997, at paras. 134, 135.

[32] *Id.* at para. 149.

[33] Committee on the Rights of the Child, Seventeenth Session, Consideration of Reports of States Parties: Initial report of Ireland, CRC/C/SR.438, 15 Jan. 1998, para. 20.

[34] See, e.g., the latest report on the implementation of the CRC by Luxembourg, which reported at length on sex education and family planning for adolescents under its obligations concerning education and the preservation of health. Committee on the Rights of the Child, *Initial reports of States Parties due in 1996, Addendum, Luxembourg*, CRC/C/41/Add.2, 11 April 1997.

[35] For example, Trinidad and Tobago reported on its poster campaign to inform adolescents about AIDS and other STDs. (Committee on the Rights of the Child, Sixteenth Session, Consideration of Reports Submitted by States Parties, Initial Report of Trinidad and Tobago, CRC/C/SR.416, 5 January 1998, para. 31.

[36] Suggestions vary from teaching the equal nature of responsibilities in family planning to offering advice on methods of communicating reproductive health information. See, e.g.. Committee on the Rights of the Child, Thirteenth Session, Concluding Observations of the Committee on the Rights of the Child, Nigeria, CRC/C/15/Add.61, 30 October 1996, para. 36; *id.*, Thirteenth Session, Concluding Observations of the Committee on the Rights of the Child, Hong Kong, CRC/C/15/Add.63, 30 October 1996, para. 6.

[37] According to a United Nations survey, of those countries recognising problems of adolescent fertility, only 22 per cent in Africa and 33 per cent in Latin America and the

Caribbean offered sex education in the State school curriculum. See note 9 *supra*. More recently, in Poland, the Roman Catholic right, in power for only four months, forced the Head of State to withdraw obligatory sex education in the school curriculum in state run schools. See 'Le président polonais sauve l'éducation sexuelle à l'école,' *Le Monde* 4 (2 Jan. 1998).

10 Health and Education: Conflicting Programmes for Sex Education

DANIEL MONK

Introduction

Sex education has provoked complex political struggles. In England and Wales,[1] both within and outside of Parliament, these struggles have taken various forms: conflicts between the rights of parents and children;[2] battles between central government and local education authorities, or between local education authorities and parents and governors; and, more generally, conflicts between conservative fundamentalists and liberal progressives.[3] Since 1986, fierce political and public debates have caused the legal provisions governing sex education to be amended and re-amended.[4] They are confusing for the professionals involved,[5] and, in some respects, as this chapter will show, are contradictory.

This chapter seeks neither to defend sex education nor to arbitrate between competing claims. It seeks neither to engage with current discourses of children's rights,[6] nor to identify 'the truth' about children's best interests.[7] Rather, it seeks to analyse the conflicting understandings of childhood sexuality which underlie current approaches to sex education. It will be argued that sex education represents not simply an attempt to liberate or to protect children, but, primarily, to govern[8] childhood sexuality, by influencing the ways in which children and adults experience and perceive childhood sexuality. Sex education serves not merely as a means of transmitting information about sex, but rather as an instrument for the cultural production of knowledge about sex and childhood.[9]

The analysis begins with an identification of how the conceptual problematisation of child sexuality gives rise to two contradictory programmes for sex education — a health programme and an education programme.[10] It examines how these programmes have been enacted and continue to coexist, both within and outside of schools. While focusing on concerns about childhood sexuality, rather than on children themselves, this chapter does not assume a position of relativistic unconcern,[11] nor that political or rights-based debates and strategies are irrelevant or ineffective. It seeks only to examine the extent to which current approaches rely upon claims upon 'the truth' about childhood sexuality, and thus objectify children throughout the process of legal and social policy formation.

Problematising Child Sexuality

Underlying the political conflict surrounding sex education is a deep social and cultural unease about child sexuality.[12] This unease can be identified not only in debates concerning sex education but in a wide range of recent controversies: the explicit nature of young girls' magazines;[13] the sensational journalistic coverage of school-age fathers and 'abusive' female teachers;[14] child rapists and children who abuse other children;[15] the regulation of 'pornographic' images of children;[16] the homosexual age of consent;[17] and the 'unacceptable' number of teenage pregnancies.[18] What is noticeable about approaches to these issues is the enduring nature and, simultaneously, the instability of innocence as an essential defining characteristic of childhood. The tensions surrounding child sexuality are reflected in an ongoing redefinition of childhood in which the boundary between adult and child is destabilised and repositioned.[19]

This crisis regarding the status of childhood is particularly evident in the context of sex education. Sexuality represents a crucial distinction between adults and children. Sexual innocence has been a key component of romantic or ideal notions of childhood since the seventeenth century.[20] Resistance to the 'knowing' sexual child animates much of the conservative opposition to progressive sex education policies, which are perceived as a dangerous form of permissive indoctrination and corruption.[21] Yet the child's need for protection also motivates progressive sex education policies. There are 'two versions of protection, one of sexual beings from harm because of their immaturity and ignorance, the other of the non-sexual being from the "perversity" of sexual indoctrination.'[22] It is the conceptualisation of children as either non-sexual or potentially sexual that informs calculations as to how best to protect them. Sex education is thus cast in stark, binary terms as both dangerous and protective. The broad concern, for example, that current rates of teenage pregnancies are too high does not translate into a consensus regarding sex education.[23]

This binary conceptualisation of child sexuality has given rise to two conflicting programmes of sex education: the education programme and the health programme. The education programme emphasises traditional moral values. It seeks to protect the 'natural' status of the child as non-sexual. It excludes all reference to practical sexual information and perceives sex education as a cause of teenage pregnancies. By contrast, the health programme allows for the possibility of sexual children. It, too, seeks to protect children, but by providing information about sexuality. These two programmes clearly conflict. Both of them, however, lay claim to a knowledge of childhood, thus yielding conflicting truth claims. That conflict demonstrates how, in the development of public policies, the 'solutions for one programme tend to be the problems for another.'[24] Despite this conflict, an examination of the structure and content of sex education identifies how the education programme and the health programme coexist.

The Law and Sex Education

The legal regulation of sex education is complex. The legislation has been subject to frequent amendments. In addition, the statutory duties on head teachers, governors and teachers are often framed in highly discretionary terms. As the courts have not been called upon to test the limits, or the legality, of certain activities, there is uncertainty as to what the law actually allows. The legislation has recently been consolidated and is now contained in the Education Act 1996. In addition to the statute, guidance is provided to schools by means of the current circular *Education Act 1993: Sex Education in Schools*[25] ('the Circular'). The legal status of government circulars is a matter of debate. While they do not have the weight of statute, they cannot be ignored without reasonable cause.[26] This is a matter of some importance in the context of sex education, for the Circular has 'had a significant impact on the way in which school sex education was and continues to be perceived.'[27] It has been argued that the Circular fails to make clear the distinction between an interpretation of law and a statement of the Secretary of State's view of good practice.[28] In effect, the statute and the Circular combined provide for sex education in three distinct locations: the National Curriculum for science, sex education in the basic curriculum, and individual advice provided outside the classroom.

National Curriculum

The National Curriculum[29] was introduced by the Education Reform Act 1988. It radically altered both the content and the structure of control over the curriculum as a whole.[30] It is compulsory and its content is determined centrally by the Secretary of State for Education and Employment. Sex education within the National Curriculum is contained in the biology section of the science curriculum. This aspect of sex education is often perceived as unproblematic, its emphasis being largely on body parts and the facts relating to human reproduction as opposed to human relationships. However, in 1991 Kenneth Baker, the then Secretary of State, used his discretionary powers to amend the National Curriculum for science in order to include the study of the 'ways in which the human body can be affected by HIV/AIDS.'[31] The resulting political storm led to the Education Act 1993, which established the current legal structure for sex education.[32] The Parliamentary debates indicate that it was not so much the subject matter of HIV/AIDS that was considered inappropriate, but the way in which it was presented. Implicit, and at times explicit, within the objections to Baker's action, was the fear that teaching about HIV/AIDS would involve children being taught about homosexuality. As Baroness Elles argued, 'some people believe that there is a moral code which children should be brought up to observe. If they are taught the kind of sex education of which we are being given examples that will undermine and deny the moral code.'[33]

This conflict resulted in information about HIV/AIDS being specifically excluded from the science curriculum. It is significant for a number of reasons. First, it reflects the lack of consensus as to the purpose of sex education, clearly revealing the tension between the education and health programmes. Second, it suggests the contingent uses of the concept of 'biology.' The debates revealed that biology is not simply a matter of incontrovertible scientific truth, but rather that, in the context of sex education, biology could be defined in such a way as to legitimate either the education programme or the health programme. Removal of HIV/AIDS from the science curriculum ensured that biology lessons were restricted to human reproduction, excluding reference to non-reproductive sex, such as sex for pleasure, masturbation, homosexuality, as well as practical advice about contraception and sexually transmitted diseases. These exclusions support the traditional moralist's aim that sex education be a programme of moral education. The exclusion of child sexuality, homosexuality, and non-reproductive sex from 'biology' reinforces the discursive construction of these aspects of sexuality as problematic, deviant and unnatural. As Epstein and Johnson observe, 'sex education which starts with the biology of reproduction is inherently problematic because it cannot be anything other than heterosexist and therefore sexist.'[34]

Curiously, contraception, albeit in a highly restricted way, is considered appropriate for inclusion in science lessons, whereas HIV/AIDS has been excluded. This disparity reinforces the contingent construction of biology. Contraception is legitimated in a way that safer-sex programmes are not. A possible reason for this disparity is that contraception does not challenge monogamy and marriage. The euphemism 'family planning' is used as a legitimating strategy precisely for this reason. The promotion of safer sex is problematical, for it is more closely perceived as condoning and even abetting activity that conflicts with social and legal norms or ideals, particularly because of its association with homosexuality, drug use, and prostitution.

The restrictive definition of 'biology' represents a particularly successful technique for the marginalisation of child sexuality and of other problematic sexualities within the classroom, due to the privileged position that the National Curriculum occupies within the curriculum as a whole. Not only is it compulsory; in addition, assessment of achievement in National Curriculum subjects determines a school's standing in school league tables. It thus has a significant detrimental impact on the time and resources available to schools for subjects positioned outside of it.

The Basic Curriculum

The Basic Curriculum[35] is controlled by school governing bodies. While governors may exercise their discretion as to its provision in primary schools, it is now compulsory in secondary schools. Parents, however, have an absolute right to withdraw their children from this part of the curriculum. The statute requires that it be 'given in such a manner as to encourage pupils to have regard to moral considerations and the value of family life.' Since 1993, it has required that 'reference to HIV/AIDS and other sexually transmitted diseases' be included.[36]

One might expect to find here a more progressive form of sex education. With control based at a local level[37] and the statutory provisions being open to a wide interpretation,[38] there exists a great diversity of provision. However, the Circular makes clear that the education programme is favoured. It presents an interesting contrast with the Department of Health's policy document, entitled 'The Health of the Nation.' The Circular endorses the Health Department's aim to reduce the rate of conceptions among the under sixteen-year-olds by 50 per cent by the year 2000 and of lessening the incidence of HIV, AIDS, and other sexually transmitted diseases[39] and states unequivocally that 'Education has a vital part to play in achieving these targets.'[40] However, the Circular does not endorse the Health Department's recommendations of 'better access *for everyone* to family planning information and services' or that 'safer sexual practices, including the use of condoms to reduce the risk of infection, must be encouraged.'[41] Instead it implicitly rejects the health programme in favour of the moral education programme. It states that sex education can make a 'substantial contribution' to the Department of Health's targets by being taught 'within a clear framework of values and an awareness of the law on sexual behaviour.'[42] While values are open to a pluralistic interpretation, the reference to the criminal law implicitly suggests that practical information about sexual activity to children below the age of consent is inappropriate. Consequently, in place of advice on contraception and safer-sex practices, a 'just say no' policy is favoured, which serves to bolster the moral education programme with its insistence on the non-sexual conceptualisation of childhood.

Individual Advice

The legal position regarding advice to individual pupils outside the classroom is not clear. This aspect of sex education is not referred to directly by statute, nor has the issue been brought before the courts. However, once again, the Circular provides detailed guidance and suggests a restrictive approach. It advises teachers that their pastoral interest in the welfare and well-being of pupils 'should never trespass on the proper exercise of parental rights and responsibilities'[43] and that advice to pupils on such matters as contraceptive advice 'without parental consent or knowledge would be an inappropriate exercise of a teacher's professional duties.'[44] The language used here, in particular the word 'trespass,' suggests that caution by teachers is required not on the basis of the interests of the child but that to act in any other way would be an unacceptable interference with the proprietory rights of parents over children. Not surprisingly, this approach has been much criticised and its legality has been challenged.[45]

While the Circular advises a cautious role for teachers, it suggests quite a different role for health professionals located outside of the school. It advises teachers that if approached on matters of personal sexual behaviour, in particular when a pupil 'has embarked on or is contemplating, a course of conduct which is likely to place him or her at moral or physical risk or in breach of the law,' they should 'wherever possible, encourage the pupil to seek advice . . . from the relevant health service professional . . . and the Head Teacher should arrange for the pupil to be counselled.'[46] The role of the health professionals is significant because it is only in this context of sex education that there is an open acknowledgement that children are sometimes sexual and that as a result explicit advice about safer sex and contraception is made available. In this respect it contrasts dramatically with curriculum — and school-based sex education and represents an example of the pragmatic health programme being enacted.

However, the extent to which pupils are encouraged to use such services, or indeed made aware of their availability, is dependant on the attitude of school governors and head teachers. Furthermore, it is significant that the Circular does not envisage these health services being provided to all pupils but only to those who as a result of their sexual behaviour are 'at moral or physical risk or in breach of the law.' This has the effect of marginalising those pupils and also problematises their sexuality to the extent that a sexual pupil is in this way constructed as having a moral, health, or legal problem as opposed to an educational right to information. In this way advice from health professionals operates in binary opposition, but simultaneously reinforces, the construction of 'biology' within the National Curriculum. Biology, considered essential for all pupils, refers to sex which is 'natural,' 'functional,' 'moral' and 'legal' and consequently excludes any practical advice to children and any mention of non-reproductive sexual activity. In contrast, advice from health professionals, restricted to a minority of pupils, is associated with illness, illegality, and immorality. Consequently, while the role for health professionals enables the provision of practical sex education, its location outside of the curriculum and indeed the school itself, simultaneously reinforces the norm of the child as ideally non-sexual.

Education and the Construction of Citizenship

The foregoing analysis of the regulation of sex education demonstrates that, within the school curriculum and in the context of the teacher/pupil relationship, the construction of the child as non-sexual dominates. The existence of the sexual child is problematical and often 'denied.' An example of this is the experience of pregnant, teenaged schoolgirls who are in effect excluded from school during pregnancy[47] — such is the seeming incompatibility of a highly visual child sexuality and the mainstream classroom as a location for 'normal children.' This denial of the possibility of child sexuality indicates the success of the traditionalists' campaigns and their insistence that sex education within school be a programme for moral education as opposed to the more pragmatic health programme. This serves to uphold the distinction between adult and child sexuality. Indeed a stark indication of this is the fact that, while in connection with adults Government HIV/AIDS campaigns have used the expression 'ignorance = death,' in the context of school sex education the resistance to safer-sex campaigns suggests that in connection with children, ignorance is equated not with death but, rather, with a state of blissful childhood innocence.[48]

One of the reasons for this stark distinction, and the success of the education programme in general, is that children and adolescents, to the extent that they are denied sexual autonomy by contemporary legal and social norms, are not *sexual citizens* and, consequently, traditional moral discourses, with their emphasis on sexual prohibitions, have had far greater influence in sex education than they currently have in matters of adult sexuality. Restrictions on child (sexual) behaviour are not perceived as challenging liberal-democratic principles.

Many writers have commented on the fact that children have very few, if any, autonomous rights in education. Sex education is often cited as a prime example.[49] This situation is contrasted with the position of children in child law, and in particular the position of children under the Children Act 1989, which requires children's wishes and feelings to be taken into account and recognises the possibility of a conflict between the views of children and those of their parents.[50] While this is perhaps regrettable, it is not surprising. Rather, it reflects the fact that education is primarily *productive*, which is to say that its purpose is the *construction* of a particular type of future citizen. Consequently, an insistence on the adult/child distinction in education matters and a disregard of children's own opinions is implicit in education as a social practice.[51] This perspective serves to challenge dominant perceptions of the curriculum, in particular, that the curriculum is a response to the needs of children, or is a result of politically neutral calculations as to their best interests. Focusing on the aspirational nature of the curriculum enables it to be best understood as a site of cultural conflict. In debates concerning such areas of the curriculum as English and History, the fact that the underlying questions have been 'What type of society are we?' and 'What type of adults will the knowledge taught at school produce?' has been quite explicit.[52] Yet in the context of sex education the belief in the fixed or natural state of sexuality and human relationships has precluded such openness. This is regrettable, for, as Jeffrey Weeks has commented, issues of sexuality frequently occupy a 'front line in the battle for the future of Western society.'[53] The resistance to acknowledging the sexuality of children within schools reflects an attempt to resist a cultural and social redefinition of childhood and, additionally, a more complex and general resistance to non-traditional gender roles and alternative patterns of domestic relationships. In this way the political concern and conflict surrounding sex education reflects not so much children's problems but, rather, adult anxieties for the future.[54]

Health: Protecting Children?

Sex education outside of schools, under the auspices of health professionals as opposed to teachers, appears dramatically different. Most notably, the child as a potentially sexual being is acknowledged. This conflict has a number of implications.

First, the discrepancy between the constructions of children in the two locations demonstrates how the conflicting objectification of children enables opposing practices or expertise to operate simultaneously.[55] In the health context, the child is constructed as a patient, independent and potentially sexual — which legitimises the provision of practical advice about sexual activity and recognises the potential conflict between the interests of parents and children. However, in the context of the education programme, the child is a pupil, dependant and non-sexual until adulthood — which in turn legitimises upholding sexual prohibitions and traditional images of childhood innocence.

Second, as already noted, the marginalised status of the health programme in effect constructs the sexual child as a problem child. While the education programme reinforces the adult/child dichotomy, the health programme constructs a good child/bad child dichotomy. It is the deep cultural attachment to the normative construction of the child as non-sexual which necessitates the creation of the 'other' sexual child as a 'problem' child. Alternatively, the marginalisation of the health programme and the construction of the child within this category can be understood as excluding the sexual child from the social category of childhood itself, thereby protecting the traditional construction of the child as a non-sexual innocent. As Jenks comments, in connection to responses to extremely violent children, 'by refusing children who commit acts of violence acceptance within the category of child, the public was reaffirming to itself the essence of what children are' and that 'the system of classification stays intact by resisting the "defilement" of the abhorrent case.'[56] This approach can equally be applied to sexual children and demonstrates how the status of the child as non-sexual is clearly socially constructed and not a matter of nature.

Third, the legitimation of the involvement of health professionals in effect constructs a dichotomy between good parents and bad parents. Parental rights are, to a certain extent, removed when the child is transferred from the location of education to health; and this suggests that when a child is sexually active, and especially if a girl becomes pregnant, the parents have failed to carry out their duties responsibly and it is this failure that legitimises the surveillance and intervention of health professionals, as well as doctors and social workers. Parental responsibility is in this way defined in accordance with the traditional constructions of the sexual child as morally and socially problematic.

These critical perspectives are significant as they challenge the progressive narrative inherent within the health programme. They suggest that the involvement of health professionals is legitimised not so much by a desire to 'liberate' children from parental rule or from the restrictive construction of the traditional 'ideal' norms of childhood, but rather that the health programme serves a normative function, in that it serves to protect children from the consequences of a failure of the moral education programme, and from irresponsible 'permissive' parenting. It is significant that supporters of practical sexual advice to children frequently legitimise their demands by seeking to demonstrate that this form of sex education is the most effective way to reduce teenage pregnancies and the spread of sexually transmitted diseases.[57] They make strategic use of research demonstrating explicit sex education actually delays rather than encourages sexual activity among children.[58]

Health programmes can thus serve a moral or political purpose with an explicitly normalising intent in the same way as the school curriculum. However, 'health-based' programmes are less explicitly political than the sex education curriculum. The language of health draws on a common-sense claim to truth, which serves to hide its normative intent.[59] In other words, the health programme is presented as politically neutral, incontrovertible and uncontroversial, in contrast to education within the curriculum, with its more explicit political and moral concerns. Consequently, the involvement of health professionals and the subsequent acknowledgment of the sexual potential of children *may* result in children having more choice and autonomy over their lives. However, it is important to be aware of the disciplinary potential of health programmes, particularly in the context of sexually active children. Health-based calculations within the medical and 'psy-' discourses as to what is in a child's best interests may often conflict with a child's own wishes and developing sense of sexual identity.[60] Put simply, while the health programme effectively decriminalises sexual children, it does not liberate them. Rather, they become pathologised through an alternative, medical, adult gaze.[61]

Conclusion

> *Always already framed by language and inherited views, children nonetheless are embodied, sticky, ticklish, intense beings who change and grow. No wonder they become repositories of societal fears as well as hopes, regulations as well as dreams.*[62]

Sex education provokes staunch opposition and equally passionate support. It is described, simultaneously, as a form of moral indoctrination and corruption and as an essential and basic human right. Rather than enter this debate and attempt to identify the 'truth' about sex education, what this chapter has attempted to do is to demonstrate that sex education is in essence neither 'good' nor 'bad' but, rather, reflects a desire to regulate or govern the sexual behaviours and attitudes of children and, indeed, those of the adults of the future.

Reiss identifies the aims of sex education as including stopping girls getting pregnant, reducing the incidence of sexually transmitted disease, decreasing ignorance, decreasing guilt, embarrassment and anxiety, enabling students to make their own decisions, develop assertiveness, challenging gender roles in society, and providing an ethical framework for the expressions of sexuality.[63] These aims inevitably give rise to a number of conflicts, in particular, conflicts between children's rights of autonomy and adult calculations as to their best interests, and between opposing ethical and moral values. Sex education is, consequently, complex, highly ambitious, and in England has resulted in two broad and distinct programmes — traditional moral education within the school curriculum and a health programme located outside of the classroom.

Acknowledging the complexity of sex education is important. It requires national and international legal and political debates to focus not so much on whether or not children should have more, less, or any sex education or whether they have a 'right' to sex education or, indeed, whether it is an infringement of parents' rights, but rather to define what 'sex education' means and what its purpose is. Claims about children's best interests are contingent upon shifting social and cultural definitions of childhood. Programmes for sex education are not so much responses to the activities of 'real' children, but attempts to uphold particular images of childhood. For example, the programme for moral education attempts to resist challenges to non-sexual childhood innocence and to traditional moral values and gender stereotypes. Similarly, the health programme also produces and protects an 'ideal' childhood, albeit one that acknowledges child sexuality. Both the traditional innocent child of the moral education programme and the progressive, responsible sexual child of the health programme are contingent and normative constructions. Sex education is not simply motivated by a concern for individual child welfare, but is simultaneously interconnected with adult concerns, anxieties and projections, both progressive and reactionary, for a particular form of social and sexual order. Epstein and Johnson comment that 'to teach thoughtfully about sexual matters is to accept change in yourself.'[64] Acknowledging these adult concerns is an essential precursor for developing a form of sex education that responds genuinely and openly to the wishes and experiences of children, and enables the possibility of a plurality and fluidity of sexual identities.

Notes

[1] This chapter refers only to sex education in England and Wales. However, similar debates have taken place in other Western countries. For Canada, see, e.g., M.L. Adams, *The Trouble with Normal: Postwar Youth and the Making of Heterosexuality*, ch. 6 (1997). For the United States, see, e.g., S.E. McNay-Keith, 'AIDS in Public Schools: Resolved Issues and Continuing Controversy,' 24 JLE 69-80 (1997); P.S. Ramos, 'The Condom Controversy in the Public Schools: Respecting a Minor's Right of Privacy,' 145 UPLR 149 (1996).
[2] The concept of children's rights, in this context, includes both rights to autonomy and rights to protection. The distinction is important, particularly in the context of sexual activity, as the latter depend upon adult calculations of children's best interests, which often conflict with children's own wishes. See, e.g., *Children, Rights and the Law* (P. Alston *et al.* eds., 1992).
[3] See K. Jones, 'Cultural Politics and Education in the 1990s,' in *Education after the Conservatives* (R. Hatcher & K. Jones, eds.,1996).
[4] See R. Thomson, 'Unholy Alliances: The Recent Politics of Sex Education,' in *Activating Theory: Lesbian, Gay, Bisexual Politics* (J. Bristow & A. Wilson eds., 1993); R. Thomson, 'Prevention, Promotion and Adolescent Sexuality: The Politics of School Sex Education in England and Wales,' 9 SMT 94 (1994) [hereinafter 'Prevention']; P. Meredith, *Government, Schools and the Law* (1992); M. Durham,

Sex and Politics: The Family and Morality in the Thatcher Years (1991).

[5] See G. Lenderyou, 'Sex Education: A School-Based Perspective,' 9 SMT 127 (1994).

[6] But see C. Packer, 'Sex Education: Child's Right, Parents' Choice or Societal Obligation?' in this collection.

[7] Some would argue that the socially constructed nature of childhood renders this task impossible. See, e.g., M. King, *A Better World for Children? Explorations in Morality and Authority* (1997).

[8] 'Govern' in this context refers not to the explicit actions of state institutions or agents, but to Foucault's concept of governmentality – the 'tutored mediation of the intimate.' See A. McGillivray, 'Governing Childhood,' in *Governing Childhood* 1, 2 (A. McGillivray, ed., 1997). The concept thus encompasses a range of practices and techniques which regulate the actions of individuals, and by which individuals simultaneously regulate themselves. See also N. Rose, 'Government, Authority and Expertise in Advanced Liberalism,' 22 ES 283 (1993); *The Foucault Effect: Studies in Governmentality* (G. Burchell *et al.*, eds., 1991).

[9] See D. Monk, 'Sex Education and the Problematisation of Teenage Pregnancies: A Genealogy of Law and Governance,' 7 SLS 239 (1998); D. Epstein & R. Johnston, *Schooling Sexualities* (1998).

[10] The term 'programmes' refers to concrete public policies. However, the terms health and education in this context do not refer to the Government departments of those names, despite the fact that the Department of Health and the Department of Education (and now Employment) have at times advocated conflicting programmes — a situation which is now changing under the new Labour government. See, 'How Do You Make Sure Everyone Is Doing It?, *Times Education Supplement* 14 (31 Oct. 1997).

[11] See, e.g., D. Monk, 'Beyond Section 28: Law, Governance and Sex Education,' in *Legal Queeries: Lesbian, Gay and Transgender Legal Studies* (L. Moran *et al.*, eds., 1998).

[12] See, e.g., W. Stainton Rogers & R. Stainton Rogers, 'What is good and bad sex for children?' in *Moral Agendas for Children's Welfare* (M. King ed., 1998); Epstein & Johnson, *supra* note 9; D. Gittens, *The Child in Question*, ch. 6 (1998); D. Archard, *Children, Rights and Childhood* (1993); D. Evans, *Sexual Citizenship: The Material Construction of Sexualities* (1993).

[13] See P. Pinsent & B. Knight, *Teenage Girls and their Magazines* (1998).

[14] See, e.g., 'Teacher Jailed for Affair with Schoolboy,' *The Guardian* 1 (18 July 1998).

[15] See A. Higonnet, *Pictures of Innocence: The History and Crisis of Ideal Childhood* (1998).

[16] See *id.*

[17] See, e.g., *Sutherland v. the United Kingdom*, App. No. 25186/94, Eur. Comm'n H. R. DR (1997) <http://www.dhcommhr.coe.fr/eng/25186R31.E.html> visited 1 Oct. 1999).

[18] A. Phoenix, *Young Mothers* (1991).

[19] Higonnet note 15 *supra*; C. Jenks, *Childhood* (1996); M. Minow, 'Governing Children, Imagining Childhood,' in *Governing Childhood,* note 8 *supra*.

[20] See C. Piper, 'Historical Constructions of Childhood Innocence; Removing Sexuality,' in this collection; Higonnet, note 15 *supra*.

[21] See 'Marriage and Family at Risk,' *Times Education Supplement* 14, 31 Oct. 1997.

[22] Evans, note 12 *supra*, at 216.

[23] See Monk, note 9 *supra*.

[24] P. Miller & N. Rose, 'Political Power beyond the State: Problematics of Government,' 43 BJS 173, 190 (1992).

[25] Education Act 1993: Sex Education in Schools, Department for Education and Employment Circular No 5/94.

[26] It falls beyond the scope of this chapter to discuss this point of public law in depth. See *R v. North Derbyshire Health Authority*, ex parte Fisher QBD, reported in *The Times* 38 BMLR 76 (1998); *Grandsen & Co Ltd v. Secretary of State* 54 PCR 86, 93-94 (1985); *Bristol District Council v. Clark* 3 AER 976 (1975). See also D. Foulkes, *Administrative Law* 76-79 (1995).

[27] Thomson, 'Prevention,' note 4 *supra*, at 20.

[28] See A. Blair & C. Furniss, 'Sex, lies and the DFE Circular 5/94: The Limits of Sex Education,' 7 EL 197 (1995); J. Bridgeman, 'Don't Tell the Children: The Department's Guidance on the Provision of Information about Contraception to Individual Pupils,' in *Sex Education and the Law* 45 (N. Harris, ed., 1996); Jones, note 3 *supra*.

[29] The relevant provision is Education Act 1996 sec. 356 (9).

[30] N. Harris, *Law and Education: Regulation, Consumerism and the Education System* (1993); P. Meredith, *Government, Schools and the Law* 77-88 (1992); J. White, *Two National Curricula — Baker's and Stalin's: Towards a Liberal Alternative*, 36 BJES 218 (1988).

[31] Education (National Curriculum) (Attainment Targets and Programmes of Study in Science) Order 1991, SI 1991/2897.

[32] Thomson, 'Prevention,' note 4 *supra*.

[33] Hansard 10/5/93 col. 1103, HL.

[34] Epstein & Johnson, note 9 *supra*, at 194.

[35] The term 'basic curriculum' refers to those aspects of the curriculum outside of the National Curriculum and the curriculum for religious education. The relevant provisions are Education Act 1996, secs. 252, 352, 371, 372, 403, 405.

[36] *Id.*

[37] For a more detailed theoretical analysis of the politics and consequences of local control, and, in particular, of parental power, see Monk, *supra* note 9, at 248; A. Barron, 'The Governance of Schooling: Genealogies of Control and Empowerment in the Reform of Public Education,' 15 SLPS 167 (1996).

[38] With respect to the requirement to include reference to HIV/AIDS, there is no indication as to how this should be done. Consequently, nothing prevents schools

from teaching about HIV/AIDS from a traditional moral perspective, excluding reference to safer-sex practices. This situation is, to an extent, encouraged and legitimated by the Circular, which states that 'where schools are founded on religious principles, this matter will have a direct bearing on the manner in which such subjects are taught.' See the Circular, note 25, *supra,* at para. 9.

[39] Department of Health, Health of the Nation, paras. 94, 95 (1992).

[40] The Circular, note 25 *supra*, at para. 9.

[41] Department of Health, note 39 *supra,* at paras. 92, D10 (emphasis added).

[42] The Circular, note 25 *supra*, at para. 8.

[43] *Id.* at para 38.

[44] *Id.* at paras 39, 40.

[45] See Blair & Furniss, note 28 *supra*; Bridgeman note 28 *supra*; M. Beloff & H. Mountfield, *Sex Education in Schools* (1994).

[46] The Circular, note 25 *supra*, at para. 40.

[47] N. Dawson, 'The Provision of Education and Opportunities for Future Employment for Pregnant Schoolgirls and Schoolgirl Mothers in the UK,' 11 CS 252 (1997).

[48] D. Monk, 'Sex Education and HIV/AIDS: Political Conflict and Legal Resolution,' 12 CS 295 (1998).

[49] See M. Freeman, 'Children's Education: A Test Case for Best Interests and Autonomy', in *Listening to Children in Education* 29 (R. Davie & D. Galloway eds., 1996); T. Jeffs, 'Children's educational rights in a new ERA?,' in *The Handbook of Children's Rights: Comparative Policy and Practice* 25 (B. Franklin, ed., 1995).

[50] A. Bainham, 'Sex Education: A Family Lawyer's Perspective,' in *Sex Education and the Law* 24 (N. Harris, ed., 1996).

[51] See D. Monk, 'Failing Children: Responding to Young People with 'Behavioural Difficulties,' in *Moral Agendas for Children's Welfare* 212 (M. King, ed., 1999); J. Finch, *Education as Social Policy* (1984); White, note 30 *supra*.

[52] See Jones, note 3 *supra*; K. Crawford, 'A History of the Right: the Battle for Control of the National Curriculum for History 1989-1994,' 43 BJES 433 (1995).

[53] J. Weeks, *Sexuality and its Discontents* 17 (1985).

[54] See Jenks, note 19 *supra*.

[55] See K. O'Donovan, *Family Law Matters* (1993); L. Moran, 'A Reading in Sexual Politics and Law: *Gillick v. Norfolk and Wisbech Area Health Authority*,' 8 LLR 83 (1986).

[56] Jenks, note 19 *supra*, at 129.

[57] Epstein & Johnson observe that sex education in schools frequently emphasises dangers, but rarely refers to pleasure. See Epstein & Johnson, note 9 *supra*. See also M. Reiss, 'What Are the Aims of School Sex Education?' 23 CJE 125 (1993); Sex Education Forum, *Highlight 158 — Sex Education* (1998).

[58] See K. Wellings, 'Provision of Sex Education and Early Sexual Experience: The Relation Examined,' 311 BMJ 414 (1995); D. Kirby *et al.*, *School-Based Programmes to Reduce Sexual Risk Behaviours: A Review of Effectiveness* (1995).

[59] C. Smart, *Feminism and the Power of Law* (1989); D. Gastaldo, 'Is Health Education Good for You? Rethinking health education through the concept of biopower,' in *Foucault, Health and Medicine* 113 (A. Peterson & R. Bunton, eds., 1997).
[60] P. Gordon, 'The contribution of sexology to contemporary sexuality education,' 9 SMT 171 (1994); C. Lind & C. Butler, 'The Legal Abuse of Homosexual Children,' 7 JCL 3 (1995).
[61] See Smart, note 59 *supra*; Gastaldo, note 59 *supra*; Rose, note 8 *supra*.
[62] Minow, note 19 *supra*.
[63] Reiss, *supra* note 57.
[64] Epstein & Johson, note 9 *supra*, at 195.

11 Seeking a Gendered Adolescence: Legal and Ethical Problems of Puberty Suppression among Adolescents with Gender Dysphoria

CATHERINE DOWNS & STEPHEN WHITTLE

Introduction

Changes in attitudes have encouraged increasing numbers of young people to identify as gender-dysphoric.[1] In order to reduce the distress caused by the onset of puberty, young people with gender-dysphoria are increasingly seeking pubertal-suppression therapy. Health care professionals must then confront a variety of clinical, ethical and legal issues. This chapter examines three therapeutic approaches to adolescent gender dysphoria, and, in particular, the responsibilities of health care professionals towards young people requesting pubertal-suppression therapy.

Psychological, Social and Therapeutic Issues

In typically shocked tones, the *Sunday Times* recently reported that '[c]hildren as young as 14 are receiving sex change treatment on the National Health Service.' The article noted an estimated 600 girls and boys in Britain — some as young as seven — who suffer from gender identity disorders. The disclosure that growing numbers of children were seeking treatment for gender dysphoria had sparked intense debate among medical specialists: 'While some psychiatrists believe children should be helped to change sex early, others insist that they should only take that decision after reaching maturity.' The article cited the views of one psychiatrist, Russell Reid, who believes that children as young as 13 should be offered preliminary drug treatment to prevent puberty.   Reid's approach contrasted with that of Dominic Di Cegli, who runs the Portman Gender Identity Development Clinic.   Di Cegli admitted that up to one in four of the teenagers who, at 14, seemed convinced of their desire to change sex, would later decide against the change.[2]

Such reports must always be read with caution.   Nevertheless, the last two or three years have seen a rise in the number of adolescent children who, with the support and guidance of their parents, have sought medical help to deal with perceived gender dysphoria.   These young people are increasingly expressing a desire for medical intervention, in the short term, for the following purposes:

1. Preventing the development of secondary sexual characteristics.   (1) Female-to-male gender-dysphoric adolescents will seek to avoid the traumatic experience of menstruation. They will also seek future avoidance of major surgical procedures to remove breasts, which will have developed with puberty. (2) Male-to-female gender-dysphoric adolescents will seek to avoid having their voice break. They will also seek future avoidance not only of electrolysis to remove beard growth that will develop with puberty, but also of the social problems of having to live as an adult woman with a masculine voice.

2. Enabling them to continue their education in a more congenial gender role. Adolescents may not be entirely comfortable in a new gender role. With the support of their schools and colleges, however, they may be able to spend significant parts of their education being socially accepted by their peers as young transsexuals.

3. Allowing them time, without having to face the unwanted (and often hated) effects of puberty, to decide whether gender reassignment is the appropriate course of action in the long term.

In the United Kingdom, awareness of gender identity disorders has increased in recent years. There is a growing understanding that gender identity disorders can be experienced by anyone, from any social group, and at any age. Much of this awareness has been achieved through the news coverage of recent campaigns undertaken by groups such as Press For Change and the Gender Trust. There has also been increased access to resources and information through helplines and websites such as those of the Gender Trust.

For young people, there have been three significant developments. First, the creation, in 1989, of a clinic providing services for young people with gender dysphoria, initially located at St George's Hospital in London, and led by Dr. Di Cegli.[3] Second, in 1996, British television's Channel 4 screened a two-part film in a series entitled *The Decision*.[4] The film concerned three female-to-male transsexuals and their trip to the Netherlands to learn about treatment and services provided by the Gender Clinic at the Free University of Amsterdam. It included a young female-to-male transsexual, 'Fredd,' aged 13, showing his parents as they sought to provide Fredd with support through his adolescence. It also showed several young female-to-male transsexuals who had begun pubertal-suppression treatment at the ages of 13 and 14 in order to prevent the emergence of unwanted secondary sexual characteristics. By the age of 16 or 17, these young people went on to begin active hormone therapy in order to change their secondary sexual characteristics to those of their chosen gender role. They commenced surgical gender reassignment surgery from the age of 18. The film portrayed them as content and handsome young men. A third important event has been the creation of a support group, Mermaids, for children and teenagers with gender identity disorders. The group provides support for their families, their friends, and for professionals who work with them. It has facilitated networking among young people and their families, helping them to understand that their experiences are not unique. Mermaids has also enabled young people and their parents to compare the various approaches taken by doctors in this field. As a result of these three developments, gender-dysphoric adolescents increasingly form part of a well-informed patient group who know what they are seeking before attending a clinic. These patients enjoy the support of their parents in their request for a plan of medical intervention which will culminate in gender reassignment.

Generally, clinicians treating gender-dysphoric youth define their therapeutic task in terms of preventing later problems through early intervention. They can achieve this aim by developing a framework in which the family, the young person, and other interested parties (for example, the school) can find ways of understanding the child's behaviour so that it does not pose an excessive burden to the child or the family.[5] The fundamental question for the clinician is: what is the right treatment to give a child with such a syndrome? This question does not merely arise from the clinician's duty to care for the patient. Due to the many social stigmas still associated with gender dysphoria and gender reassignment, clinicians may also find themselves facing a personal crisis as to the best treatment for the young person.

There are three possible methods of treating young people with gender dysphoria, which may be categorised as follows (although they may be combined):

1. The clinician may attempt to 'cure' young persons of the problem, ensuring that they do not grow up into transsexual adults.

2. The clinician may help reconcile the young persons and their families to the behaviour and to the social stigmas that can result. This approach seeks to enable the young persons to have a good experience of adolescence, but postpones active intervention until adulthood. It often involves other involved parties, such as friends or school authorities, so that young persons' alternative gender behaviour, while not actively encouraged, will not be treated punitively.

3. The clinician may provide active medical intervention, through puberty-suppression therapy, thus allowing the young person to undergo hormonal or gender reassignment therapy more easily at a later stage, should that be the chosen path.

While some clinicians may still attempt to 'cure' patients with gender dysphoria, this approach is becoming outmoded. In the case of adults requesting gender reassignment treatment, there is increasing awareness that 'it is exclusively and primarily the person himself or herself who will decide for sex reassignment.'[6] Thus, while clinicians can participate in the diagnosis of gender dysphoria, it is the patient who decides whether it is appropriate to proceed to full gender reassignment. The primary role of therapists and counsellors is to ensure that the patient is fully informed of the possibilities and risks of gender reassignment, so that they may make an informed decision.

When considering young people, however, some clinicians feel that the role of the therapist is not merely to provide information, nor merely to provide liaison psychiatric services to deal with the social stigmatisation processes that are linked with cross-gender behaviour. They feel they have a role in preventing transsexualism in adulthood. For Zucker and Bradley, this approach is manifestly valid and ethical, thus justifying therapeutic intervention,[7] despite their observation, in the same book, that treatment to prevent adult homosexuality is more problematical. They note the absence of studies demonstrating that therapeutic intervention in childhood can alter the developmental path to transsexualism or homosexuality. Yet they do not equate the two conditions with respect to the clinician's therapeutic goal.

This inconsistency sums up the problem faced by young people seeking intervention from clinics. Clinicians are gatekeepers to the hormonal and surgical reassignment sought by many young people with gender dysphoria While the adult transsexual is, at least nowadays, acknowledged as being someone who decides whether or not to undergo reassignment, young people are faced with a clinical situation in which doctors still feel a cultural imperative to 'cure' them. A significant amount of their clinic experience (and of the experience of parents who accompany them) is perceived as 'stalling tactics' and even 'lies' on the part of doctors. Such delays are perceived as a tactic for delaying the individual's quest for active treatment leading to gender reassignment, whilst the doctors instead seek to cure them.[8] Such stalling is also experienced even when clinicians are aware of the futility of attempting to cure their patients and instead are seeking to help with the social problems associated with gender identity problems. The adolescents and their parents suffer considerable distress as puberty advances and nothing appears to be happening to prevent the inevitable onset of adult transsexualism and its associated problems.

It is acknowledged that hormonal or other medical interventions are inappropriate in pre-pubertal children.[9] Nevertheless, there may be medical options for young people under the age of majority. By adopting the second possible method of treatment — because adolescence is viewed as a time when many aspects of identity are still being developed — professionals often fear that 'interference' with gender identity formation and gender role performance may cause more problems than it can resolve.[10] The doctor decides that gender-dysphoric adolescents are 'simply not old enough' to make up their own minds about whether pubertal-suppression or active hormone therapy would be appropriate. These adolescents are deemed unable to consent to such treatment until they are at least 18 years old. We will see that this is a problematical approach, in view of young persons' rights to consent to treatment.

The third method, in the cases of those children who have shown consistent and extreme patterns of gender dysphoria with a strong cross-gender identification, provides an alternative that leads to hormonal and gender reassignment in early adulthood. Some early form of active intervention can help prevent feelings of hopelessness for young persons who must wait for the onset of adulthood in order to undertake full gender reassignment. It also improves the prospects of an enhanced physical appearance in the new gender role, and prevents the onset of permanent secondary sexual characteristics, such as a deep voice in male-to-female transsexuals. In numerous follow-up studies, it has been shown that the earlier gender reassignment is commenced, the greater the chance of a favourable post-operative outcome.[11] In the Amsterdam clinic, this approach is offered only to young people who are determined to be psychologically stable, to function well with family and social support, and to have a lifelong, extreme and complete cross-gender identification. The initial treatment afforded to an adolescent who meets these requirements involves providing pubertal-suppression hormones which block the actions of sex steroids in a reversible manner, followed by full non-reversible hormone treatment at the age of 18. If, in the meantime, the patients have concluded a favourable 'real-life test' (i.e. lived in their new gender role successfully and happily for at least one year), then consideration is given to requests for surgical reassignment. This model of treatment has been tried with several adolescents in the Gender Clinic of the Free University Hospital in Amsterdam, with reported success. However, there have been calls for more prospective and follow-up studies.[12]

Legal and Ethical Problems

Which legal and ethical questions, then, should doctors consider when choosing among these three methods? In the event that the physician should choose either to attempt a 'cure' of the patient or to delay active treatment, what are the legal consequences if patients or their families choose, at some later stage, to sue the clinician because they deem the treatment to have caused unnecessary suffering? Such a scenario is entirely plausible in a world where hormonal and surgical gender reassignment is increasingly accepted as the only solution to transsexuals' plight, and in which the medical profession's own follow-up studies have shown a high success rate (97% to 99%) in the case of persons reassigned.[13] Where young people, with the support of their parents, seek active intervention, doctors who choose either of the first two routes may be subject to litigation, unless they have clarified the questions regarding clinical judgement leading to refusal. In some situations, for example, female-to-male transsexuals may decide that, because of a refusal to treat them when they were younger, they were forced to undergo unnecessary breast reduction surgery, and thus deserve compensation for their pain and suffering. Similarly, male-to-female transsexuals may sue for the costs incurred in obtaining beard reduction through electrolysis. Parents may even sue if their children were among the small percentage of untreated young people who commit suicide. Doctors may then be called upon to justify the action they took.

    Of particular concern is the view that people aged 14 to 17 are not old enough to decide whether they are transsexual. In our opinion, this view may be legally insufficient as a basis for withholding pubertal-suppression treatment. The dilemmas confronting doctors in these circumstances are undoubtedly difficult, as the patient is desperate and social pressure is great. It is precisely for these reasons, however, that clinicians must consider carefully the problems involved in providing, or refusing to provide, pubertal-suppression treatment, and for ensuring that they have not only safeguarded their patient's best interests, but also have made clinical judgements of the highest standards.

The Problem of Consent

In the United Kingdom, children under 18 are generally deemed incapable of giving consent to treatment because of their minority. Health professionals must rely on consent being given by their parents or under the inherent jurisdiction of a court, following an application. In the case of older children who are still under 18, there are two main ways in which they, if they have full mental capacity, can consent to treatment. For the age group of 16 to 18, section 8(1) of the Family Law Reform Act 1969 lowers the age at which an individual can consent to treatment, from 18 to 16. For the purposes of consent to medical treatment, consent by a minor aged 16 or above 'shall be as effective as it would be if he were of full age.' The minor can only consent to certain kinds of treatment, namely surgical, medical, or dental treatment including according to sub-section (2) diagnostic and ancillary procedures.

The sub-sections do not make clear whether the treatment must only be therapeutic or whether it also includes non-therapeutic treatment, which is arguably the definition of treatment for transsexuals.[14] The only case in which section 8 of the Family Law Reform Act has been discussed is *re W*[15] In this case, the suggestion by Nolan L.J. was that the phrase 'surgical medical or dental treatment' in the Act should be construed in a narrow sense because of the need in sub-section 2 to elaborate by including, for clarification, diagnostic and ancillary procedures. If section 8 is limited by this narrow approach to therapeutic treatment, then there may be restrictions on the treatment to which those aged 16 to 18 can consent. It is unclear, however, whether this restrictive interpretation is correct. These patients may still be able to give effective consent under section 8.

Minors under the age of 16 can consent to treatment following the decision in *Gillick v. West Norfolk and Wisbech Area Health Authority*. The court in this case held that children under 16 can give valid consent to medical treatment without parental knowledge or consent, provided that the doctor treating them is satisfied that they understand the nature of the proposed treatment.[16] There are no clear-cut grounds as to the age at which this independent right comes into existence. The test put forward by Lord Scarman is that a child must have 'sufficient understanding and intelligence to enable him or her to understand fully what is proposed.'[17] There are problems in putting the *Gillick* test into practice because of its subjectivity and the lack of clarity in the House of Lords decision as to the actual test to be applied. Lord Scarman indicated (at least in relation to contraceptive treatment, although the test must apply to other kinds of treatment) that the minor must understand not only the nature of the medical advice regarding the treatment, but must also be mature and understand the family, moral and social issues involved. Lord Fraser indicated that the patient must be capable of understanding the doctor's advice. These tests are often hard to satisfy. Adults of full capacity do not have to show the same level of understanding when they consent to treatment.

It is possible, then, that if the patients are 16 or older, they can give consent to treatment in exercise of their statutory right under the Family Law Reform Act 1969. If they are under 16, they may be '*Gillick* competent' and still be able to give effective consent to treatment under the common law. Even if they are under 16 and not assessed as *Gillick* competent, their parents can give consent to treatment on their behalf. Lack of parental consent should not affect the validity of the consent given by the minor either under statute or the *Gillick* test. Difficulties with regard to the issue of consent will only arise in cases where the patient's parents do not consent to the treatment *and* the patient is under 16 *and* not assessed as being *Gillick* competent. In most of the cases involving gender-dysphoric adolescents, the parents of these patients support their children's desire for treatment. In many cases, they are prepared to pay for the treatment abroad, if necessary.

Even if consent to treatment is not a real problem, decisions about whether to treat at all, and about the kind of treatment to be administered, are difficult. They depends on the doctor's professional judgement. In *Re J* it was held that doctors can never be forced by the courts to administer a particular kind of treatment contrary to their professional clinical judgement.[18] In this case, as a result of an accident, a baby had become acutely handicapped. The medical staff did not want to place the baby on a ventilator, but the mother did. The mother tried unsuccessfully to force the medical staff to give her baby the treatment she wanted, even though she had a medical expert who supported giving that treatment. Lord Donaldson believed that doctors should be free to treat in accordance with their best clinical judgement. For the court to intervene 'would require the practitioner to act contrary to the fundamental duty which he owed to his patient . . . which was to treat the patient in accordance with his own best clinical judgement.'[19]

In contrast, the Court of Appeal has recently decided against overruling the decision of a mother concerning medical treatment for her child. In *Re T* the mother of a small child did not want him to undergo a liver transplant even though medical opinion favoured such treatment. This involved a slightly different issue, as the mother did not want access to treatment. Rather, she wanted to be able to refuse a certain kind of treatment on behalf of her child. Lord Justice Butler-Sloss held that the child's welfare must be the paramount consideration, even if, in this particularly acute case, that meant allowing the mother to decide on her child's future treatment rather than automatically making a decision to prolong life.[20] This decision affirms the welfare of the child test. If followed, it may require greater recognition of parents' wishes. In general, however, patients must largely depend on whether a doctor is willing to administer a certain kind of treatment. The courts do not usually intervene to force doctors to administer any particular treatment, or to administer one form of treatment in preference to another, in any way that would disregard the wishes of the patients or their parents.

In cases of gender-dysphoric adolescents, the problem is not access to treatment *per se,* but access to a *specific form* of treatment. Specific forms of treatment must be recommended and administered by the patient's doctor. If a doctor refuses to provide treatment that a patient wants, the patient may seek a second opinion. If there is no doctor available in this country who is prepared to treat gender-dysphoric adolescents by the third method, the patients are left with no choice about their treatment. There are doctors in the Netherlands, however, who may be willing to administer the treatment. Patients may be able to challenge the clinical judgement of doctors in this country who are unwilling to provide such treatment when colleagues abroad have offered it for a number of years.

Patients seeking to establish negligence must show that their doctor owes them a duty of care. Once a patient has been accepted (in the case of the specialist) or has been registered with a general practitioner and sought treatment, this duty of care is established. The law of negligence requires that health care professionals must exercise reasonable care in the performance of their duties. The standards expected of a reasonable professional were set forth in *Bolam v. Friern HMC.* The professional is expected 'to act in accordance with a practice accepted as proper by a responsible body of medical men skilled in that particular art.'[21]

If there are different views about the appropriate mode of treatment, health care professionals will not be condemned by acting in one way, rather than another, provided that they can justify the approach they have taken.[22] The practice adopted must be accepted as proper by a body of skilled and experienced doctors.[23] While the paternalism of the *Bolam* test can be criticised for allowing doctors to set the standard of treatment that they are to give, it still sets a high standard. Doctors needing to show standards of excellence within their field of specialisation must demonstrate an awareness of current practices. That showing may include research and work conducted outside the United Kingdom. The introduction of evidence-based medicine, which requires compliance with treatment on the basis of research evidence, may further make it difficult to justify failing to follow up-to-date procedures and treatments which are supported by research findings. Doctors may be justifiably cautious in providing new forms of treatment; however, if a new approach to treatment is supported by research, it may be difficult to justify not following this new approach.

In the Netherlands, the different and novel kind of treatment for gender-dysphoric adolescents has been shown to be successful over a number of years in cases that have been carefully selected on the basis of prognosis and individual circumstances.[24] In the United Kingdom, actions in negligence could be taken if a doctor or National Health Service (NHS) Trust had failed to provide the most effective and up-to-date treatment. Patients suing for compensation for medical negligence would have to establish causation. They would have to produce evidence that failure to treat in a way that they allege would have been more effective has caused or contributed to their medical condition and thus caused them loss. This causation may be difficult to establish. However, doctors should be aware of the possibility of legal actions for negligence, and must ensure that they have considered the most appropriate treatment for each patient.

Hospital ethics committees may also have a role to play in the decision-making process concerning available treatment. In *R v. Ethical Committee of St. Mary's ex parte Harriott,* the judge found that the role of an ethics committee is not to decide on particular cases, but to provide a forum for discussion amongst professionals in an informal context. The only situation in which the advice given by the ethics committee would be subject to legal scrutiny would be if it were to advise that a section of the population should be refused treatment based on, for example, race or religion.[25] In cases of treatment for gender-dysphoric adolescents, ethics committees must ensure that doctors can explain the clinical rationale for their decisions to provide or to withhold the treatment in question. Prudent doctors should be able to justify the clinical approach taken in the light of current practice. They must take into account recent developments, research and treatment in other countries and at other clinics. Failure to act in accordance with successful new techniques may become more difficult to justify as more evidence becomes available to support these new approaches to treatment. Patients rely on their doctors to give them the most appropriate and effective treatment for their condition and their personal circumstances. Doctors must be able to demonstrate that they have considered what is the most relevant treatment for each patient. The obvious risk in failing to demonstrate that each patient has been considered individually, and that there is a blanket ban on treatment, is of being sued for negligence if the patient suffers harm as a result of the policy.

Recall, then, the three methods of treatment already discussed. We have seen that the first does not work. It should never be recommended by a doctor or endorsed by a hospital ethics committee. The second approach, which delays any active intervention and treatment, should only be used if it can be shown to be therapeutically beneficial for the individual patient. If the third method is requested, it is unnecessary to wait until the patient has attained the age of 18 to obtain effective consent to treatment. In order to reach decisions as between the second and third methods, hospital ethics committees may have to develop guidelines, bearing in mind the overall requirement to consider the welfare of the child. Let us now turn, then, to guidelines which should be considered.

Proposed Guidelines

When considering whether to undertake pubertal-suppression treatment, doctors should ask the following questions:

1. What is the preferred treatment of the patient and the patient's parents? Is there a clinical reason not to follow their choice?

2. What is the likely prognosis for the patient? Is there a clear indication that the patient is unlikely to want to proceed to gender reassignment as an adult?

3. Can the doctor justify delaying access to pubertal-suppression treatment in the particular patient's case, bearing in mind the psychological and social pressures of adolescence, and the fact that pubertal-suppression treatment is reversible?

4. Would the non-provision of pubertal-suppression treatment prove genuinely beneficial for the particular patient?

5. Has the clinician ensured that the correct procedures will be followed if pubertal-suppression treatment is not given?

Such decisions must, of course, consider the age of the child and the likely support he or she will receive for a cross-gender life-style from parents, family members, peers, and school or college officials. Nevertheless, in our view, pubertal-suppression treatment should be used in all cases unless there are positive reasons for choosing the second method.

Before turning to an ethics committee for advice, we would recommend that clinicians evaluate the three available methods in the light of the following observations:

1. Is there any clinical basis for refusing treatment because the individual can be cured of gender dysphoria? The answer, at present, is *no*. Severe gender dysphoria is currently assessed as not being susceptible to any treatment other than hormonal (and surgical) gender reassignment.

2. Has valid consent to treatment been given by the adolescent or the adolescent's parents? If a parent consents to pubertal-suppression treatment, then, regardless of the child's level of competence to consent, treatment should not be refused, unless there are specific contra-indications. If parents refuse to consent, then an adolescent's competence, under the rules in *Gillick*, should be assessed if they are under 16. If over 16, their competence should be assessed according to section 8 of the Family Law Reform Act.

3. Are there specific contraindications to pubertal-suppression treatment? These might be that the adolescent does not have an extreme cross-gender identification, or does not function well socially (apart from any anxiety or depression caused by the social stigma resulting from their cross-gender identification). If no, then pubertal-suppression treatment should be provided. It is reversible, it relieves anxiety and distress and, perhaps importantly for the clinician involved, it removes the threat of possible future litigation as a result of the consequences of failing to provide such treatment.

Conclusion

Doctors and ethics committees must consider the implications of refusing pubertal-suppression treatment to gender-dysphoric adolescents who have a good prognosis for future gender reassignment. In deciding what path to take in the treatment of these adolescents, clinicians must also consider the possibility of future litigation as a grounds for refusal to treat. The well-documented experiences of the Dutch model of treatment have shown that this treatment can provide an effective approach for young people experiencing gender dysphoria.[26] The alternatives, to date, have been shown to prolong distress and to allow the development of secondary sex characteristics, which require extensive, painful and expensive medical intervention in later life.

Gender reassignment treatment is no longer a medical practice in its infancy. It was initiated at the end of the 19th century, and has been provided regularly since the late 1960s. The prognosis for patients is excellent. The younger they are allowed to commence some sort of treatment and cross-gender lifestyle, the better. Nevertheless, the social stigmas associated with gender reassignment, and the resulting concerns of clinicians who provide it, are still significant. Doctors must assess the best long-term medical interests of adolescent patients before refusing active intervention. Seeking guidance from their ethics committee would ensure they have shown why they have chosen a particular method of treatment. In the long term, this process of consultation can safeguard the clinician and health authorities from litigation, and can safeguard individual patients, ensuring that they receive the treatment best suited to their clinical and social needs.

Notes

[1] The terms 'gender dysphoria' and 'transsexualism' denote the experience of a gender identity opposite to that of one's anatomical sex, commonly characterised by a desire to undergo medical gender reassignment. See, e.g., *Blending Genders* (R. Ekins & D. King, eds. 1996); B.L. Hausman, *Changing Sex* (1995); D. King, *The Transvestite and the Transsexual* (1995).

[2] 'Children of 14 Get Sex Change Treatment on NHS,' *The Sunday Times* 6 (12 Oct. 1997).

[3] See D. Di Cegli, 'Conference Proceedings: Gender Identity and Development in Childhood and Adolescence,' (Child and Adolescent Section, Department of Mental Health Sciences, St. George's Hospital, London, 1992) (on file with author).

[4] *The Decision* (Channel 4 television broadcasts, 6 Feb. 1996, 13 Feb. 1996).

[5] K.J. Zucker & S.J. Bradley, *Gender Identity Disorder and Psychosexual Problems in Children and Adolescents* 269 (1995).

[6] F. Pfafflin, 'Revision of the Harry Benjamin Standards of Care in Progress,' in *Gender Blending* 337, 342 (B. Bullough & V.L. Bullough, eds., 1997).

[7] Zucker & Bradley, note 5 *supra*, at 269.

[8] L. Howse, 'Children with GID versus the Medical Profession,' (12 Feb. 1998) (unpublished report, on file with author).

[9] See, e.g., R. Green, *The 'Sissy Boy Syndrome' and the Development of Homosexuality* (1987); B. Zuger, 'Early Effeminate Behaviour in Boys: Outcome and Significance for Homosexuality,' in 172 JNMD 90 (1984). See also Zucker & Bradley, note 5 *supra*.

[10] See P.T. Cohen-Kettenis & S.H.M. van Goozen, 'Sex Reassignment of Adolescent Transsexuals: A Follow-Up Study,' 36 AACAP 263 (1997).

[11] *Id.* at 264.

[12] *Id.* at 271.

[13] F. Pfafflin, 'Regrets after Sex Reassignment Surgery,' in *Gender Dysphoria: Interdisciplinary Approaches in Clinical Management* 69 (W.O. Bockting & E. Coleman, eds., 1992).

[14] See M. McMullen & S. Whittle, *Transvestism, Transsexualism and the Law* 85 (1994).

[15] *Re W (a minor)* 4 AER 627 (1992).

[16] AC 112 (1986).

[17] *Id.* at 189 (Scarman, L.J.).

[18] *Re J*, 4 AER 614 (1992).

[19] *Id.* at 615.

[20] *Re T*, 1 WLR 242 (1997).

[21] *Bolam v. Friern Hospital Management Committee*, 2 AER 118 (1957).

[22] *Maynard v. West Midlands Regional Health Authority*, 1 AER 635 (1985).

[23] *Sidaway v. Board of Governors of the Bethlem Royal and the Maudsley Hospital*, 2 WLR 480 (1985).

[24] P.T. Cohen-Kettenis & S.H.M. van Goozen, 'Pubertal Delay as an Aid in Diagnosis and Treatment of a Transsexual Adolescent,' (1998) (on file with author).

[25] *R v. Ethical Committee of St. Mary's ex. p. Harriott* 1 FLR 512 (1988).

[26] See P.T. Cohen-Kettenis & S.H.M. van Goozen, note 10 *supra*; P. T. Cohen-Kettenis & S.H.M. van Goozen, note 24 *supra*; L. Cohen *et al.*, 'Psychological Functioning of Adolescent Transsexuals: Personality and Psychopathology,' 53 JCP 187 (1997).